11 Change as aesthetic
experience
12 Suffering: followed by a
revelation of its meaning.
2 f Homo Sapiens' capacity
to apprehend beauty & for
religious awe — elements of
survival.
— combined obj.
• 37 Ulro, negation
...
157 music of humanity
140 Dreams occur all the
time.
149 Leading w/ Awe

THE AESTHETIC DEVELOPMENT

THE AESTHETIC DEVELOPMENT

The Poetic Spirit of Psychoanalysis
Essays on Bion, Meltzer, Keats

Meg Harris Williams

KARNAC

Published in 2010 by
Karnac Books Ltd
118 Finchley Road, London NW3 5HT

British Library Cataloguing in Publication Data

A C.I.P. for this book is available from the British Library

ISBN 978 1 85575 617 5

Edited, designed, and produced by The Studio Publishing Services Ltd
www.publishingservicesuk.co.uk
e-mail: studio@publishingservicesuk.co.uk

www.karnacbooks.com

CONTENTS

ACKNOWLEDGEMENTS

I would like to thank Irene Freeden, Dorothy Hamilton, and Neil Maizels for generously diverting attention from their own work to scrutinize mine, enabling me to correct some of its infelicitations; the colleagues who attended my series of talks of the same title and whose response likewise helped with last-minute clarifications, and especially Jonathan Bradley for chairing them; and above all my husband, Adrian Williams, who, as always, read every draft of the book as it came along. I would also like to thank Meriel Gold and Morag Donnelly for their inspiration in the life-drawing studio, and all my wonderful models.

I also thank the editors of the periodicals in which sections of this book were first published: *The British Journal of Psychotherapy*: "Inspiration: a psychoanalytic and aesthetic concept", Vol. 14(1), 1997, pp. 33–43; "Psychoanalysis; an art or a science?", Vol. 16(2), 1999, pp. 127–135; "The three vertices: science, art, religion", Vol. 21(3) 2005, pp. 429–441; "Psychoanalysis as an art form", Vol. 25 (3), pp. 381–392; *Encounter*: "'Knowing' the mystery: against reductionism", Vol. 67, June 1986, pp. 48–53; "Looking with the mind: psychoanalysis and literature", Vol. 74, May 1990, pp. 33–38; *Journal of Melanie Klein and Object Relations*: "The aesthetic perspective in the work of Donald Meltzer", Vol. 16(2), 1998, pp. 209–218; *The Psychoanalytic Review*: "The role of incantation: lifedrawing as an analogue to psychoanalytic process", Vol. 95(3), 2008, pp. 463–472.

Meg Harris Williams is a writer and visual artist with a lifelong psychoanalytic education; her mother was Martha Harris of the Tavistock Clinic, and her stepfather Donald Meltzer. She read English at Cambridge and Oxford universities and her first book to marry poetic and psychoanalytic epistemologies was *Inspiration in Milton and Keats* (1981). Since then she has continued to write on the poetic origins of psychoanalytic thinking and the aesthetic implications for psychoanalysis in many books and articles including *A Strange Way of Killing* (1987), *The Apprehension of Beauty* (1988, with Donald Meltzer), *The Chamber of Maiden Thought* (1992, with Margot Waddell), *A Trial of Faith: Horatio's Story* (1996), *The Vale of Soulmaking* (2005) and *Bion's Dream* (to be published in 2010). She has also written and illustrated a book of Shakespeare stories for children, *Five Tales from Shakespeare* (1996). She is editor of the Harris Meltzer Trust publications. Websites: www.artlit.info and www.harris-meltzer-trust.org.uk

To my ancestors

Between fulfilment and its prophecy
We live, between worlds unborn and dead;
Growth is the principle of our beauty,
Striving to speak the inward sense of things . . .
[Roland Harris, "The schoolroom
empties"]

One day men will learn to think of sanity as an aesthetic achievement. [Adrian Stokes, "Living in Ticino"]

Introduction

> We are so familiar with psychoanalytic theories that we tend to forget the basic points; so much so, that it is difficult to say what the fundamental points are. Free associations—sometimes we hear of analysis in such a way that we think what a wonderful time we are all having, wandering about amongst the weeds, plucking the wild and beautiful flowers, admiring the brambles, the bushes, and not getting anywhere near to disturbing the sleep of the sleeping beauty—the wisdom that lies fast asleep somewhere in the thickets. [Bion, 1997, p. 37]

The study of "aesthetics" as a particular means of gaining knowledge began formally in the later eighteenth century. It never lost its original Greek derivation of being grounded in sense-based awareness, so differing from purely rational or analytic cognitive procedures; this has remained important for its place in psychoanalytic thinking, where it plays an increasingly prominent role. Modern philosophers recognize that the aesthetic and the ethical—our intimate knowledge of values—are inextricably intertwined.[1] And, since Bion's emphasis on the limitations of our scientific knowledge of the mind and on the need to improve our observational tools to learn to perceive and ingest the small amount of knowledge that is accessible to our consciousness, the realm of the aesthetic in psychoanalysis has begun to come into its own. This book reflects my own lifelong preoccupation with developing the aesthetic affiliations of psychoanalysis, and with suggesting through literary analogy the kind of poetry that is innate or implicit in the psychoanalytic method, as well as the poetic influences on its model of the mind.

There are three main senses in which psychoanalysis can be said to have acquired an aesthetic dimension. These are: the psychoanalytic model of the mind; the nature of the psychoanalytic encounter as an aesthetic process; and the evolution of psychoanalysis itself as an art-science. These things are, of course, interdependent, but it is also useful to remain aware of their distinctness.

According to Meltzer, the model of the mind that is employed in the clinical setting serves as both a holding-place for well-known clinical phenomena and as a jumping-off point for new phenomena that make their appearance. It is what makes observation—not just interpretation—possible. In my own previous writings, when trying to marry the epistemologies of poetry and psychoanalysis, I have focused on the literary roots of this psychoanalytic model of the mind: in particular, the dramatization of the struggle between developmental and anti-developmental forces in the search for self-knowledge. In the present book, I would also like to consider in more detail the second aesthetic area—the psychoanalytic dream-encounter—and its relation to some traditional forms of aesthetic response. The examples I shall provide include poems, both well and little known, some passages of art appreciation, and a discussion of the practice and philosophy of life-drawing.[2] All these forms are founded on establishing a dialogue between two minds in relation to an aesthetic object. Bion and Meltzer both lamented the impoverished vocabulary available to psychoanalysis for describing psychic reality; and the potential for improving on this is one major benefit of the link with literary forms.

To set this investigation in context, I shall briefly note here the essential nature of the modern psychoanalytic model, followed by a sketch of some key features of the wider philosophical background from which it has emerged, for, as Meltzer reminds us,

psychoanalysis has its "historic roots more in philosophy and theology than in nineteenth century science" (1978a, Vol. III, p. 94).*
The aesthetic development in the model of this new science allows
us to see much more clearly the evidence of its belonging in fact to
a very ancient tradition, whose central concern is the Delphic
"know thyself"—"introducing the patient to himself" as Bion puts
it.[3] The first step in this internal communion is the Socratean
acknowledgement of ignorance. The psyche needs to be built
through ingesting thoughts, and this makes the picture of healthy
"learning from experience" both more problematic and more interesting than that of psychopathology alone. "Normal" psychic
development is not automatic, but is an earned and worked-
through evolutionary process. This is a model which makes psychoanalysis more open to analogies with artistic modes of knowing,
including "aesthetic criticism" of the various arts, in so far as this
depends on both expressive and on self-analytic capacities: that is,
on the internal dialogue that takes place in response to an aesthetic
object such as, in traditional poetic terminology, the Muse.

To Bion's emphasis on the nature of psychoanalytic observation
and the observer–observed, Meltzer added the psychoanalytic
method as aesthetic object—the fundamental object of observation.
Our aesthetic responses in all areas are founded on the original, primordial knowledge attained by the infant's first perception of the
beauty of the world as seen in the mother or breast-as-combined-
object: "In the beginning was the breast and the breast was the
world" (Meltzer, 1986, p. 204). So, the goal of the psychoanalytic
encounter becomes that of restoring or reshaping any points of
thwarted or stunted growth (Money-Kyrle's "misconceptions").[4] As
Roland Harris puts it:

> Growth is the principle of our beauty,
> Striving to speak the inward sense of things.
>   [Harris, "The schoolroom empties . . ."][5]

---

*The remainder of this chapter is based substantially on "The aesthetic per-
spective in the work of Donald Meltzer", *Journal of Melanie Klein and Object
Relations* (Williams, 1998).

This quest to reconnect with the "inward sense" that makes our lives beautiful is achieved not through direct action on the part of the analyst, but, rather, by facilitating renewed contact with the mind-feeding roots of the psychoanalytic method as aesthetic object. Thwarted development, mental illness, dis- and un-integration, can all be seen in a new light: that of emotional failure to maintain this aesthetic contact. The "principle of beauty" requires to be re-established. This switches the focus from the minute variations of psychopathology to the mysterious complexities of aesthetic reciprocity, which regulates the individual's ethical development in a way analogous to poetic "inspiration". This is the "psychoanalytic spirit" that Bion says he hopes will "endure for hundreds of years" (1997, p. 34).

The third aspect of the aesthetic development—psychoanalysis as an evolving art-science—has been the subject of Meltzer's *The Kleinian Development* and other works. The modern origins of psychoanalysis in this sense could be said to have begun with the Enlightenment, with its concern with the nature of "man as a symbol-making animal", as described by philosophers such as Cassirer, Whitehead, Wittgenstein, and Langer, and philosophically developed for psychoanalysis by Money-Kyrle and others. The general pattern of this cultural background could be summarized as follows.

By the later eighteenth century (a period whose thinkers greatly interested both Bion and Meltzer), the static "Chain of Being" model of man's relation to God and the universe was crumbling, and the way was being paved towards the concept of evolution. The essential nature of man was no longer conceived in terms of the fixed co-ordinates of angels and beasts, but of the progressive ones of source ("origin") and direction. Man needed to be reminded of his origins in order to redirect himself towards the true goal of his innate humanity. The new emphasis was on the individual, who needed to be educated to become himself—"for his own sake, not that of society"—Rousseau insisted; yet, only then could he constructively take part in society, the march of humanity. The question was asked, what really distinguishes man from the animals? Certainly not (as Swift satirized through the Houyhnhyms) his veneer of civilized living. This was rather, said Rousseau, a perversion or obscuring of his natural talents. Like the "state of nature" propounded by Rousseau, myths emerged which might formulate the mystery of the essence of humanity, and these came to focus on what appeared to be his most distinctive characteristic, the faculty of speech.

In this context the question of the "origins of language" was fiercely debated, and Dr Johnson was the first to recognize that language was not inventable:

> When once man has language, we can conceive that he may gradually form modifications of it. I mean only, that inspiration seems to me to be necessary to give man the faculty of speech; to inform him that he may have speech . . . [Boswell's *Life of Johnson*, quoted in Jain, 1991, p. 36]

He saw that a new perspective on the debate was required. In saying language had to come from "inspiration" not "invention", Johnson made a distinction analogous to Bion's between "thinking" man and "toolmaking" man with his clever capacity to modify his environment. Thinking is painful, Bion believed, not because of its results, but because it is, in evolutionary terms, only a very recent function of animate matter (Bion, 1980, p. 31). Not the "truth" alone, but the process of acquiring it, is stressful, which is why the human animal is tempted to prefer action. As a first step towards understanding this, Johnson saw, in effect, that signs that could be manipulated were of a different order from the principle of learning itself, for which only the poetic–religious term "inspiration" was suitable.

The direction of this inquiry entailed a resurgence of interest in Plato, the father of aesthetic philosophy; once again his myths were reinterpreted. Plato was a symbol-maker and he generated further symbols. Despite his banishment of the artists for their hubristic attempts to shadow reality (his personal recoil from aesthetic conflict), he has always been the poets' philosopher. Apart from Blake, who angrily accused Plato of "confuting himself", poetic thinkers have generally ignored Plato's moralism and focused instead on his aesthetic, myth-making practice. C. M. Woodhouse (1982) has pointed out the flexibility of Platonism through the ages, by contrast with Aristotelianism, which remained rather a fixed system. It was once again considered of interest that the relation between beauty and knowledge was both significant and problematic. Michael Podro writes how Diderot looked for "rapports" outside the reach of propositional thought, and for ways of uniting object and subject; Kant likewise showed the possibility of "reflection without the duty of cognition". Kant adopted the term "aesthetic" (originally coined by Baumgarten in his *Aesthetica*) and made it indispensable thereafter; poetry showed that nature could be used as a "schema for the supersensible" (Podro, 2003, p. 65). As a result, aesthetic judgement has been seen as "by nature value charged" (*ibid.*, p. 51). In his interpretation of Platonism, Kant defined "pure reason" as an aesthetic attainment inseparable from ethics, and this, it could be argued, has remained the main line of forward thinking to the present day, despite various wobbles in the directions of either decadence (sloppy, self-indulgent views of the aesthetic) or behaviourism (rigid, mechanical, and pseudo-scientific notions of the aesthetic).[6]

Cassirer describes how the term "symbol" was coined by Goethe in response to the Kantian view of an "ideal" not as something remote from reality, but as "a moment, a factor in the process of experience itself" (Cassirer, 1953, p. 74). Rather than referring to something above and beyond the experience of the moment, it actually gives shape and unity to the particular experience. It is "constitutive" not "regulative"; it enters in, rather than directing out. Knowledge that is imbibed directly through the senses, outside conscious manipulation, maintains links with our animal origins while, at the same time, providing an Platonic orientation to more evolved—possibly infinitely evolved—forms of knowledge.[7]

Coleridge's enthused adoption of German Romantic philosophy made it available to all the English writers of the era (see Holmes, 1982; Stephenson, 1995): he distinguished between "mechanic" and "organic" ways of being and of knowing, recognizing (like Bion with his "vertices") that it was necessary to focus on "the relations of things" not just one or other single factor in an equation, and stating emphatically that "An idea cannot be known except through a symbol". The poets were clear that the way in which these personal ethical ideas took earthly or sensuous shape and became "known" was an aesthetic process. Keats speaks of "the knowledge of contrast, feeling for light and shade, all that information (primitive sense) necessary for a poem" (letter to Brown, 30 November 1820; 1970a, p. 398). The primitive and the poetic are ends of a single cognitive spectrum, and represent the type of knowledge that is not arguable but is, none the less, demonstrable—that impresses itself "on the pulses". In this, we see the genesis of Bion's distinction between "knowing" and "knowing about". And Croce, as Bion avowed, established the importance of the aesthetic as a "universal linguistic".

In this way, the innate capacity for symbol-making—rather than just language—came to be recognized as the faculty that identified the essence of humanity. Language itself had evolved from pre-verbal forms of expression that came closer to demonstrating the essential nature of symbol-formation (Sparshott, 2004, p. 278). All the same, it took another century for the confusion between signs and symbols, which had befuddled the "origins of language" debate, to be decisively tackled. In the field of philosophy, this was done by those like Langer who—Meltzer said—"focussed attention on problems of symbol formation, notational systems, modes of thought, uses of ambiguity, the meaning of silences, the role of the musical versus the lexical level in communication" (1978a, Vol. III, p. 21). The symbol-making capacity is an innate function of human mentality, as Wittgenstein saw it, and therefore demands realization. Thinking is the logical consequence of speech, music, art, and dance, and perhaps also, in the same tradition, the logical consequence of psychoanalysis.

This sketches the philosophical background to the present-day concern with the aesthetic qualities of the transference–countertransference. When we turn to this it becomes clear that the concept of symbol formation has still not had its full impact on the psychoanalytic model of the mind, and that the idea of psychoanalysis as an aesthetic experience requires much more distinctness before its place at the heart of the modern model can be recognized. Symbol formation, in the Coleridgean sense, is a function of clinical work with its quest for the meaning of emotional experiences. But, as Meltzer has frequently pointed out, Freud and many subsequent psychoanalysts use the term synonymously with "word" or "sign", in the mechanical dictionary sense of a system of referents. This is a problem not just of terminology, but of appreciating the nature and value of psychoanalysis's aesthetic qualities. It is related to the account given in The Kleinian Development (Meltzer, 1978a) of Freud's internal struggle between clinician and theoretician. In Meltzer's view, Freud was hampered by his reluctance to abandon the explanatory, psychopathographic features of his model. His detective-style approach looked for "signs" that would allow the past roots of a neurosis to be deduced, rather than for symbols of a present emotional situation in the inner world. At crucial moments, Meltzer says, the "poet" takes over from the neurophysiologist (*ibid.*, Vol. I, p. 27), and Freud as clinician becomes "an artist at work", able to follow the method and the patient and to tolerate not understanding what was happening (p. 62). By contrast, both Freud-as-theoretician and Freud-as-romanticist represent "enforcing" aspects of himself (p. 25). Enforcement employs the language of signs; exploration employs the language of symbols.

It is significant that both Meltzer and Bion considered the science of psychoanalysis to be very much in its infancy, so there will be a lot more to be said in the future than we can say now. Its birth-myth, in the Meltzer–Bion view, takes psychoanalysis to be "a thing-in-itself that existed in the world prior to its discovery by the mystic genius of Freud . . . who gave it form" (*ibid.*, Vol. III, p. 104). That was the aesthetic intersection of "O" with a thinker.[8] Then, as if responding to the demands of the psychoanalytic spirit itself, Melanie Klein found an inspired way to dispense with Freud's reconstructive diagnostic route. She saw the evidence of children's concrete inner worlds and their present phantasies expressed primarily through play, and deduced that "symbolism is the basis of all talents" (Klein, 1930, p. 220). That is, she observed symbol formation, the origins of human mentality, continuously regenerating and redirecting itself then and there in the dynamic process of the transference. Psychoanalytic learning-from-experience began to converge with poetic learning-from-experience and its underlying model of the mind. Until, finally, by the time of Bion, or, as Bion would say, "why finally?" (1991, p. 527), the aesthetic psychoanalytic process resembles "thought sitting amazed in Plato's cave" (Meltzer, 1978a, Vol. III, p. 2). To paraphrase Plato's *Meno*, the soul of psychoanalysis pre-exists as the thought which requires its thinkers to realize it.

Meltzer saw the embryonic science as pursuing its own internal logical development, rather like the "natural history" of the psychoanalytic process itself (1967). This internal inevitability of evolution is, in fact, he says, his "faith" (1978a, Vol. I, p. 27). To describe the evolution of its "logically necessary propositions", he borrowed a metaphor from Freud of winding a garland of flowers about a wire (*ibid.*, p. 4). The wire is the poetic spirit of "becoming" and it leads, in the Bion–Meltzer model of development, to the domain of aesthetics, which Meltzer saw as constituting the ultimate category of Bion's Grid for categorizing the development of thoughts.[9] Not only do aesthetic features and preoccupations play an increasingly prominent role, they do in fact become *logically necessary* to sustain the psychoanalytic development. In Meltzer's exposition of the logical advance of psychoanalysis, the method and the model of the mind interdigitate and adjust themselves step by step to the Platonic Idea of Psychoanalysis.

To suggest, therefore, that psychoanalysis is entering an "aesthetic" phase of development, or, rather, of conceptualizing its own ontology, is to be concerned with such things as how containers for meaning (symbols) become shaped, with the subtleties of "conversations between internal objects"[10] as a form of aesthetic response, and with the spiritual problems of relating to the aesthetic object in mediating our contact with the Platonic realm of ideas. In Meltzer's view, artist and scientist were never separated in Bion's mind, by contrast with Freud (1985 lectures; Meltzer, 1994a, p. 523). The only thing that changed in Bion's account of psychoanalytic evolution was his use of metaphor, which increasingly aligned itself to the world of art and fiction. Bion compares this evolution to the way that algebraic geometry lay "implicit" in Euclidean geometry: "that implicit truth was a kind of sleeping beauty waiting to be rescued . . . the truth hadn't altered, it had become explicit" (2005a, p. 92). Analogously with Meltzer, Bion speaks of the "implicit" thinking of Melanie Klein as something that existed in her practice rather than her theory, awaiting a more formal articulation (1991, p. 628). This again relates directly to the need to consider more closely the nature of psychoanalysis as an art form, with a capacity for generating unconscious meanings not only about its individual participants but also about itself as an evolutionary science. Such meanings may only become formulable "centuries later".

Bion, when feeling pessimistic about the survival of Freud's brainchild, saw the "Sleeping Beauty" of the "psychoanalytic spirit" as often overlooked by those circling in the thickets and brambles around its perimeter (1997, pp. 34–37).[11] However, aesthetic considerations are becoming increasingly formulable, so more widely discussed as a matter of interest to psychoanalytic epistemology in general, not only the post-Kleinian. It is impossible to pay comprehensive attention to the varied linkages between psychoanalysis and the arts, which are now burgeoning in ways that go far beyond the dogmatic substitutions of early "applied psychoanalysis". In focusing on the work of Bion and Meltzer, I would like to take my cue from Money-Kyrle when he explains that he concentrates on the ideas which he "believes to be the most progressive, at the cost of perhaps missing much good work which may be found elsewhere" (1961, p. 8). It is in line with Keats's view, expressed in a letter to Reynolds dated 3 May 1818, that there *is* a "grand march of intellect" with a logical progression, built upon the durable qualities of previous ideas (Keats, 1970a, p. 96). My own approach to these ideas is better described as applying poetry to psychoanalysis than as applying psychoanalysis to poetry—but only in the sense that poetry, with its centuries of experience in symbolizing mind-to-mind queries and revelations of the type we call "self-analytic", can help direct attention to the poetic spirit that exists within psychoanalysis itself, and, thus, enhance its operation. As Bion puts it in his *Memoir*, in the context of discussing with "Myself" what Kant meant by his formulation "concepts without intuition are empty and intuitions without concepts are blind":

BION: I know the quotation to which you refer, of course, but—is *that* what he meant?

MYSELF: I have no idea what he meant, but I am using *his* "concepts" to match with *my* "intuitions" because in this way I can bring together a concept and an intuition, making it possible to feel that *I* know what *I* mean. [Bion, 1991, p. 194]

In this book, which was originally conceived as a collection of reprinted essays, I have attempted to weave into a coherent narrative extracts from my work over the past thirty years, matching Bion's and Meltzer's concepts with my intuitions in order to understand better "what *I* mean". The Kantian idea, which I am relying on to unify the material, is that of the psychoanalytic method as an aesthetic object. I see this as the poets saw poetry, as one of those many "shapes divine" in which the "idea of the beautiful" becomes manifest.[12] In such shapes, as Meltzer said, the artist, lover, and scientist aspects of the personality become one. As Plato says, in his myth of the incarnations of the soul, the most difficult problem is to use "present experience" to "recollect the world of reality"; and in this context, "The soul that has seen the most enters into a human infant who is destined to become a seeker after wisdom or beauty or a follower of the Muses and a lover" (*Phaedrus* 248; Plato, 1975, p. 54).

By implication, the most progressive part of the mind - the part that can "see the most" - employs all these aspects to the limits of their capacity, and so does "progressive" psychoanalysis. With this in mind, I hope not to lose sight of the Sleeping Beauty while tracking in the undergrowth some of the many openings into the complex nature of psychoanalysis as an art form.

Notes

1. Although this is variously interpreted. Sometimes, the "ethical" is simply applied to the subject matter or theme of an artwork (Gaut, 2004, p. 283). The ethics that applies to psychoanalysis, however, is more complex and is related to the nature of the deep symbol in art—to its untranslateable value-system (see Chapter Three).

2. Originally, I had intended to include a section on Bion's autobiographical narratives in this book; however, it outgrew its allotted shell and became a separate book, *Bion's Dream* (2010).

3. As Bion puts it, "Know thyself—the oracle at Delphi. Nowadays we don't say anything quite so simple as that, it's got a much longer word like psychoanalysis attached to it but the principle of it is much the same" (1977, cited from tape transcript of Tavistock seminar).

4. Money-Kyrle, educated as a philosopher, derives the concept of misconception from Aristotle's of memory mis-fitting the Platonic idea-as-image (*eikon*) (see also Ricoeur, 1977, pp. 8–48)

5. For information on Roland Harris, see "Afterword" to this book.

6. Even analytical aesthetics (which might be thought a contradiction in terms, since its methods are those of logical proof, and aesthetic apprehension is non-arguable) is gradually and somewhat painstakingly following in the footsteps of the imaginative philosophical tradition (see Lamarque & Olsen, 2004).

7. Bion stresses the sensuous qualities of psychoanalytic intuition by means of an analogy with the senses used by the physician (1970, p. 7), and the need for a permeable caesura between psychic (including psychotic) and somatic.

8. Bion's formulation of "O" in the body of his later work (first in 1965a, p. 17) refers to the "underlying idea" or "ultimate reality" of an emotional situation; this is ineffable so can never be fully known (in the sense of "absolute truth"), but can be "aligned with". It is known by means of its "evolutions" (see 1970, pp. 26–27). For further types of "evolution", see, for example, Bion, 1991, pp. 36, 209. Associations such as "object" and "godhead" accrue to the sign—the "one and all alone"; also, through assonance, it embodies a musical equivalent to the word "awe"—which is the same vowel sound with a touch of vibrato.

9. Bion's Grid (1963, 1977) was his inspired attempt to map along two axes the process by which thoughts originate and develop, beginning with the formation of "alpha elements". He compared it to Kant's Matrix: "what I call the Grid and what Kant called the Matrix. In practice it is difficult because the conversation is really as it were written in water. The water closes in immediately on top of it. So it does depend on having some system of recording it, mentally", and the Grid was intended to provide "a matrix into which you can fit your various ideas and then they begin to have a meaning and the pattern begins to emerge" (Tavistock seminar of 1977, cited from tape transcript). Bion made clear it was not intended as an explanation, but, rather, as an aid to observation (Bion, 1970, p. 3). The Grid was first discussed by Meltzer, in *The Kleinian Development*, as "an extraordinarily graphic way of representing the necessary movement of thoughts as they progress through the hypothetical apparatus for thinking that Bion wishes to construct" (Meltzer, 1978a, Vol. III, p. 59), with its implied Negative or "anti-Grid" being a "mirror image" for lies (*ibid.*, p. 87). For Meltzer's further thoughts on the Grid and its aesthetic qualities, see Meltzer, 1995b, 2005a. For further discussions of the Grid see, among others, Grotstein (2007) and Sandler (2005).

10. This was Meltzer's definition of the psychoanalytic method in his final years, given informally in various talks. See also 1983, p. 46.

11. As Bion also puts it, "I feel that most people reach an age where they have so much knowledge that they cannot penetrate through to the wisdom—it's a new kind of forest that you can't see for the trees" (2005b, p. 42).

12. Milton, for example, in a letter to Diodati dated 23 September 1637, described his vocation in Platonic terms as "seeking for the Idea of the beautiful . . . throughout all the shapes and forms of things ('for many are the shapes of things divine')" (cited in Williams, 1982, p. 76); similarly, Keats, in a letter to Fanny Brawne of 1820 (undated), said he had been faithful to "the principle of beauty in all things" (Keats 1970a, p. 361).

CHAPTER ONE

Psychoanalysis: an art or a science?*

This chapter is intended to map out the epistemological background to the field of inquiry of the present book, with its focus on the artistic qualities of psychoanalysis. In subsequent chapters, I shall go into more detail over some of the features touched on here—in particular, the nature of symbol-formation, inspiration, the psychoanalytic (or self-psychoanalytic) dream encounter, and I shall also say more about the central aesthetic concepts of Bion and Meltzer.

The modern answer to the question "art or science?" must be "both". As Meltzer says, "The great artist and scientist has always been the same person" (1975, p. 221).[1] The interest of the question lies in the way artistic or scientific aspects interrelate in the quest for knowledge of the mind; and the way this quest is perceived (as well as performed) will be dependent on one's model of the mind.

---

*This chapter amalgamates sections from two previous papers: "Psychoanalysis: an art or a science? A review of the implications of the theory of Bion and Meltzer", *British Journal of Psychotherapy*, 16(2), 1999: 127–135; and "The three vertices: science, art and religion", *British Journal of Psychotherapy*, 21(3), 2005a: 429–441.

Just as Aristotle defined man as a "political animal", which accounts for his lying and manipulative propensities, so Bion sees man in his truth-seeking capacity as a scientific, artistic, and religious animal. These are all orientations concerned with reality, whether external or internal, and Meltzer would say they all focus on the "aesthetic object", whether this be an internal object, an artwork, or the world itself. In the domain of psychic reality, the interdependence of the domain and the instrument for investigation places knowledge about the mind beyond the reach of single-vertex science; therefore, the spirit of scientific inquiry needs to be modified by these other "vertices". It is the tension and overlap between them that is important:

> It would seem absurd if the tension between these three groups—science, religion and art—which are all fundamentally devoted to the truth, was either so slack or so tense that it was unable to further the aim of truth. [Bion, 1973–1974, Vol. I, p. 96]

Science and art merge into one another through observation and exploration of the sensuous world; art and religion through reverie and inner focus; religion and science through their respect for the idea of a reality that is neither invented nor imagined, but that exists beyond our desire or control. The disciplines conflict when they become propagandist, single-vertex, and, to some extent, self-caricaturing. Any single-vertex approach tends in the direction of the lie (covering-up of a truth once glimpsed); elsewhere, Bion calls this "calcification" (2005a, p. 11), and he regards it as endemic to psychoanalytic thinking. The links between the vertices need to be not too slack, not too tense; they need to come under the category of communication, not of denial or action to remove the unpleasantness of the tension. An initial mutual suspicion may stimulate in the direction of "the truth", but neglect or obliteration will not.

Although the artistic element was present in psychoanalytic practice from the very beginning, it has only recently begun to become explicitly valued. The emotional composition of the mind is traditionally the field of interest of artistic disciplines such as music and poetry, which employ sensuous means to convey mental abstraction. For, as Bion keeps stressing, we do not know what the mind is, or even if its boundaries correspond to an individual's body. Do mental transactions take place somewhere "in the air", as poets have often described the arrival of inspiration? Part of the endeavour of Bion, Meltzer, and others has been to establish psychoanalysis's links with the humanist disciplines which already have a language of their own to describe this suprasensuous exploration. It is this that has helped to make the formal designation of "psychoanalysis as an art form" a convincing and useful proposition.

The distinction between scientific and artistic ways of knowing is at least as old as Plato and Aristotle, and probably marks a dualism as ancient and innate as the human species itself. A list of pairings which seem to derive from this fundamental dichotomy would include the following: the classical one of *doxa* (opinion) *vs. episteme* (truth); the quantitative (measurable) *vs.* the ineffable (suprasensuous); practical and contemplative; right and left sides of the brain; reason and intuition; discursive *vs.* presentational forms; analysis and synthesis; conscious and unconscious; masculine and feminine components of the personality; and so on. Each of these cognitive pairings has, at some time, been taken to reflect the dualism between science and art, often with descriptive plausibility, and sometimes with practical application to techniques of learning and teaching. Nonetheless, any humanistic discipline, when pursued to a degree of depth, will find itself forging complementary links between these modes of knowing and will probably discover that they support rather than undermine one another.

In the history of psychoanalysis, the possibility of its being an art form began to emerge when mind and brain were recognized as different entities and, in particular, when Freud realized that transference and countertransference were not screens which clouded true scientific vision, but, rather, the tools of intuition. Here, if anywhere, was the "truth" about the mind to be found. This makes psychoanalysis a "presentational form" (in the jargon of aesthetics) rather than a discursive one, an art more than a science. Nonetheless, the idea of psychoanalysis actually being an art form would have been received with incomprehension at that time, and is even now likely to be resisted and distrusted. There are both intellectual and social reasons for this. People fear that "scientific rigour" may be replaced by "artistic licence" (as in "wild analysis"): there would be no standardization of procedures or results, no consistency, no reliability, no respect for academic hierarchy. As Meltzer points out, science is respectable, art is not (Meltzer & Williams, 1988, p. xii). Social problems—disguised as organizational problems—arise, such as: how can assessment of analysands or trainees take place? What meaning can be given to the "qualification" of being either a trained therapist or a trained analysand? Is there any difference between a "qualified" person and any other type of bourgeois acceptability, and does not this cynically undermine the spiritual purposes which are the very *raison d'être* of psychoanalysis? Or, as Bion frequently puts it, the label is not a reliable guide to the contents.

These social aspects of the question are more to do with the image of psychoanalysis than with the thing itself: would it look better as an "art" or a "science"? Much of the academic debate revolving around the "scientific" qualities of psychoanalysis reads like a disguised attempt to evaluate its social status, giving the impression that some apology is needed for its foundation in subjective emotional contact. It is subtly derogatory and pessimistic. Psychoanalysis is seen, in effect, as a pseudo science or, at best, a second-rate science struggling conscientiously with an unfair endowment of irrationality. The approach of Bion and Meltzer, by contrast, focuses on the concept of "the truth of an emotional experience", which is seen as a fact in itself, to be apprehended with all the attendant joy and trepidation of the quest. They regard the non-sensuous nature of the mind's existence not as a hindrance, but as a stimulant; indeed, an object of awe and wonder which genuinely awakens scientific curiosity of a descriptive orientation, but which cannot be explored by solely scientific means.

The limitations of Promethean science

Meltzer writes that "the history of science could be written as a constant wrestle with the unexpected" (1975, p. 220), but the problem occurs with our emotional reception of the unexpected, which can arouse childish delusions of omnipotence and "supernatural power". If science is by nature sense based, rational, progressive, categorizable, then it is but a short, seductive step to translate this into "explicable": "truth modified to lie within man's comprehension" as Bion's religious vertex (Priest) puts it in the *Memoir* (1991).

This is the characteristic hazard of the scientific vertex when it loses touch with the other vertices of knowledge.

Bion and Meltzer continually stress the dangers of trying to explain the mysteries of the mind. In addition, says Bion, "addicts'" of psychoanalysis have a "curiously two-dimensional quality" (1973–1974, Vol. II, p. 56). They do not partake of the peculiar capacity to make human beings and situations look real, which is conferred by artistic methods. It would be a relief, says Bion, if scientific papers could somehow remind us of real human beings, so that they were not such a pain to read. Aesthetic theory, from Aristotle onwards, recognizes that this realistic capacity is something necessary to human identification and participation in what is essentially an abstract process: a meeting of minds. It is the prescriptive role of interpretation that holds psychoanalysis back in the straitjacket of pretending to be a science. The novice or overly rigid analyst believes his task is to seek out a correct interpretation and communicate it, or coerce the patient into accepting it. Bion recounts wryly how he first realized the inadequacy of this pseudo-scientific approach:

> One of the painful, alarming features of continued experience was the fact that I had certain patients with whom I employed interpretations based on my previous experience with Melanie Klein, and, though I felt that I employed them correctly and could not fault myself, none of the good results that I anticipated occurred. [Bion, 1991, p. 559]

He explains that "mechanical thinking" and "mechanical interpretation" have their place, but should not be used in such a way as to "preclude the development of the ultra- or infra-sensuous, even though I may not know what that is or even if it exists" (ibid., p. 204). Correct interpretation does not make the clinical situation one of learning from experience. Scientific accuracy is not sufficient. It is, in effect, two-dimensional; it does not remind one of real life; it does not promote growth. Some other type of communication between analyst and analysand is necessary, some other process needs to be activated: not the acquisition of knowledge, but the getting of wisdom. "Wisdom or oblivion," says Bion starkly, "take your choice" (ibid., p. 576). Or, as he frequently formulates the problem, how do you change an activity that is "about psychoanalysis" to one that "*is* psychoanalysis"? (1970, p. 66). Being right is not the same thing as telling the truth. Rightness is a function of the self (the ego), whereas telling the truth involves interaction between internal objects of both analyst and patient.

The scientific mind in its most primitive form was modelled for Bion by the tomb-robbers at Ur, a Freudian archaeological model. It is what Meltzer terms "Promethean science", as distinct from "inspired science" (1986, p. 183). The Promethean steals the fire of knowledge from heaven, rather than being smitten by the lightning command to "know thyself" (see Coleridge, *Biographia Literaria*; 1997, p. 152). It does not ignore religion so much as override it. After many centuries, the robbers broke through the invisible restraints of a religion that had fossilized into superstition in the form of the guardians of the tomb, the "ghostly sentinels of the dead and their priestly attendants" (Bion, 1973–1974, Vol. I, p. 11). The tomb-robbers, he says, must have been "brave men"; and they are "the patrons of the scientific method". This primitive type of scientific research (unalleviated by art or religion) will lay open some aspects of the truth while obscuring others: it is not, in itself, a sufficient model for "thinking for oneself". Science has overcome superstition, but at the expense of making the link with religion too confrontational, too tense, just as in Freudian psychoanalysis it is too slack. The "scientific, psychoanalytic" view of religion, says Bion, "flattens out" religious feeling (1973–1974, Vol. I, p. 52).

Milton describes science-as-robbery in his great epic, *Paradise Lost*, when the fallen angels, led by Mammon (the "least erected spirit to fall from heaven"), "ransack the centre" of Mother Earth and "rifle her bowels" in search of gold and riches (*Paradise Lost*, I: 684–686). This mentality sees the aesthetic object as containing secrets to be possessed, rather than a mystery to be apprehended and respected for its richness and otherness. The intellectual counterpart of Mammon-man is Belial, the pseudo-thinker, who leads the little devils in academic theological debates about "Fixed fate, free will, foreknowledge absolute". Their "false philosophy" has no emotional reality, owing to its divorce from the knowledge of God. It embodies the lie-in-the-soul, which looks like the real thing but is, in fact, a Negative Grid imitation of it: "cannot we his light / Imitate as we please?" In Bion's terms, they perform mental "monkey-like tricks"; they are clever, but not wise. (When asked what was the difference, he said, "wisdom takes longer" [Bion, 1973–1974, Vol. II, p. 54].) We cannot understand the nature of thinking without understanding the nature of not thinking: "We have to use a method which includes not only understanding but also misunderstanding" (Bion, 1973–1974, Vol. 1, p. 40; see also 1980, pp. 68–69).

The operation of Promethean scientific method in this non-sensuous domain encourages the operation of infantile omnipo-tence, the sterile imitation of God. It is associated with premature claims to scientific status and the desire for respectability. Blake, in his poem *Milton*, said we needed to cast off the "rotten rags of Memory" and replace them by "Inspiration" (Blake, 1966, p. 533), one of those terms that, as Bion says, need to be revitalized in order to rediscover its meaning (see Chapter Three). Projective identifica-tion alone is not sufficient. The fruits of thinking are scientific only in so far as they are the result of real experience, not the inventions of fancy or memory, which are types of rationalization. The scien-tific vertex needs the influence of art and religion to ensure that the experience is a real one, that it is discovery, not invention, in the distinction continually emphasized by Meltzer.

To remind ourselves of the feeling of "discovery", we may invoke Keats's poetic formulation in his sonnet "On First Looking into Chapman's Homer":

> Then felt I like some watcher of the skies
> When a new planet swims into his ken; . . .

The discovery is of an old idea (Homer) but it is still a "new planet" to the astronomer-poet. Bion uses Keats's phrasing to convey the first encounter with a proto-mental element (beta-element), saying that all we can do is to provide "boxes" for such categories "in case that strange creature should exist and should it swim into my ken" (1997, p. 29). The "new planet" feeling of science-as-discovery is illustrated by Milton in *Paradise Lost*. His picture of the newly-fallen Satan, finding his way through "darkness visible", is based on his admiration for Galileo and his new instrument of discovery, the telescope. The unfamiliar universe of hell represents the realm of an "unpremeditated" experience which has been "won from the void and formless infinite", in the phrase much admired and often quoted by Bion (*Paradise Lost*, III: 12). As Satan moves tentatively over the "burning marl", prefiguring twentieth-century landings on the moon, he bears an aura of magnificence, his shield cast behind his shoulder like the moon itself:

> The moon, whose orb
> Through optic glass the Tuscan artist views
> At ev'ning from the top of Fesole,
> Or in Valdarno, to descry new lands,
> Rivers or mountains in her spotty globe.
> [*Paradise Lost*, I: 287–291]

The moon on Satan's shoulder is like the viewing glass (telescope) itself, an attribute of the poet-scientist. Satan swims into the poet's sight with the moon on his shoulder, extending the imagination, and saying: "Space may produce new worlds" (l. 650). Milton's identification with Galileo (the "Tuscan artist") underlies his own venture into the unknown spaces of the mind, to give birth to previously unknown facts of feeling, giving form to the formless. *Paradise Lost* is full of imaginative conjecture about outer space, the infinite source of ideas not yet thought into existence.

It is also worth noting that although, for Blake, Newton represented the devil himself, most Romantic poets and philosophers looked optimistically towards an eventual unification of the types of knowledge. Keats, for example, kept his medical books because he regarded every "department of knowledge" as being "part of a great whole" (letter to Reynolds, 3 May 1818; 1970a, p. 92). The Romantic poets were, in general, fascinated by new scientific developments, and used the language of physics and chemistry metaphorically to enhance their expression of psychic realities (atoms, molecules, magnetism, valency, electricity, particles, matter, ethereal, gaseous, decomposition, etc). Coleridge, indeed, coined the word "scientist" for his personal discussion group; he attended Humphry Davy's lectures and hailed him as "the man who born a poet, first converted poetry into science".[2] Bion's usage of scientific and mathematical language to convey metaphysical speculation is analogous.

According to Bion, therefore, the single-vertex approach of the pure scientist is, in the context of psychoanalysis, a type of philistinism. He is scathing about "scientifically prejudiced people" and persists in seeking for mental contortions to subvert such attitudes, such as the idea of a "beam of darkness", because when knowledge is "too thick" it is impossible for any new insight to penetrate (1980, p. 121). Galileo's telescope, with its poetic history (and its context of persecution by institutionalized religion), is often invoked by Bion as the sensuous counterpart of the faculty of "intuition" to illustrate the type of mental instrument for which the thinker or psychoanalyst needs to find a suprasensuous analogy. We need to develop a "psychoanalytically augmented intuition" to be the equivalent of the physician's "see, touch, smell, hear" (Bion, 1970, p. 7); in other words, an aesthetic dimension, in the sense that the term "aesthetic" was coined originally, as that which then gives rise to the subjective experience of beauty. Bion reminds us that the heliocentric movement of the earth was first imagined by Aristarchus centuries before the instrument to prove it was built. And, as Blake says in *The Marriage of Heaven and Hell*, "what is now proved was once only imagined" (Blake, 1966, p. 151). For Milton, blindness became the equivalent of the telescope; it augmented his intuition so he could see the heroism in Satan. It was not what he wished or intended to see; indeed, like the fall of man later, the vision cruelly contradicted the tenets of his doctrinal allegiance. Watching the skies, like watching the shadows on the wall of Plato's cave (as in Meltzer's description of the consulting room [Meltzer & Williams, 1988, p. 200]), represents science-as-discovery, as distinct from science-as-explanation or science-as-invention. If we watch the skies with sufficient patience and Keatsian negative capability, then—Bion says—"a pattern will emerge". A new planet will swim into our world of knowledge.

Artistic openings

Bion was fond of quoting the passage in which Milton's blindness metamorphoses from a state of mental imprisonment to one of facilitating inner vision:

> Shine inward, and the mind through all her powers
> Irradiate, there plant eyes . . . that I may see and tell
> Of things invisible to mortal sight. [*Paradise Lost*, III: 51–54]

In this passage, Milton describes how his pre-existing "book of knowledge" is replaced by, first, the agony of nothingness (corresponding to his blindness), a "universal blank", "quite shut out", and then how, outside his own power of comprehension, the inner light dawns and forcefully irradiates his mind. The natural scientist provides the basis for the religious artist: his sensuous knowledge is mirrored on another plane of existence. Bion was profoundly impressed by the mental reorientation embodied in these lines. Many of his own metaphors for alternative ways of knowing derive from it, such as the sculpture whose solid structure acts as a "trap for light"; the tennis-court which leaves an after-image of glowing reticulated holes; or the rough and ugly surfaces in which an "idea might lodge", by contrast with the smooth continuum of scientific logicality. Artistic awareness has to find a way in through the tensions, the links, the spaces in between, the holes in existing knowledge. These can catch some aspect of the truth if they can escape the vigilance of conscious control and commonsense.

This is "learning from experience", in Bion's loaded sense. It incorporates something of the "religious vertex", which he said had been neglected in psychoanalytic inquiry ever since this replaced religious problems with sexual ones. When he was asked, "How about defending the right to make up our own minds?", he made the characteristic reply, "It's a nice idea; otherwise we would have to consider the possibility that our minds are made up for us by forces about which we know nothing" (1980, p. 69). In Bion's view, it would be necessary for the different "vertices" represented by science, religion, and art to combine in some sort of constructive tension for any real investigation of that suprasensuous entity—the mind—to take place. He asks:

> How is a proper balance to be achieved between a scientific vertex, which could be said to be devoted to truth or the facts, and a religious vertex, which could equally be said to be devoted to truth? Similarly, the sincere artist is also concerned to depict truth. If Vermeer can paint the little street in Delft and, if people can look at it, then they will never see a street in the same way again. The painter has brought about a change in the individual which makes it possible for him to see a truth that he has never seen before. [Bion, 1973–1974, Vol. I, pp. 95–96]

We see from this that what Bion admires about artistic method —and what he hopes it could contribute to psychoanalytic practice—

is, first, that it reminds us of actual human existence (Vermeer's little street) and, second, that it unobtrusively engineers a radical change in the human mind. *If* the observer is able to really "look" at Vermeer's street, his mind will never be the same again; he will view the streets of life in a different light. When he walks out of the gallery he will be a different man. This may sound an exaggerated claim, but it is no more than we expect, and have always expected, from "great" art, and is fully appreciated in philosophical aesthetic theory. This is the structural change that Bion calls "catastrophic change", which, in his model, marks every step forward in self-knowledge.

In Bion's view, this change is, by its very nature, an aesthetic experience. It is, in fact, the Kantian traditional realm of aesthetic investigation. But the sense-based phenomena which carry through this type of knowledge are the "facts of feeling", which are intuitively discovered by the light of "attention", as in the analogy with Galileo's telescope. "What matters is the unknown and on this the analyst must focus his attention" (Bion, 1970, p. 69). These intuited phenomena begin to take shape when some facet of the noumenal truth, some new idea, begins to press upon the mind. If the modern aim of psychoanalysis is to "introduce the patient to himself" (as Bion often puts it), and to activate those emotional conflicts which will set the growth of his mind in motion, then it must somehow provide these aesthetic encounters. For, in Bion's view, the essence of the psychoanalytic process lies not in reviewing past experiences, but in *having* present experiences. Thinking does not consist in organizing feelings through hindsight (as in "secondary process"), but in gaining access to feelings, which are then "transformed" through alpha-function into symbols, a complex and many-layered process for which the Grid imaginatively conjectured a route-map, gradually permeating sense with abstraction.

In this, the Grid is inherently Platonic in its origins, as well as mathematical: it has many poetic forebears. Donne wrote:

> Love's mysteries in souls do grow,
>   But yet the body is his book.
> And if some lover, such as we,
>   Have heard this dialogue of one,
> Let him still mark us, he shall see
>   Small change, when we are to bodies gone.
>   ["The Extasie", ll. 71–76]

"Souls that have seen the most" (Plato) take the earthly form of lovers, or the mind in love, and the knowledge transubstantiates. Milton had a Grid in which the five senses and compartments of the brain are linked via a neo-Platonic ladder of "transubstantiations", and, as Raphael explains to Adam, literal food is transformed into intellectual "by gradual scale sublimed", giving rise to both discursive and intuitive types of reason (human and angelic): "Discourse is oftest yours, the latter most is ours, / Differing but in degree, of kind the same" (*Paradise Lost*, V: 487–489). Keats likewise spoke of the "regular stepping of the Imagination towards a Truth", in which the mind could achieve "a fellowship with essence . . . / Full alchemized and free of space".[3] The fellowship with essence is, like Donne's souls that flow in and out of their bodies, a species of "passionate love", which, in Bion's terms, equates with alignment with O.

Feelings congregate at a caesura between vertices. The presence of a "feeling" thus initiated may, in Bion's view, result either in "pain" (which causes symptoms) or in "suffering", which is accompanied or followed by a revelation of its meaning (1970, p. 18). Bion's idea of suffering develops from his recognition that we should "neither fight nor run away" (1961, p. 65). Instead, we try to locate the feeling's origin:

> This sad event, this experience of sadness—where did it originate? Could it be located in some geographical place? Or could it originate in the mind of the analyst? Or could it originate in the relationship between two people? [Bion, 2005a, p. 64]

In order to suffer the meaning and learn from the present experience, memory and desire must be set aside. With patience (negative capability), "a pattern will emerge":

> I think that a revised Grid—not to take the place of the first one— would be useful for a practising analyst to be able to consider how "a pattern emerges". I find it useful to consider that the stages are an imaginative conjecture, a rational conjecture, a pictorial image— the sort of thing you can see in dreams . . . A minute later the shadowy impression might become more solid, "three-dimensional". You can invent this grid for yourself—the one which seems to come closest to your actual experience in analysis. It could also be applied

to a scientific paper or a lecture. The criterion, whether it is true, should also apply, but this time to something which is more aesthetic, as if you were engaged on a work of art. A scientific paper should remind you of real people; it should not be so boring, so unaesthetic, that it becomes a pain in your mind to read it. We have a difficult job; even the impromptus in the analysis, the interpretations that we give, would be all the better if they stood up to aesthetic criticism. [Bion, 1980, p. 127]

This invitation to review his Grid emphasizes that it was Bion's attempt to provide a model for genuine "psychoanalytic talk", as opposed to "talking about psychoanalysis" (1970, p. 66). The invitation is to review, not replace; that is, to ingest its central aesthetic idea by means of a sympathetically aesthetic response: "The spirit of it", as Meltzer put it in one of his late talks (Meltzer, 2003). A human science becomes more real and, hence, more accurate if its various modes of communication can stand up to aesthetic criticism. Indeed, in order to fulfil this therapeutic aim, psychoanalysis must become, in some sense, an art form. It is the triumph and the wonder of art forms that they can make emotions accessible. "What sort of artists can we be?" (Bion, 1980, p. 73). The implications of this question are considered in Chapter Five.

The real-life situation that shines through all transactions of the transference is, in the post-Kleinian model developed by Bion and Meltzer, the baby and mother-in-reverie. There, the metabolization of projected anxieties is a natural and artistic process, not even, in the first instance, a conscious one. The origins of symbol formation and thinking lie in this (internal) relationship, which is simply given a specific usage in the analytic setting. Following Wittgenstein, as well as Melanie Klein, Bion and Meltzer begin by considering the capacities of man as a human animal, a fact of nature who happens to have a certain genetic inheritance termed a "mind", and, having got a mind, what on earth is he to do with it? This is a descriptive–scientific approach, which can incorporate what Bion calls "imaginative conjecture" and find satisfaction in the coherence of human nature as it reveals itself, as opposed to the more omnipotent type of scientific urge to manipulate nature or appease it by means of "sublimations", etc., which accompanied early psychoanalytic theory and is still the basis of behaviourist and semiotic styles of psychoanalysis.

In the descriptive or phenomenological view, psychoanalysis might be regarded as an attempt to bring man more in harmony with his natural features, including those which are undesirable, disturbing, or unpleasant. Man is seen as a creature who has an innate desire to know the truth about himself. This follows from the feature termed a "mind"; it is part of his natural inheritance. Individual morality—namely, ethics—evolves in proportion to the degree of self-knowledge. Although minds are individual, this underlying principle applies to all of them. The thinkers of the neo-Platonic tradition always emphasize that it is the capacity for self-knowledge that gives life to all the other types of knowledge and makes the world meaningful. As Money-Kyrle puts it: "The morality of different individuals does approximate to a common type as their inner worlds approximate to truth. And this type is humanistic" (1961, p. 130). He explains that

> I claim only that people who are wise in the Greek sense of knowing themselves would tend to have the same humanistic *type* of morality—irrespective of the mores of the society in which they happen to have been nurtured. But many of the specific obligations accepted by them as moral would still be relative to their membership of this society. [*ibid.*, n. 1]

The morality of a culture is manifest in specific types of behaviour; the ethics of an individual, however, relate to the private motivation behind such manifestations: the logical pattern of growth indicated by the Grid, the poetic spirit of humanism. Merely following a moral code allows for the possibility of "doing the right deed for the wrong reason" as T. S. Eliot put it in *Murder in the Cathedral* (1935). Morality is relative; ethics are of the essence, and are object-inspired. Morality can also be a vehicle for lies, when tyrannically applied, as Bion examines in *Attention and Interpretation* (1970, pp. 102–105); "The lie is a falsity associated with morals" (p. 117).[4] The nature of the mind, unlike the body, is that it appears to have infinite potential for growth, and could, therefore, be said to *need* to grow in order to keep its essential humanity in a healthy condition. The patient in analysis is one whose capacity for growth—for ethical evolution—has got stuck, and the analyst also needs to grow from this experience.

This reformulates the possibility of "cure" in analysis, not in terms of something ever achieved or achievable, but in terms of the patient's new contact with himself being of sufficient quality and *Cure* endurance to be able to continue. Cure, according to Bion, is a Siren song that avoids contemplating the significance of the "journey": the analytic process itself (1985, p. 52). Analytic "success" depends on the patient having sufficiently introjected a capacity for learning from experience to be able to carry on his self-analysis. This is to be distinguished from social adaptability, normality, or relief from symptoms, and it is dependent on a particular type of learning from example: that is, learning from the analyst's capacity to think about the patient. This, like the mother and baby, is an artistic mode of cognition: identification with an inspiring process, rather than a fact. Meltzer writes:

> If the practice of psychoanalysis is an art, as I firmly believe, and its findings are those of a descriptive science, it is essential that it be done by individuals who can think for themselves . . . It is not possible to make observations and find a language for transformation without there being a Model of the World in the back of the mind. The process of discovery of new phenomena is completely dependent on the explicit and conscious use of a model in order to recognize the emergence into one's awareness of phenomena which cannot be described by the existing model. The evolution of the science is of this inductive–deductive spiral nature, that novel phenomena require an extension of the model, and this extension opens to view other phenomena which not only could not be described before, but could not even be recognized. [Meltzer & Williams, 1988, p. 204]

In this model, the scientific knowledge gained by psychoanalysis and the artistic mode of attaining it are interdependent. Together, they result in a spiral progression. This is owing to the peculiar nature of the mind as an ever-growing, suprasensuous, but still natural, domain, in which the instrument of observation is the same as the object that is observed, making it the "perfect science" (Meltzer, 1983, p. 164). Bion writes, "However prolonged a psychoanalysis may be, it represents only the start of an investigation. It stimulates growth of the domain it investigates" (1970, p. 69).

This view of psychoanalysis's function aligns it more closely with traditional poetic philosophies such as that of Coleridge, who talks about the "shaping spirit of imagination" and how to stimulate the stalled personality by reactivating the "principle of growth" within the mind, as discussed more fully in Chapter Three. This is the same principle that, according to Wordsworth, man brings with him as an infant "trailing clouds of glory" as part of his innate inheritance from those Platonic realms of truth. He described the infant mind's suckling at the fountain of truth as "what we half perceive and half create", indicating not the child's omnipotence but the rhythm of introjection and projection. As Money-Kyrle said, the goal of psychoanalytic theory is "to envisage and describe, as it were from within, the way in which [the child] both discovers and in a sense creates the world he lives in" (1961, p. 61). Psychoanalysis tries to re-establish the process of learning from experience by means of the transference relationship between patient and analyst. It is one activity in a wider world-view in which man is perpetually searching for the next "idea" to feed his mind and fulfil his nature.

The new idea

What is this idea, this principle that attends the infant mind in clouds of glory? Both Bion and Meltzer distinguish between the *feeling* of newness that accompanies a reinvigorated idea, and the age-old treasury of human consciousness which has already come across that same idea in some form or other. "'Tis new to thee", as the jaded Prospero informs Miranda—the old scientist speaking to the ever-renewed faculty of wonder and admiration that is successor to his outgrown island mind. Recognition, founded on Platonic pre-conception, replaces invention as the cornerstone of creativity, recognition being "the basic act in cognitive development" (Money-Kyrle, 1978, p. 422). As Bion writes:

> It is most unlikely that any of us will discover something new. I have never found out anything which has not already been discovered ... the desire to believe in the creative person obscures the capacity to discriminate between uniqueness and originality or creativeness. [Bion, 1973–1974, Vol. II, p. 58]

Indeed, the wisdom of Solomon, as cited by Bacon himself, was that "there is no new thing upon the earth" (*Essays*, 1625; Bacon, 1985,

p. 228). Bion stresses that creativity is not to be confused with "uniqueness" and, in fact, depends on acknowledgement of one's internal "ancestors". Meltzer, like Bion, suggests that "creativity does not seem to mean new ideas" but rather the ability to

> develop the received ideas to . . . levels of aesthetic and spiritual values. From this point of view science and art are completely indistinguishable and the great peril is in the area of implementation, of action. [Meltzer, 1995b][5]

He thinks these categories should replace Bion's "scientific deduction" and "algebraic calculus" in the Grid, as the culminating phases of thought production; and that Bion himself implicitly confirmed this modification of the Grid in the *Memoir*. The aesthetic–spiritual level is dominated by the ethos of internal objects, and communication takes over from action: for "the concept of experimental action as a necessity when thought has reached its limit belongs to the computational world" (Meltzer, 2005a, p. 422).

This makes the new idea more fearful or awesome, not less. It is reinvigorated by its roots in that basic, fundamental constellation of emotions that Meltzer, pursuing Bion's implications, calls "aesthetic conflict" (see Chapter Two). In Bion's philosophy, the "new idea", which is always on the horizon in any analytic session, is feared. It causes premonitions of catastrophic anxiety. Like the new baby, it can appear a "monster" to the established complacency of the personality. In Meltzer's extension of this philosophy, it is feared for *the impact of its beauty*:

> If we follow Bion's thought closely, we see that the new idea presents itself as an "emotional experience" of the beauty of the world and its wondrous organization, descriptively closer to Hamlet's "heart of mystery". [Meltzer & Williams, 1988, p. 20]

Meltzer describes the impact of Bion's thinking on his own in similar terms (1986, p. 204). The beauty is an essential function of its relationship with the unattainable truth, the noumenon, the mystery. As Keats described the threshold of knowledge:

> The Chamber of Maiden Thought becomes gradually darkened and at the same time on all sides of it many doors are set open—but all dark—all leading to dark passages—We see not the balance of good

and evil. We are in a Mist—We are now in that state—We feel the "burden of the Mystery". [Letter to Reynolds, 3 May 1818: Keats, 1970a, p. 95]

In Keats's image, as with Milton's "things invisible to mortal sight", the effect of a "sharpening vision" is, paradoxically, to experience the clouded mist-mystery, owing to the marriage of darkness and brightness and the conflicting simultaneous emotions of love and hate: the "aesthetic conflict". According to Keats, this is how "the thinking principle" is born within us. When Bion, in his later work, begins to write of aesthetic impact, it is likewise to emphasize the strangeness and discomfort of the idea that this could lie at the heart of the poetic spirit, the "O" of both psychoanalysis and the truth of the session: "I cannot support this conviction by evidence regarded as scientific. It may be that the formulation belongs to the domain of *aesthetic*" (Bion, 1965, p. 37).

A certain discomfort and puzzlement appears to adhere to this strange transition. Is it the "mental pain" that, according to Meltzer's interpretation of Bion, "arises at that point in growth of a thought where it becomes fixed in dream-myth" (1978a, Vol. III, p. 64). This "fixing" is the point at which a preconception is formed, ready to seek a reciprocal realization in the world or the consulting room, a thought. It is a process of aesthetic organization.

Clinical work by Meltzer and others with whom he has worked has illustrated the principle that, if the baby cannot introject the idea that it is experienced by its mother as beautiful, it will imagine itself to be the product of an ugly secret parental union (like Edmund in *King Lear*) and, guided by this, be unable to become beautiful, that is, to develop as a human being. Nowhere is this more poignantly illustrated than in Romana Negri's work with premature infants, in which she concludes, "We can see clearly how a child's 'beauty and weight' are directly related to its viability" (Negri, 1994, p. 19). In the clinical experience here referred to, it is suggested that the primal, mutual experience of "beauty" between mother and child is essential to the baby's ability to develop, and, in the case of premature infants, even to its ability to survive.

The concept of the aesthetic conflict is a particular leap in psychoanalytic theory that would not have been possible without assimilating the implications of Bion's instruction to forgo memory and desire and to enter into a state of "reverie" which enables the analyst to focus only on the present experience. In other words, he has to put aside his "knowledge"—what he knows about the patient, what he knows about psychoanalytic theory—and, for that period, he has to become an artist rather than a scientist. Instead of searching for knowledge, he must wait for inspiration. As Martha Harris writes:

> Like Keats and many another poet [Bion] seems to regard truth as inevitably linked with beauty, and became in later years increasingly concerned with the problem of giving some fitting expression to the poetry of intimate personal relationships. [1980; 1987a, p. 341]

She quotes Bion on how psychoanalytic interpretations would be much improved if they "stood up to aesthetic criticism", meaning, they would be *closer to the truth*. It is the feeling of beauty which is growth inducing, inspiring. This is what organizes the different vertices, the conflicting emotions, into a meaningful pattern; this is what enables "alpha function" or symbol formation to take place. The feeling of psychoanalytic conviction belongs to the domain of the aesthetic, or, as Keats said, "I never feel certain of any truth but from a clear perception of its Beauty" (letter to G. and G. Keats, December 1818–January 1819; 1970, p. 187).

Bion and Meltzer both stress the strenuous quality of the psychoanalytic reverie; although imaginative, it is work, not holiday. The pattern emerges from the work in some sensuously apprehensible yet intuited form that parallels the physician's literal sensory apparatus. Probably, it takes the form of a dream-like image—the analyst's dream—that contains the reflected meaning of the patient's emotional experience. The therapeutic potential of psychoanalysis depends on this actually happening at the present time in the session. Remembering or reconstructing infantile memories on behalf of the patient would be a different thing: organizational (via hindsight), but not in itself growth inducing. It is part of the scientific nexus of interpretation. This accumulated body of knowledge is also necessary, but it has to be kept in abeyance ("forgotten") while reverie is operating. Reverie gives interpretations a different status in the texture of the analytic process, less dogmatic even when "correct", since they are known to be only a limited expression of the scientific truth. One function of interpretation is to maintain the verbal medium, to keep it going, along with its musical or non-lexical aspects. For the emotional truth of the situation is captured by artistic means, in the dream resulting from reverie.

It is the artistic imagination that can discern patterns in the void and infinite, despite its darkness, chaos, and ugliness. This is where, given the right degree of tension, it overlaps with the scientific vertex. It is in the nature of art to find a structural way into the meaning by seeking out the existing contrasts and contrary linkages: delighting in the "light and shade necessary to a poem", as Keats said (1970, p. 398). Hazlitt called this "gusto"; Blake called it "energy", something that "exists", while the smooth "negations" of correctness and conventional beauty do not really exist, in psychic reality. Where a beautiful or smooth surface presents itself, the artistic orientation feels the urge to roughen and uglify it in order to reveal the idea that is imprisoned underneath or within it (as in Michelangelo's famous description of stone-hewing). In Coleridge's terms, it "dissolves in order to recreate" (1997, p. 175).

Bion notes, on various occasions, that art can make something beautiful out of something ugly or frightening (e.g., 1980, p. 18). It has also been noted by others. What precisely is meant? It is often said that the beauty of art consists in providing a containing form for ugly or intolerable facets of mentality so that they are no longer frightening: they can be held at arm's length as it were, without threatening a personal attack on the beholder. This may indeed be one of the services provided by art, but it is of a very limited nature and is not at the heart of Bion's vision, which is tied to his concept of catastrophic change (to be discussed in more detail in Chapter Two).

Probably we should take it that anything that has meaning is beautiful. It appears ugly when the meaning is not known. There is a beauty in Oedipus's self-blinding, or Cleopatra's suicide, which has nothing to do with self-violation but, rather, has to do with self-transcendence. Beauty relates to the aspirational function of the object, rather than to its comforting or consolatory aspect. Art, therefore, does not seek to beautify, to impose order on chaos, but to uncover or discover the hidden beauty of the subject: the "golden world" of ideal forms as Sidney expressed it in 1580 in his "Defence of Poesy". The aspirational search differs from the "idealization" of psychoanalytic jargon, which is essentially a form of narcissism.

The hidden beauty of ideas is imagined, but not known. Essentially, it entails condensation (narrowing down, selecting, focusing under pressure of the medium and its enforced limitations), destroying the open-endedness of the situation. In other words, symbol formation. Art responds to the "selected fact" that can organize all the other elements, pulling them into order, so that meaning shines out from within. Yet, the new idea always carries with it an ambiguous aura: "Did it come from God or the Devil?", as Emily Brontë posed the question about her satanic hero Heathcliff in *Wuthering Heights*. One of Bion's characters in the *Memoir* (another "little devil") calls it "psyche-lodgement". Milton and Blake say it happens in microscopic "moments" of sleep or dreaming.

If mental illness may be considered ugly, then the attraction of both analyst and patient may be considered to be the hidden truth, the beauty of the latent idea or symbol which has been covered up or "reversed", made negative. The idea awaits reversal of this claustrophobic negative state. In order to reveal it, analysts generally agree on the need to find a private language that makes communication possible, which means, says Bion, being "some kind of a poet" as well as a scientist or religious person (Bion, 1973–1974, Vol. I, p. 32): treating psychoanalysis as a complex artistic or presentational form rather than a simple discursive or didactic procedure.

Artistic intuition, reverie, counter-dreaming, is a sharpened attentiveness that overrides the tendency to omnipotently explain that can hamper the scientific vertex, or the tendency to moralize that hampers the religious vertex. It has no interest in those unaesthetic types of smoothness; in fact, it relishes the contrast in vertices. Art can hold the uncomfortable roughness of contradiction and incomprehensibility, and can readjust the tension between science and religion in a way that makes their contrary qualities constructive, delighting in their "light and shade" without the need to smother them in grey compromise. The mental expansion facilitated by art has been conjectured to derive from its prehistoric "decompartmentalization" of existing forms of knowledge (Mithen, 1996, p. 222), in particular the fundamental ones of science and religion, thus making metaphor and analogy possible, and the possibility of simultaneous existence in different worlds. "Metaphor" means, like transference, to bear or carry meaning, and implies an increase of meaning beyond that of its separate components. The new idea, as Coleridge said, arrives in the shape of a symbol and has a life of its own, with the consequence that (as Bion pointed out) it can also be "killed": "A foetal idea can be killed, and that is not a metaphor *only*" (Bion, 1991, p. 417).

In conclusion: if psychoanalysis is an art form, with a scientific (as well as a humanitarian) objective, the following factors are worth bearing in mind.

1.   The artistic "reverie" encourages speed and depth in thinking, making connections beyond conscious control.

2.   It strengthens the tolerance of not understanding, since this is an accepted part of artistic method. So, there is less temptation to fill gaps in knowledge with omnipotent or authoritarian explanations.

3.   Many interdisciplinary possibilities open up which a single-vertex analogy with physical science would have closed.

4.   Of course, in so far as "artistic" analysis is "real", it involves the danger inherent in any real situation to end in disaster, as when repressed conflicts emerge which the personality of either analyst or analysand is not strong enough to endure. As Bion constantly reiterates, any analyst who is going to see a patient the next day should experience fear. It might plausibly be claimed that a purely scientific mode is safer because nothing really happens. But this has its corresponding dangers, or at least disappointments, if it results in failure of development. Bion asks, indeed, what is "the price" for *not* engaging in the dangerous flood of life, such as that required by "helping one's fellow men", and reminds us: "For though the Soul should die, the Body lives forever" (1991, p. 257). As Martha Harris reminds us: "The personality is ossified by identification with closed minds and can be preserved alive only through developing and risking itself"(1978; Harris, 1987c, p. 178).

5.   Allowing the clinical participation to be artistic enables a distinction to be maintained between "thinking about" (outside the session) and experiencing scientific and artistic modes of inquiry. If these are recognized as being different paths towards knowledge, they can interdigitate more fruitfully and support one another.

This should enhance both enjoyment of the beauty of the method and the personal advantages which derive from regarding one's workplace as a "Chamber of Maiden Thought" (Keats) rather than as one of horrors.

Artistic method, unlike scientific method, cannot be taught, only imbibed. It is learnt by example. The way to learn artistic method is to identify with (introject) a model of the mind in which the aesthetic has a central place; the implications of this will be discussed in Chapter Five. The theory of the aesthetic conflict makes the psychoanalytic method itself the aesthetic object: in the religious vertex, the godhead, or noumenon (see Meltzer & Williams, 1988, p. 23). This it is which governs the process and guides the analyst in his search for meaning. It is not the analyst who is conducting the analysis; rather, it is being conducted by his objects in communion with the internal objects of the patient. It is imperative that the emotional drama should be a *present* experience, otherwise this communion cannot take place. Psychoanalysis would still be two-dimensional, a "talking about" rather than a "becoming". In this way, Bion's emphasis on eschewing memory and desire provided a missing link, which was necessary before Meltzer could elucidate the function of "beauty" in clinical psychoanalysis, through the concept of the aesthetic conflict.

This enabled a new structural link between psychoanalysis and art forms such as literature, which has, as yet, only begun to be developed. For psychoanalysis is, according to Meltzer, "a new method as old as religion and art but less pretentious than Baconian science, less authoritarian than the Church, more poorly implemented than the arts which have developed their craft for several millennia" (1980; 1994b, p. 473). The huge amount of knowledge about the mind that has come to be stored in artforms over the centuries takes on a new relevance for psychoanalysis, while, correspondingly, psychoanalytic ideas and practice have the potential to help with our problems in accessing the knowledge that is stored in art. In acknowledging their place in this ancient tradition, and pursuing its implications, "the analysts of today may be laying the foundations of a science of great grandeur in the future, in the way that the alchemists laid the groundwork for modern chemistry and its astonishing accomplishments" (Meltzer & Williams, 1988, p. 23).

Notes

1. Meltzer's original view of psychoanalysis as a science became (like Bion's) progressively modified by the need to incorporate its artistic qualities, first with regard to the autobiographical nature of its research (see, for example, 1983, p. 165), and then with regard to the craftsmanship of the method itself.

2. Letter to Williamson, 11 November 1823 (1956, Vol. V, p. 309).

3. Lines from *Endymion* quoted by Keats in a letter to Taylor, 30 January 1818 (1970a, p. 59). Keats said that writing that "Argument will perhaps be of the greatest Service to me of any thing I ever did—It set before me at once the gradations of Happiness even like a kind of Pleasure Thermometer".

4. Also associated in Bion with the "overpowering culture of non-conformist Protestant cant", which he felt inhibited his sexuality in his youth (Bion, 1985, p. 43).

5. See also Meltzer 2005a, where he writes of replacing Bion's final categories G and H (scientific deductive system and algebraic calculus) "by more Kierkegaardian categories of aesthetic and spiritual" (p. 422).

CHAPTER TWO

Aesthetic concepts of Bion and Meltzer

I n *The Claustrum*, Meltzer writes that the "heart of post-Kleinian psychology" consists in the addition of geographic and episte- mological aspects of mental functioning to Freud's original categories of dynamic, genetic, structural, and economic. He then adds, "Whether the aesthetic aspect will eventually take on suffi- cient distinctness to add a seventh category remains to be seen" (1992, p. 50). To help give "distinctness" to the aesthetic category is essentially the aim of this book.

In this chapter, I would like to review two of the key concepts at the heart of the Bion–Meltzer model of the mind: Meltzer's "aesthetic conflict" and Bion's "catastrophic change". They are key concepts because they structure the whole process of "learning from experience" in Bion's particular sense of that phrase: the process of mental development with all its ethical, emotional, and cognitive implications. Any vital work of art can be said to be *about* them, and they embrace all the other aesthetic concepts of Bion and Meltzer: the thought without a thinker, the observer–observed, the positive and negative Grid, container–contained (Bion), the "gener- ative" theatre of meaning, dimensionality, reciprocity (Meltzer), the "combined object" that governs the ethics of the inner world, and the relinquishment of memory and desire (Bion)—Keats's "negative capability".

In Bion's view there is no pain without imagination, and, in the absence of pain, no mental life. There is instead a "nothingness" for which many types of activity may be a "cover", ranging from the depredations of war and terrorism to the apparently civilized procedures of the debating chamber or of impeccable psychoanalytic "technique" (1991, p. 610). Bion's advice was to "stick close to the firing line", that is, to the realities of mental pain, because the bloodshed let loose by non-combatants behind the scenes can be appalling, whether internal or external (2005a, p. 95). His writings are imbued with a sense of danger regarding the very real possibility that mental life can be extinguished if imagination is not, at the very least, "given an airing" (1997, p. 47) and, it is to be hoped, involved in the disciplined process of "imaginative conjecture" that underpins both the generation of meaning in the individual psyche and the evolution of psychoanalysis as an inspired science. Failing this, psychoanalysis is likely to become "extinct", as have other non-viable or over-complicated species of animal and intellectual existence: hence, the need to learn to tolerate "catastrophic change". What is required is the aesthetic orientation to reality that both Bion and Meltzer see as poetically implicit in Mrs Klein's concept of the "depressive position".

Although "catastrophic change" was formulated first, since "aesthetic conflict" comes first generically in terms of psychic development (unless we count birth as the first catastrophe), I shall consider the concepts in that order.

Aesthetic conflict

The "aesthetic conflict", elaborated in *The Apprehension of Beauty* (Meltzer & Williams, 1988) and its metaphysical companion, *The Claustrum* (Meltzer, 1992), was first formulated by Meltzer in *Studies in Extended Metapsychology* (1986) and adumbrated as early as *The Psychoanalytical Process* (1967). Its genesis, as a concept, lies in three fields: the first is clinical work, in particular that with autistic children, which Meltzer said provided a "key" to failures in symbol formation owing to a lack of dimensionality. The second field is that of baby observation, as a result of the influence of Esther Bick and Martha Harris; the third lies in the aesthetic appreciation of poetry and the speculations of poetic philosophy. Milton's term for the phenomenon of aesthetic conflict was "the hateful siege of contraries", as experienced by Satan in response to the beauty of the earth (*Paradise Lost*, IX: 121–122); and it was Wordsworth who, in his description of how the babe "gathers passion from his mother's eye", first wrote of "that most apprehensive habitude" which is the generative ground for personality development (*The Prelude*, II: 232–40). I would like to say more about the poetic roots of the aesthetic conflict, but first, to summarize briefly the fundamental vision which the concept denotes.

In *Extended Metapsychology*, Meltzer writes that

> psychoanalytical observation and infant observation declare, as do the poets, that the "aesthetic conflict" in the presence of the object is primary over the conflicts of separation, deprivation and frustration to which so much thought has been devoted. [1986, p. 182]

It is this major reorientation towards the highly complex problems of normal development that brings psychoanalytic epistemology into line with the poets and with the mother–baby relationship. In relation to the latter, Meltzer writes in his paper on Money-Kyrle:

> Perhaps it has been the experience of listening to mother–baby observation seminars in the last few years that has so impressed on me the inadequacy of the psychoanalytic model . . . to describe the nuances and complexities of that primary relationship. [1981; 1994c, p. 503]

Meltzer associates the "daily beauty" (*Othello*) in a child's life with his or her "quest for knowledge and understanding" (Meltzer & Williams, 1988, p. 54), and believes that the beauty of a newborn baby lies not in its appearance, but, rather, in its "baby-ishness . . . which "sets us peering into its future" (*ibid.*, p. 57), though he is well aware that most mothers would disagree that a baby is not beautiful also in the straightforward sense. In *The Apprehension of Beauty*, he writes:

> No flower or bird of gorgeous plumage imposes upon us the mystery of the aesthetic experience like the sight of a young mother

with her baby at the breast. We enter such a nursery as we would a cathedral or the great forests of the Pacific coast, noiselessly, bare-headed . . . [Winnicott] was right to use that word "ordinary", with its overtones of regularity and custom, rather than the statistical "average". The aesthetic experience of the mother with her baby is ordinary, regular, customary, for it has millennia behind it, since man first saw the world "as" beautiful. And we know this goes back at least to the last glaciation. [Meltzer & Williams, 1988, p. 16]

The first known art dates from 35,000 years ago, and constitutes durable evidence of man seeing the world as beautiful, since the art-object (whatever its ostensible function) is always a response to the perception of beauty, and this indicates something special about human mentality, perhaps even indicating the evolutionary point at which mind evolved from brain. One might even speculate further and wonder whether it was *homo sapiens'* capacity to apprehend beauty with religious awe that enabled him (by contrast with the Neanderthals) to survive the Ice Age. And, if so, whether paying attention to our apprehension of beauty rather than to our weapons of mass destruction might not be as useless as it appears.

"Aesthetic conflict" entails seeing mental growth as an aesthetic function founded on reciprocity between the internal infant mind and its internal objects, beginning with the actual infant's response to mother-as-the-world, which serves as prototype for all subsequent mental explorations. It is the complex experience of the beauty of the world together with the desire to know it that sets in motion the peculiarly human activity of symbol-making, a function of "the aesthetic level" of mentality (Meltzer, 1986, p. 200). Symbols, like intimate relationships, represent our "striving to speak the inward sense of things" (Harris) and are ordinary acts of homage to the principle of beauty in the world.

The godhead is initially the breast as combined object, a discovery of Klein's that, like all new (or rediscovered) ideas, she regarded with a hint of ambivalence. Rediscovered, because it is in the Augustinian tradition that the beauty of the universe was created by God as a compound of opposites. The "combined object" (male–female internal parents in conjunction) was discovered by Klein through her work with children; and although she was initially impressed by its persecutory potential, she later came to see in it "a quality not clearly visible in the external parents—

namely, its essential privacy and perhaps sacredness" (Meltzer, 1991; 2005c, p. xvi).The combined object is the source of trust and also of distrust, so Klein felt it could be overwhelming to the infant mind (Meltzer, 1978a, Vol. II, p. 113). Its beauty is the source or governing quality from which emotional richness and ethical qualities such as goodness and strength are derived, and it is in relation to this combined object with its potentiality for "passionate love" (Bion, 1991, p. 183) that ultimately, "all work is sexual in its meaning" (Meltzer, 1973, pp. 94, 130). Yet, although the very first response is to "the dazzle of the sunrise" (Meltzer & Williams, 1988, p. 29), founded on the impact of sensuous beauty, this is almost immediately clouded by the ambiguity of the mother's unknown and unknowable insides. Her mental contents—the human face of Bion's "O"—arouse a "tormenting uncertainty" (Meltzer, 1992, p. 61). This is the ugliness that sharpens the perception of beauty in the *presence* of the object. Consequently, the twin emotions of love and hate come into being, and the fluctuations in tolerability of their combined impact set into perpetual oscillation the value orientations of Ps (paranoid–schizoid) and D (depressive).[2] The stability of the depressive position lies not in the achievement of a comfortable stasis, but in the strengthening of the personality through an improved capacity to withstand envy and destructiveness.

When the impact of beauty is too overwhelming, it may be modified not by containment, but by vulgarity, which has its uses. See the poem "Switzerland" by Roland Harris:

It is a relief to descend to the towns . . .
Hotels and public buildings indistinguishable;
A certain grossness of piety, unaware
Of the terrible aspect of the godhead.

A relief, a balancing truth, that leaves
The immaculate mountainry; so that it would be torture
In Spring with all her blossom, to the implacable

Glory of winter, to see so much perfection—
The magical hills, made "rather recently,
Geologically speaking, of fish bones"—and decorated with
                            frozen water.

Not all turnings-away from the impact of the aesthetic object are pathological; they may also be a dilution necessary to making everyday living tolerable. As Keats said, "a man should have the fine point of his soul taken off to be fit for this world" (letter to Reynolds, 22 November 1817; 1970a, p. 40).

Following the birth of the apprehension of beauty, it is the creative tension between love (L) and hate (H), and the oscillation of Ps↔D in a field of value flux, that governs the development of thought processes. It can be seen that this flux has both structural and ethical implications. The tension sets in motion the desire to *know* the aesthetic object, and this, in turn, affects the way the mind is formed and structured. Beauty, as Bion says, "aids formulation" (1991, p. 588). It is growth inducing, and, reciprocally, "growth is the principle of our beauty" (Roland Harris, "The schoolroom empties").Yet, as with any dominant drive, the infant mind can rebel against its very dominance: hence, Bion's interpretation of self-murder as rebellion against the impulse to exist (1991, p. 609), or Meltzer's description of "mindlessness" in autistic children—a state which absolves itself from the pain of aesthetic conflict, but also from the undesirability of attacking the mother, by substituting an adhesive identification for a projective one.

For it is not just the epistemophilic urge that is by nature dangerous, painful, ugly, and monstrous, which led Melanie Klein to be wary of its potential destructiveness, and to see it as a type of attack on the mother or aesthetic object. The withdrawal from the epistemophilic urge is equally dangerous, as Bion points out in his oft-recounted fable of Virgil's Palinurus, who falls asleep at the rudder owing to his lack of curiosity about the apparent smoothness of the Mediterranean (latency). "What has happened to the storm?" It has "no features" (2005a, pp. 101–102). But the storm is *there*, whether you can see it or not. Sleeping can be either an opportunity to meet the truth of one's psychic condition, or it can be an attempt to escape from it. The latter is far more catastrophic—in the sense of disaster—than simply acting-out like the rest of the adolescent fleet. The rudder of attention is torn from its sub-thalamic keel.

Bion and Meltzer, therefore, affirm the healthy necessity of the epistemophilic urge: "Inquiry", or "Oedipus", as Bion first termed it in his Grid. They see it as the source of both scientific and artistic paths to knowledge: the scientific by means of exploration of the interior, and the artistic by waiting for the voice from the interior to speak out. These represent two complementary types of attention, the "penetrating" and the "passive" (Meltzer, 1986, p. 181), and they relate to the tension between knowing the inside and the outside of the object. Both are distinct from the intrusive identification that seeks to control the inside of the object (as in "Promethean" science), associated with magic and violence. It was the need to restore value to the epistemophilic urge that led to this differentiation between communicative and intrusive types of projection. The inspired types of both art and science come under the aegis of the depressive position, attained through communicative projective identification (*ibid.*, p. 191). This has the balancing quality of the "religious vertex" in Bion's formulation of the "three vertices" of science, art, and religion; when these engage in a tension which is neither too loose nor too slack, they act together to "further the aim of truth" and lead the personality into the unknown realms of its future being (Bion, 1973–1974, Vol. I, p. 96). The mind has engaged with "becoming".

Science, art, and religion are thus complementary facets of every mind, and need to be deployed simultaneously once the epistemophilic instinct has been aroused through aesthetic conflict. The vertices constitute a creative tension, but not a value flux. The value flux relates to the different types of identification that prevail in relation to the aesthetic object; these may be either growth promoting, or growth retarding. The infant mind, whatever its given attributes, then sets forth to prove itself and to develop its individual ethics in the context of alternative orientations to the aesthetic object. Meltzer describes this as "breasting the current", meaning, resisting the temptation to either conform or to rebel (1986, p. 20); Keats described it as turning a "world of circumstances" into an opportunity for "soul-making" (1970, p. 249).

The struggle between intrusive and communicative types of projection in relation to the aesthetic conflict is nowhere better illustrated than in *Hamlet*, as the protagonist searches for the "undiscovered country" of his future self and becomes caught in a play-world where internal mystery is treated as political secrecy, and there is no space for symbolic reciprocity. The idea of "playing" becomes a byword for manipulation, rather than for discovery through art.*

---

*For a full discussion of *Hamlet* (from which this paragraph is taken) see "The Undiscovered Country" (Williams 1988a).

In *Hamlet*, all types of acting and action tend to be false moves rather than fictions about revelation; they are all "actions that a man might play". Instead, playing is contrasted with the idea of "holding"—the capacity to observe without interpreting, which comes to focus substantially on Hamlet's relationship with Horatio, as in, "If thou didst ever hold me in thy heart", or:

> Give me that man
> That is not passion's slave, and I will wear him
> In my heart's core, ay, in my heart of heart,
> As I do thee. [*Hamlet*, III.iii. 71–74]

Balanced against this prototype of a psychoanalytic "holding" space is the ambiguous lobby of dreams, in which Hamlet makes vain attempts to symbolically contain his own thoughts about the aesthetic object that may or may not be embodied in Ophelia. His knife-edge internal struggle is not helped by parental figures from the court (Horatio is an outsider) but is instead aggravated by their intrusive curiosity, as brought to a head in the "lobby" scene. The Lobby is partly open to the sky, making a sort of artificial outside within the claustrophobic heart of the court; it is the place where Polonius and Hamlet discuss the shapes of the clouds, and Hamlet implies that the shape of the prince he is looking for is not that of a camel or a weasel or a whale; a place which Hamlet regards as but one step from the grave, as when Polonius asks him: "Will you walk out of the air, my lord?" and he answers "Into my grave?" The Lobby as a space also echoes the Ghost's "prison-house" of purgatory, whose "secrets" he is "forbid to tell". All in all, it is ambiguous as to whether the Lobby is a chamber of dreams or a prison for nightmares. In it the prince is "bounded in a nutshell", rehearsing the interaction between infinite space and bad dreams.

The turbulence which disturbs the narcissistic yet unformed shape of the adolescent mind is described in the following poem by Roland Harris:

> There is a stream quite near to me,
> I thought I knew it well,
> But tonight as I stared down to its depths
> I didn't recognise myself.
> The above me broke up loud
> Into a thousand places and smashed my face

In the stream, and for my life
I couldn't fit me together again.
My nose was sunk and out of view
My eyes twisted and apart
My mouth turned down upon a wave.

Yet all I long for is calm clear water
And life to survive around
Me. For love to grow well through my veins
And peace forever after.
To be left alone with those I love
For this endless turmoil to cease, to cease.
I'm afraid that the only way
To find this previous life
Is to run a knife right through my heart
And end the confusion emotion presents.
                    [Harris, "There is a stream", unpublished]

The "confusion emotion presents" shatters the self-image of the adolescent who, like the original Narcissus, sought confirmation of his identity in a reflection in a stream, but like Humpty Dumpty, finds he cannot put the pieces together again. Confusion is the key to developmental change; for turbulence, in Bion's terms, is where O "intersects" with the human condition (Bion, 1973–1974, Vol. II, p. 30); it makes the invisible visible. One of his frequent and favourite symbols of such turbulence is the swirling lines of hair and water drawn by Leonardo:

I would not be able to see a stream which was flowing smoothly without any obstacle to disturb it because it would be so transparent. But if I create a turbulence by putting in a stick, then I can see it. Similarly, the human mind may set up a turbulence, and some sensitive, intuitive and gifted mind, like the one we call Leonardo da Vinci, can draw pictures of turbulence reminiscent of hair and water. He can translate this turbulence and transform it by making marks on paper and canvas which are clearly visible to us. But we may not so easily "see" this turbulence in the world that we call the mind. [Bion 1973–1974, Vol. I, pp. 41–42]

As in Bion's favourite story of Palinurus, the steadfast helmsman, the adolescent mind (the mind on the verge of catastrophic change) may hope for "calm clear water" but cannot avoid the pain of the emotional crux: the stick–knife–keel that pierces the cloudy, watery surface of his latency intentions and reveals the reality of the mind.

The aesthetic conflict replaces the Freudian–Kleinian duality of life and death instincts with a polarity between vital emotional conflict, and cynical avoidance of emotional conflict. Klein saw this fundamental tension as beginning to operate immediately after birth, and Bion and Meltzer place its primitive prototypal origins even earlier. The tension between love and hate, when fully experienced "on the pulses" (as Keats would say) leads to truthful self-knowledge. This composite, complex life-force differs distinctively from the idea of a love or life "instinct" and from the idea of pleasure *vs.* unpleasure. It is bound up, as Bion often points out, with "linking" and the capacity to tolerate emotional links. Evil or anti-developmental forces are no longer considered as hate or envy, but, rather, as the negation of all emotionality in the form of the non-emotions of $-L$ and $-H$, which lead to a condition of $-K$, the absence or perversion of self-knowledge (Bion's Negative Grid). Shakespeare's Iago differs from Milton's Satan precisely in his non-emotionality, his "motiveless malignancy", as Coleridge put it. Hate and love "penetrate", Bion says, whereas "banality" does not (1991, p. 618). Like the knife–keel, this unearths the pain associated with an object that arouses both aspiration and the suspicion of abandonment—the archetypal anxiety that underlies all others. The aesthetic object acts as a magnet for emotional turbulence. Turbulence is a sign of the presence of both a human personality, and a basic or fundamental reality, an aspect of O. This is why all the poets speak, either explicitly or implicitly, of "that beauty which, as Milton sings, hath terror in it" (Wordsworth, *The Prelude*, XIII: 225–226). As Bion's character Roland puts it in *A Memoir of the Future*: "I admired the great storm clouds when they towered above the fields of golden corn. 'Robin', I used to say, 'we shall have to use the scythes when this storm has laid the corn flat'" (Bion, 1991, p. 479). The nipple-within-the-breast gives and also takes away; the combined object is not a comforting one.

The idea of "beauty" here is, thus, a complex one that contains within it the sense of ugliness and monstrosity. As Shakespeare put it in relation to Caliban, "this thing of darkness I acknowledge mine" (*The Tempest*, V.i.: 275). The therapeutic capacity of the aesthetic (beautiful) object does not result from denaturing the ugliness of destructive or painful emotions (as is sometimes said); on the contrary, the object retains its dangerous qualities. The beautiful psychoanalytic process should inspire fear at the beginning of each session, according to Bion. It is not the function of the aesthetic object to tame the wild animals of the "psychoanalytic zoo" (Bion, 1985, p. 200). It is not enough for the aesthetic object to be just a container; it must also be a transformer, and the full impact of beauty has this transforming power. As Keats put it in the context of explaining his concept Negative Capability: "with a great poet . . . the sense of Beauty overcomes every other consideration, or rather obliterates all consideration" and through the "intensity" of this pursuit, "all disagreeables evaporate, from their being in close relationship with Beauty and Truth" (letter to his brothers, 21, 27 December 1817; 1970a, pp. 42–43).

This goes back to eighteenth-century aesthetics and the play between the "sublime" and the "beautiful"; pleasant beauty is counterpoised to the Longinian sublime type of beauty (*hypsos*), which has associations with fear and defamiliarization, undermining our preconceptions of what is harmonious. The hidden inner beauty of ideas seems ugly and monstrous to the existing mind that does not want to become changed into whatever subsequent shape Fate or Necessity demand. The truth itself can appear "ugly and frightening" (Bion, 1977, p. 32). This is crucial to the theological aspect of this post-Kleinian model and to the role of psychoanalytic "faith", whose significance comes to the fore in relation to catastrophic change and symbol formation. It is a feature of the model that cannot be understood without a proper appreciation of "negative links" and how these are to be distinguished from the vitality of the positive linked emotions of love and hate with their infinite variations.

In *Extended Metapsychology*, Meltzer writes that the idea of "negative links" is "deeply foreign to the western tradition in philosophy and theology, but not to the Eastern one into which Bion's childhood had dipped him, like Achilles, at the hands of his ayah" (1986, p. 26). It was a view he later modified, since, in fact, this crucial polarity has never been foreign to the poets and poet-philosophers, and he came to recognize that Bion's −K is very much "in the tradition of Milton, Blake and Coleridge" and of other English poets (Meltzer & Williams, 1988, p. 19). In addition to welcoming the poets and their treasure-house of beautiful wisdom, Meltzer (1995b) also came to consider Bion's Grid as a structure of "real beauty", which posited the ultimate aim of thinking as not action but communication, and whose final category was aiming for the "aesthetic or spiritual", though it was only in the *Memoir* that Bion's vision of this really became clear (see Meltzer, 2005a, p. 422). Certainly, Bion himself regarded mathematics as a form of poetry, not as its antithesis, and quoted Valéry on this (1997, pp. 47–48), though he had to admit it was hard to communicate to ordinary listeners his personal faith in calculus as a universal aesthetic or "language of achievement", in Keats's sense.

The distinction between positive emotionality and negative or non-emotionality is the backbone of the Grid, even though it was not part of the initial formulation. This "fundamental" idea (in Bion's loaded term) is espoused by all the great poets, but nowhere more simply and vehemently than in the writings of William Blake, so I shall borrow Blake's exposition here to clarify the issue.* As with all poetic formulations, Blake's scheme of "negations" *vs.* "contraries" is both typical and idiosyncratic. Typical in so far as it supports the underlying poetic principle of mental development; idiosyncratic in so far as he has arrived at it by means of his own personal learning from experience. Personal "yet not alone" as Milton would say (*Paradise Lost*, VII, p. 28), since it evolved in response to conversations with his internal aesthetic object.

Blake describes human creativity in terms of the cleansing of vision that takes place when the vitality of the passions is acknowledged in "the marriage of heaven and hell". To *see* infinity is to *be* human, in the Blakean sense:

> If the doors of perception were cleansed every thing would appear to man as it is, infinite.

> For man has closed himself up, till he sees all things thro' narrow chinks of his cavern. [*The Marriage of Heaven and Hell*, 1790; Blake, 1966, p. 154]

This cleansing is achieved by means of aesthetic conflict, which, neo-Platonically, pierces through sense perception and makes

---

*The discussion of Blake here is based on "Blake: the mind's eye" in *The Chamber of Maiden Thought* (Williams & Waddell, 1991, pp. 70–81).

vision imaginative, expansive, and translucent, creating the "paradise within" that Milton foretold at the end of *Paradise Lost*. Milton's poetic struggle with the "siege of contraries" becomes Blake's doctrine: "Without Contraries is no progression. Attraction and Repulsion, Reason and Energy, Love and Hate, are necessary to Human Existence" (*The Marriage*, p. 149). For Blake, "contrary" emotions such as love and hate are evidence of a vital link with internal deities.[3]

"Negations", on the other hand, are the operation of the omnipotent selfhood; they serve the "reasoning power" in man, which, in Blake's terminology (different from that of Kant or Coleridge), means a specious type of deduction that constricts and imprisons the life of feeling. If perception is not redeemed through the inner tension of love and hate, man enters a state of spiritual "non-entity" or "error", which Blake, in his prophetic books, names Ulro, his own version of hell: a condition of self-imprisonment, bounded by meaningless sense impressions; the walls of the cavern, like Bion's cloak of beta-elements or Meltzer's Claustrum. Blake's view supersedes both the Christian doctrine of sin and repentance, and rationalist empiricism. Non-entity rather than sin comprises the evil to which man is prone, and is only reversible through the spiritual dynamism of contrary passions, which endow him with a complex vision. Bion's formulation of how a "no-emotion" comes to replace an emotion is very similar: "The absent fulfilment is experienced as a no-thing . . . There is thus created a domain of the non-existent" (Bion, 1970, p. 20).

It will be apparent that the Blakean use of the term "negative", like the Bionian (1980, pp. 68–69), is different from the "realm of the negative" as employed in some other psychoanalytic theories, where it is more or less synonymous with the term "unconscious". "Negations are not contraries", insists Blake; "Contraries mutually Exist; /But Negations Exist Not" (*Jerusalem*, Blake, 1966, p. 639); In the Blake–Bion usage, the "negative" refers to the passionless world that accounts for the evil that men inflict upon themselves. It is this lack of passion, rather than excessive passion, that results in "corporeal war", and the only remedy in Blake's view is "spiritual" or internal war. The negativity of the Claustrum has to be seen in conjunction with the aesthetic conflict aroused by the primordial experience of the mother-as-the-world. Blake calls his internal mother–world Jerusalem or Jesus; from this space the "Eternal Births of Intellect" emanate forth like "Infants". The "Treasures of Heaven", he writes, "are not Negations of Passion, but Realities of Intellect, from which all the Passions emanate Uncurbed in their Eternal Glory", and men are "cast out" from heaven only if they have "no Passions of their own because no Intellect" (*A Vision of the Last Judgment*, 1966, p. 613). Keats also frequently affirmed the developmental quality of a "mixed band" of passions in such phrases as, "I have the same Idea of all our Passions as of Love— they are all in their sublime, creative of essential Beauty" (letter to Bailey, 22 November 1817; 1970a, p. 37).

In other words, the world of anti-passion, or minus LHK, restricts not just imagination but thinking power: it is essentially stupid. As Meltzer points out:

> fortunately the forces in pursuit of truth are intelligent, and those against it are fundamentally stupid, dependent on negative imitation and perversion of the truth—or the best we can approximate to it: truthfulness of observation and thought. [Meltzer, 2005c, p. xix]

"Sooner murder an infant in its cradle than nurse unacted desires", Blake wrote provocatively (*The Marriage*, 1966, p. 149), meaning that desires or passions that achieve no aesthetic organization or fulfilment are, in effect, murdered infants in the world of the mind. The "sublime" form of the passions (in Keats's metaphor) is the result of a kind of chemical reaction that brings them in line with "essential" beauty and truth, the Platonic forms.

It follows from the formulation of "aesthetic conflict" that the entire world of psychopathology can be seen in terms of retreat from it (see Meltzer, 1986, p. 208), as seen, for example, in the vacant stare of the terrorist, the complacency of world leaders, the anonymity of the committee. The temptation to retreat from the emotionality aroused by beauty was most famously expressed in Hamlet's words: "What a piece of work is a man . . . in action how like an angel, in apprehension how like a god: the beauty of the world, the paragon of animals—and yet, to me, what is this quintessence of dust?" (*Hamlet*, II.ii: 303–308).

In Blake's philosophy, the vision of Jerusalem—the internal mother-and-babies—is recovered when man ceases to worship his own manufactured lies or "errors" (*A Vision*, 1966, p. 617). As soon as a person "ceases to behold" these constructions they vanish, very much on the lines of Bion's conception of the lie as a covering-over of a truth that is already "known" (1970, p. 100). A lie is something which "does not exist", says Blake; it resides in Bion's "domain of the non-existent", which houses all the "no-emotions" (Bion, 1970, p. 20).

Blake images the beauty of the world in Platonic–theological terms of a Sun that can be viewed in two ways, either as a source for ideas or shadowed by prejudices:

> "What," it will be Question'd, "When the Sun rises, do you not see a round disk of fire somewhat like a Guinea?' O no, no, I see an innumerable company of the Heavenly host crying "Holy, Holy, Holy is the Lord God Almighty." I question not my Corporeal or Vegetative Eye any more than I would Question a Window concerning a Sight. I look thro' it & not with it. [*A Vision of the Last Judgment*, Blake, 1966, p. 617]

This is what Meltzer is referring to when he distinguishes "invention" from "discovery", and Bion when he defines a "lie" as "a falsity associated with morals" (1970, p. 117). Stupidity, therefore, consists in idolizing what Bion calls *"trompe l'oeil"* visions—the limitations of one's own cleverness:

> The truth. What does it look like? Who wants to be confronted with a *trompe l'oeil* representation of Paradise? Such confections are pardonable to an agent selling us our earthly home, but not for our eternal home—our Self. [1980, pp. 126–127]

This sort of smooth false knowing is a single-vertex art, exalting magical infantile omnipotence to the point at which it becomes a lie. The lie is inseparable from its thinker (Bion, 1970, pp. 102–103); the truth exists beyond the thinker. The *trompe l'oeil* mentality indulges its own wishes without concern for the internal or external realities demanded by the religious and scientific vertices in creative tension. It cannot "point beyond" (Bion) to see through the glass even darkly, as in the familiar Pauline metaphor, succinctly expressed by George Herbert:

> A man that looks on glass
>   On it may stay his eye,
>   Or if he pleases through it pass
>   And then the heavens espy. ["The Elixir"][4]

The *trompe l'oeil* vision confuses the mystery of the inside of the aesthetic object with a secrecy to be decoded and imitated, painted over the glass like the "covering" of lies so often described by Bion. Over-emphasis on psychoanalytic technique, for example, can be just such a "cover" for lack of inspiration (Bion, 1991, p. 610). At the same time, so can memory and desire cloud the aesthetic object or underlying O.

Milton speaks more evocatively than any of the fear of falling on the Aleian field of error, "Erroneous there to wander and forlorn" (*Paradise Lost*, VII: 20). For him, error is to be bereft of inner guidance in one's vision—to have an "empty dream"—rather than to lie directly. The poet's fear, like Adam's, is of forlornness. But his Satan, who knows the truth and starts off with the clouded brightness of "archangel fall'n", gradually degenerates into what Bion calls "nothingness" as a result of wilfully embracing the lie-in-the-soul; his original imagination calcifies and shrivels, and the poetic spirit finds a new home in the person of Eve.

These refined differences in the nature of "error" blend with Money-Kyrle's view that there is room for another category: the "mistake", or "misconception". Money-Kyrle calls lying "the emotional flight from truth" (1961, p. 83), while reserving the term "error" for defects in perception that need to be clarified. He sees ethical evolution in the individual as a process of dissolving misconceptions that can hold the mind back in infantile states of cognition. A stalled emotional situation requires a mediator—such as Blake's "daughters of Beulah"[5] who bring meaningful dreams, Milton's Urania, or Keats's Psyche. Such mediators enable the mind to look through the glass of sense and discover the aesthetic object, rather than rely on its own murky inventions or theories. Milton described this as Time "run[ning] back to the age of gold", dissolving "speckled Vanity":

> And leprous Sin will melt from earthly mould,
> And hell itself will pass away,
> And leave her dolorous mansions to the peering day.
> [Milton, "On the Morning of Christ's Nativity", ll. 138–140]

In this traditional metaphor, the "peering" day is the newborn vision that reveals the mould (shape, form) which had been covered by mould (earthly debris, projections). As Bion said, enrolling himself under the Platonic system: "Beautiful objects remind us . . .

of beauty and good once but no longer known . . . this object is a form" (1965, p. 138).

Money-Kyrle points out that it is not that people's responses are different, but that people are not looking at the same "thing" (1961, p. 113). In the case of the analyst, what is necessary is the withdrawal of projections that have covered over the thing, the O, the fundamental reality, and caused him to "miss something taking place silently in himself":

> Only after he has perceived this, can he also perceive some hitherto missed bit of the pattern of his patient's associations—a bit which he would previously have been unable to abstract from the session, however accurate his memory for the mass of detail might have been. [*ibid.*, p. 25]

The analyst may remember the "mass of detail", with the eye of the single-vertex scientist, but cannot penetrate to its underlying poetic principle. In such an instance, the analyst needs to renew his own contact with the beauty of the psychoanalytic method and follow its guidance regarding self-scrutiny and the transference. Intelligence—or wisdom, perhaps—consists in aligning our observational capacities with emanations from the aesthetic object, in hopes of illuminating "our eternal home—our Self".

> For I know then, by the lightness about me,
> That ugliness has slipped from my shoulders
> Like a boy's shirt fallen to the sand
> When he runs shining to the sea.
> [Harris, "On going into action", unpublished]

Catastrophic change*

In order for the vitality of these turbulent emotions to be maintained while at the same time "avoiding self-mutilation" (Bion,

---

*This section of the chapter includes material previously discussed in "Underlying Pattern" in Bion's *Memoir of the Future* (*International Review of Psycho-Analysis*, Williams, 1983a), "*Wuthering Heights* and catastrophic change: a psychoanalytic viewpoint" (in Williams, 1987a, pp. 119–132), "The undiscovered country" (Williams, 1988a), "A Man of Achievement—Sophocles' Oedipus" (*British Journal of Psychotherapy*, Williams, 1994), and *The Vale of Soulmaking* (Williams, 2005b).

1980, p. 97), the special type of tolerance that Keats termed "negative capability" is required. This is the link between aesthetic conflict and catastrophic change. At the head of the final chapter of *Attention and Interpretation*, Bion cites Keats on the essential quality which goes to form a "Man of Achievement": "Negative capability . . . that is, when a man is capable of being in uncertainties, mysteries, doubts, without any irritable reaching after fact and reason" (Keats, letter to his brothers, 21 December, 1817; 1970a, p. 43; Bion, 1970, p. 125).

Negative capability is the strength to tolerate the emotional turbulence of not-knowing: to forbear imposing false, omnipotent or premature solutions on a problem. It is a special formulation of the "uncertainty principle" (Bion, 1991, p. 207). This concept lies behind Bion's formulation of "catastrophic change" with its contrary emotions of Love and Hate, which need to be weathered if a true orientation towards Knowledge is to be achieved. It is, in essence, facing the experience as opposed to avoiding it. As such, it describes the nature of the quest throughout literature and life for a truly philosophical, thinking mentality that stretches beyond known didactic principles and enlarges the structure of the personality. Indeed, as Bion puts it in the *Memoir*, "I owe my continued existence to my capacity to fear 'an impending disaster'" (1991, p. 175). The fear of change" that, as Milton said, "perplexes monarchs" (*Paradise Lost*, I: 598–599) is the basis of mental life.

In *The Kleinian Development*, Meltzer writes:

> Except for the paper titled "Catastrophic Change" which [Bion] read to the British Psychoanalytical Society in 1966, and which incidentally, in its body never mentions the concept of the title, this phrase appears nowhere in the books. And yet all the books are about it, just as *Attention and Interpretation* is certainly about attention, although it is never mentioned in the text. The paper "Catastrophic Change" was a prelude to *Attention* and is virtually identical to Chapter 12. [Meltzer, 1978a, Vol. III, p. 110]

Meltzer, together with Martha Harris, were in the forefront of appreciating the importance of this concept;[6] and here, Meltzer also notes the strange quality of its almost latent nature: the way it exists implicitly in the substratum of all Bion's writings, below the level of conscious didacticism.[7] It is the sort of idea that is a guiding principle, a fount of inspiration, and, as such, is not to be argued with but simply to be known or recognized. It hardly matters whether it is acknowledged consciously or unconsciously: everything else revolves around it. Like the underlying "O" or "central feature" of a psychoanalytic situation, this concept has a structural function in Bion's internal philosophizing and, hence, becomes something to be known rather than known about by its readers. Meltzer continues with his summary:

> the truth does not require a thinker to exist, but . . . the thinker needs to find the truth as an idea which he can make grow in his mind. Among the ideas which exist in the world awaiting thinkers are certain ones which, from the religious–historical vertex, he chooses to call "messianic" ideas. The relationship of container to contained in the individual, in so far as ideas institute a conflict between thought and the impulse to action, is not so observable in the ordinary course of events, but becomes dramatically manifest when an idea of messianic significance enters. . . . [Analogously] the group, as container, must find some means of expanding to hold this new phenomenon in order, on the one hand, not to crush or squeeze or denude the messianic idea, or similarly to destroy the mystic or "sink him without trace, loaded with honours". But it must also avoid being fragmented or exploded by the mystic or the messianic idea. [1978a, Vol. III, p. 110]

The sensed awareness of the proximity of an alien, "messianic idea" arouses "catastrophic anxiety" in the mind (an anxiety which "lurks behind all lesser anxieties"); the mind is in a "critical situation", and this "calls up the image of atomic reactors".

Meltzer's view was that Bion (unlike Freud) never changed his model of the mind; he simply changed his "metaphors", in response to his audience and also as a symptom of his frustration over the difficulty of finding efficacious means of expression (1983, p. 71). Indeed, as Meltzer points out, "catastrophic change" and "transformations in O" are the same thing, just different terminology (1978a, Vol. III, p. 87). Sometimes the first term seems more appropriate, sometimes the latter—as when the emphasis is on the unknowable "beyond" rather than on its present intersection with sensuous reality. As a result of this modification of his means of expression, particularly after the period of *Transformations*, the aesthetic nature of Bion's mind-view gradually became more apparent. He shifted from talking about "invariants" and "selected facts" (after Poincaré and, also, the Gestalt model of aesthetics) to talking about the "underlying reality" and sculptural "traps for light" and other similar metaphors for conveying the process of "psyche-lodgement": finding symbols to hold ideas. This linguistic modulation shed a more aesthetic light on his earlier mathematical models, including the Grid itself, in its imaginative endeavour to map thinking in relation to a reality not dependent on human thought.

If "aesthetic and spiritual" becomes the final category of the Grid, as Meltzer surmised, this goes together with his view that the fulfilment of thought development should be "communication" rather than "action", and that this was what Bion implicitly intended. It is more useful to reserve the term "action" for acting-out: not just the muscular form of action but also the verbal forms, such as projective interpretation or persuasion. There are situations in which extreme passivity and pseudo-inquiry may actually be a form of acting-out; and conversely, there are times when incisive or decisive *doing* (even impulsively, on the spur of the moment) could best be described as communication. It depends on the inner intentions of the participants, evident perhaps only to themselves. This is the kind of aesthetic focus on the mystery of internal motivation that the Grid is designed to encompass within its boxes.

The ambiguities of action apply also to "catastrophic change". For this is essentially an aesthetic concept. Although "catastrophe theory" has an application in physics, Bion characteristically used the term as a kind of pun, in full awareness of its original literary usage (deriving from Aristotle) to denote the moment of knowledge in a dramatic work. The "catastrophe" occurs after the *peripateia*, or moment of reversal in a classical tragic drama, and refers essentially to a complete change of vision, rather like one of Plato's cave-dwellers being dragged out into the sunlight. The light is so intense that it is blinding and disorientating. It feels like death—"death to the existing state of mind" (Bion, 1970, p. 79). But in fact, it is the truth: it is food for the mind, and the mind grows thereby. It is only the self's omnipotence that has died; it has metamorphosed into a new self. This is the underlying pattern of mental growth: it is a succession of "rebirths from one state of mind into another" (Meltzer). For "mental growth is catastrophic and timeless" (Bion, 1970,

p. 108). The basic developmental "matrix", says a character in the *Memoir*, is "the ability to change" (1991, p. 163).

This is not to say that Bion does not make full use of the implications of catastrophe in its more commonplace sense as "disaster". His point in yoking the two meanings together is to emphasize the tension between the feeling of loss of identity and the fact of growth of the personality: they occur concurrently. At the same time, his point is to warn against the more literal implications of everyday catastrophe that can and will take place if we do not undergo the aesthetic, metaphorical, internal type of catastrophic change that is necessary for human evolution. It was in his personal *Memoir*, following his own advice to "abandon himself" to psychoanalysis, that he focused most explicitly on what Blake would call the "spiritual war" between negativity (disaster) and developmental passion: "We are both aware of the awe-ful experience. Many are not; they fear "going mad", some indescribable disaster, "break-down"; they may express themselves by bringing about disaster" (p. 382). "Wisdom or oblivion—take your choice" was his final message (p. 576).

The remedy is to try to catch the indescribable disaster beforehand, by making it describable: to rejuvenate the degraded meaning of "awful" in line with its etymological origin, "full of awe"; to exorcise the "indescribable disaster" in "catastrophe" by describing, through an artistic form, the original aesthetic Aristotelian implications. Bion calls this, literally, "realization". The personality's predicament is whether to "break down, up, out or through?" (*ibid.*, p. 539) and one of his humorous, yet serious, illustrations is that of a chicken's egg which wants to retain its ego-shell permanently:

> It is a nice shell; it has a nice appearance; why not be an egg-shell for ever? Suppose that in the course of development the chicken begins to hatch out; the more the person is identified with the shell, the more they feel that something terrible is happening, because the shell is cracking up and they do not know the chicken. [Bion, 1973–1974, Vol. II, p. 15]

Bion, like Milton, Wordsworth, and other poets, sees in terror "the primordial origin of mind" (1991, pp. 648, 667). As Wordsworth put it: "Fair seed-time had my soul, and I grew up / Foster'd alike by beauty and by fear" (*The Prelude*, I: 305–306). Mind has its sensuous roots in the animal and the godlike apprehension together. It is the chicken hatching from the exoskeletal shell that protects and constricts its brain—in the words of Roland Harris, "As men from knowledge strive to mysteries" ("Swans"). The fear relates less to pain than to restructuring and the Unknown. Fear modulates under aesthetic influence into awe, as in Susanne Langer's formulation of the origins of symbol formation:

> Aesthetic attraction, mysterious fear, are probably the first mani-
> festations of that mental function which in many becomes a pecu-
> liar "tendency to see reality symbolically", and which issues in the
> *power of conception*, and the life-long habit of speech. [Langer, 1942,
> p. 110]

Catastrophic change is crucial to conception and to the possibility of "an existence beyond oneself" (Emily Brontë) in which the personality itself attains a different shape. The restructuring that occurs as a result of ingesting real knowledge and participating in the process of "becoming" is attained on the basis of L, H, K. Mental development is founded on the love–hate emotions ceasing to be "commensal" and becoming "symbiotic" through interpenetration. A type of "breakdown" is thus inevitable in catastrophic change: it may be infinitesimal; it may require a period of "obscure sojourn" in imagination's hell, as with Milton (Bion, 1991, p. 663). And it need not be sudden; more often it may be gradual, as in the famil-iar hymn the tide "comes silent flooding in the main".[8] These are the implications that lie behind Meltzer's formulation of the aesthetic conflict, in line with the continued evolution of the poetic psychoanalytic spirit: "The thought proliferates and the thinker develops" (Bion, 1970, p. 118).

Meltzer asks, how can we distinguish "the revolutionary expres-sion of a new idea from the rebellion of the disgruntled who cannot master the old idea?" (Meltzer & Harris, 1976; 1994, p. 453). This is equivalent to the different types of catastrophe that the mind induces. The answer lies in the discernment of one's motivation; and this relates to the aesthetic impact of the idea as distinct from the clever manipulation of lies. Bion defines the goal of psycho-analysis, like Hamlet, in terms not of cure, but of teaching how to "suffer" ("whether 'tis nobler in the mind to suffer"). It is only at the caesura, or boundary, between worlds, vertices, states of mind, waking and sleeping, pre- and post-natal existence, that such questions arise. "In that sleep of death, what dreams may come?" (*Hamlet*, III.i.: 66). With his characteristic understatement (a way of reinvigorating everyday words), Bion describes the "patience" required in order for a pattern to emerge to contain the new experience. His loaded use of "patience" is both etymologically and theologically linked with *passio* (suffer), *pathe* (emotion) and *perturbatio* (turbulence), and, hence, is itself an indicator of a "reality beyond" the present state of knowledge and the ground for its transcendence. Somewhat confusingly, Bion links this patient-suffering with Klein's paranoid–schizoid position (1970, p. 124), though he says this is only an analogy and he does not mean in the pathological sense, but only in so far as it is a state of unintegration and frustration. It is not the "rebellion of the disgruntled", as Meltzer would say, but rather uncomfortably awaits the integration conferred by knowledge or meaningfulness: the completion of its change of state, the new idea. At this developmental crux, Bion says:

> love, hate, dread are sharpened to a point where the participating pair feel them to be almost unbearable: it is the price that has to be paid for the transformation of an activity that is *about* psychoanalysis to one that *is* psychoanalysis. [1970, p. 66]

This change of state from *about* to *being* or *becoming* underlies many great works of literature. Any tragic drama, poem, or novel which achieves catastrophic change in the aesthetic Aristotelian sense—"death to the existing state of mind"—will be just such an exercise in this complex notion of patience. Of Emily Brontë's *Wuthering Heights*, for example (a work often compared with Shakespearean or classical Greek tragedy), it was said by E. M. Forster that the emotions do not inhabit the characters but surround them like thunderclouds. The passionate love–hate relationships of its protagonists are the clouds of turbulence that prelude catastrophic change in the mind, and they gather at the caesura, or meeting point, of contrary forces, figured by the two families who inhabit opposite ends of the moor-mind.

Initially, the Linton and Earnshaw families feel no hostility because they feel no proximity; they merely know "about" one another in the social sense. Later, when Catherine Earnshaw has penetrated the other family just as Heathcliff has penetrated her own, she tries to speak of passionate interchange, and of dreams that have "changed the colour of [her] mind". But her dreams find no external resonance, no canvas to receive the changing colours in creative form. Nelly Dean, the housekeeper–mother, feels unable to listen to her dreams, and they rebound destructively, shattering her mind. Each time a boundary between non-reacting or "commensal" realms is brought to notice, and each time a separateness is felt, there is an impulsive move to turn it back into a parasitic mode of communication—the false, deathly romance, or self-destroying revenge. The death-like associations of the dark stranger personified by Heathcliff penetrate the quiet "commensal" condition of the mind, so that it becomes open to the possibility of either destruction or development. For, as Bion suggests (and as is traditional in tragedy), the idea of death gives a "sense of direction" (1991, p. 604). Only when Catherine leaves the "shattered prison" of her body and becomes a kind of dream herself can her image be received artistically and her ghost become "soul". Until her spirit is found by a receiving mind, she exists in the minds of others as an assemblage of dead, disparate elements, a "collection of memoranda" (Brontë, 1972, p. 255). The process requires more than one generation, more than one transformation of its dream-elements. This is the process of catastrophic change: a tension between previously non-reacting worlds is set up, studded with explosions of feeling, which at first threaten only chaos, and resolved only when a symbolic language of some sort is formed that is capable of receiving them aesthetically as a new mental state.

To conclude with what could be considered the prototype for catastrophic change as played out in literary form: Oedipus himself. Sophocles' Oedipus, not Freud's, or even Bion's. By this, I mean the picture that emerges from the play as *poesis*, as art symbol, not the play as representation of a myth that was then adopted into psychoanalytic theory to become part of Freud's "tomb furniture", as Bion dismissively describes the famous complex (1980, p. 114). *Oedipus Tyrannus* (Oedipus the King) was, in fact, the very play upon which Aristotle based his theory of *poesis*, and thus the seminal originator of the very concept of aesthetic catastrophe. If we are able to read the play, as Aristotle maintained, for the meaning of its poetic structure (a more abstract pursuit than simply reading it for its characters and their pathology), we can rediscover the heroic humanistic achievement that it symbolizes, and that is responsible for the play's continuing stature at the heart of western civilization.

The impressive psychoanalytic theory with which we are all familiar treats the play as being about a little boy who is punished for his Oedipal destructive phantasies and consequently warns us about our own universal Oedipus complex. There is no question the Oedipus complex is a real thing; but it is probably overweighted by the succession anxieties of a patriarchal culture, and is certainly only an incidental feature of the greater drama of catastrophic change that Sophocles presents for us. If we give too much prominence to this moral tale (the complex), we are allowing our eyes to rest on St Paul's or Herbert's glass, where vision will be halted by the opacity of our own cleverness ("homosapiens!", as Bion would joke). If we look through the glass we can identify with the eternal infant in all of us: the infant who achieves insight (imaged, as is traditional, by blindness) as a result of suffering the catastrophic change of weaning. It is the pattern of all development at all stages in life. We might say, in everyday parlance—as do the Chorus of basic assumers—that the meaning Oedipus discovers is "dreadful", so dreadful, in fact, that he is better off dead, rather than hanging on being a burden to society. But, as Kierkegaard pointed out, "The most dreadful meaning is not so dreadful as meaninglessness" (*Stages on Life's Way*, 1845; 1940, p. 329), and dread (a type of awe) is one of the key links in the traditional trio that eventually settled into Bion's LHK. Shelley, for example, has his quester Rousseau invoke the example of Dante: "him whom from the lowest depths of hell . . . Love led serene, and who returned to tell / In words of hate and awe the wondrous story" (*The Triumph of Life*, ll. 474–475). Dread, in tension with love and hate, is the antithesis to negativity, meaninglessness, or banality. It "penetrates", as Bion reminds us; its knife–keel plumbs the unconscious depths.

It is, in fact, the poetic spirit of psychic development that drives Oedipus onwards: his passionate nature rooted in his "drunken dream" of parental intercourse and developed by means of his inherited intelligence, his "mother-wit". He should be not the butt but the god of psychoanalysis, a model for all to follow. His negative Teiresian temptations (pessimistic and death-instinctual) are cast aside and his riddling "clever" mentality is superseded by a new inspired dream about the two breasts that fed different aspects of his character, the Theban and the Corinthian. When in a triumph of internal integration he finally recognizes that these belong to the same mother, he is able to discover his own identity—expressed through the will of Apollo—and to wean himself by means of the two nipple-eye-pins that upheld his mother's breast-cloak, a container that would otherwise have become a claustrum. These eyes take on new life through the next generation, in the form now of his "daughters", who will guide him onwards. And, ultimately, in the last play Sophocles wrote about the Oedipus cycle, Oedipus's death in old age becomes a metaphor for the birth of an idea.

In conclusion, we can say that all imaginative works that achieve transformation via an Aristotelian *peripateia* illustrate for us the process of catastrophic change. They metaphorically *think through* the turbulence of the aesthetic conflict to gain "a new heaven and a new earth": a vision, that is, which transforms an old mentality which had reached the limits of its containing and expressive power, and that, if it continued, would have stifled or ossified the mind's development. The shell has "a nice appearance—why not be an egg-shell for ever?" In each great literary metaphor the theme of catastrophic change is interwoven with that of symbol formation; for poetry is itself self-analytic regarding its own creative processes. Concepts such as "aesthetic conflict" and "catastrophic change" did not need to be imposed on literary works in the form of psychoanalytic exegesis; they simply fitted the organic structure of the works. This is because they had, in a deep sense, originated in such works in the first place, and found their way circuitously into the aesthetic concerns of new psychoanalytic thinking. Thus, they made for a very different attitude to art-forms from that of either Freudian psychopathography or Kleinian moral tales. This does not mean that "catastrophic change" can be used to explain literature; it means that literature can be consulted with a view to giving vividness and distinctness to the concept of catastrophic change.

Bion says, "A foetal idea can kill itself or be killed, and that is not a metaphor *only*" (1991, pp. 417–418), meaning that a nascent idea will manifest itself first as a symbol or metaphor, and, when noticed, it has the potential to either develop or be smothered over by lies. Through his ambiguity, Bion tried to reverse the assumptions implied by the everyday language of "only metaphor" or "only poetry", and to make it clear that these are, in fact, the "only" way to begin thinking. The great poets were masters of metaphor and in this sense "legislators of the world". A truer and more literal appreciation of this statement—whose power derives from the fact that it is *not* a metaphor, just something hard to believe—is crucial to the aesthetic development in psychoanalytic thinking. Our own problem, Bion reminds us, is to find a way of gaining access to ("reading") the poets' storehouse of knowledge of the mind; a capacity for self-analysis (rather than literary interpretation) is one of the necessary tools in this never-ending, eternally rewarding investigation. When he says that arrogance is "not becoming" to a psychoanalyst (1973–1974, Vol. I, p. 52), his wordplay calls to attention the unaesthetic qualities that hinder psychic evolution. It is arrogant of us to apply psychoanalytic theories to literary or artistic forms from the outside, to regard them as material for exposition and moral judgement. Any genuine lover of poetry knows, like Bion, that poetic works have been too often "victimised" by psychoanalytic interpretation (1991, p. 588). But, if we can learn to read their symbolic structure by means of a self-analytic search for aesthetic reciprocity, we can participate in the beauty of the "underlying idea" that is being expressed.

Notes

1. This would be the opposite fantasy from that so convincingly portrayed in Golding's *The Inheritors*. We now know the Neanderthal brain was larger than that of Sapiens and their tools and technology more efficient, not less, but this did not save the species. Evidence of Neanderthal tools has survived (single-vertex science), but not of art. Perhaps it was Sapiens' aesthetic sensibility—his capacity to see meaning in things, and form symbols—that enabled him to physically survive that crisis in his evolution. (Bion, indeed, always satirizes "clever toolmaking man" as an omnipotent delusion liable to lead to his doom.)

2. Perhaps owing to the moralistic way in which the formulation of the two value states has often been applied, there has been a reaction against the idea of the depressive position as a therapeutic goal. The term itself is perhaps unfortunate, since it suggests depression and even a hierarchical state of subjection. However, it is simpler to retain

the existing jargon, and remind ourselves that, in terms of values, the "depressive" state is actually the one in which happiness and creativity are located. Meltzer felt it had unlimited potential as a descriptive phenomenon.

3. Sometimes the question is raised of what are "bad internal objects". With the distinction between negatives and contraries in mind, one could define these as unreal objects; instead they are projections of the selfhood which have been deified. Real internal objects are always ethically in advance of the self. In other words, there is always room for improvement.

4. Francesca Bion (1985, p. 242) tells us that Herbert's poem "Virtue" was a favourite of Bion's.

5. Blake's word for the Muses, Beulah being a Hebrew word, also used by Bunyan to describe the earthly paradise.

6. In "The individual in the group: on learning to work with the psychoanalytic method", Martha Harris discusses it in the context of the child psychotherapy training (1978b; 1987b). See also "Bion's conception of a psycho-analytical attitude" (1980; Harris, 1987a).

7. Meltzer's *Kleinian Development* was based on a course for students at the Tavistock Clinic, contemporaneously with Martha Harris's invitation to Bion to give a series of talks there in the late 1970s.

8. Bion cites another line from this hymn by Clough in *Taming Wild Thoughts* (1997, p. 43).

CHAPTER THREE

The domain of the aesthetic object

B ion first speaks of "the domain of Aesthetic" in *Trans-formations*, where it appears as the new Idea on the expand-ing horizon of psychoanalytic thinking, accompanied, like all preconceptions about to find their "realization", by a sense of puzzlement, yet, at the same time, inevitability (1965, p. 38). It is the place where the "real psychoanalytic experience" with its "depth-stirring qualities" lies buried, like the Sleeping Beauty, among the myriad turbulences of the oceanic unconscious. It is the "void and formless infinite" where, as Bion often quotes, Milton made his difficult descent and discovered his insight, "up led" by the heavenly Muse. Bion said that he, like Milton, "visited the bottom of this monstrous world beyond the stormy Hebrides" (1985, p. 17)—a reference to the "whelming tide" in *Lycidas*—and discovered he knew even less than Palinurus about the "stormy seas of sex": a metaphor for the generative, yet overwhelming, idea of the combined object from which all the Platonic forms emanate. In Marvell's terms:

> The Mind, that Ocean where each kind
> Does straight its own resemblance find;

> Yet it creates, transcending these,
> Far other Worlds and other Seas
> Annihilating all that's made
> To a green Thought in a green shade.
> ["The Garden", ll. 43–48]

The domain of the aesthetic is the unconscious transformed. It is transformed through strangeness, then surfaces for conscious recognition. Here, it is somehow possible for the "multitudinous seas" (*Macbeth*, II.ii.: 59) to undulate into significant forms, provided negativity does not incarnadine the contents. Here, if we can align ourselves with the "fishy origins" of primordial mind (Bion, 1997, p. 38), can take place the sea-change that Shakespeare described in *The Tempest*: "those are pearls that were his eyes" (I.ii.: 399). Sensuous apprehension, as Bion is always saying, can point to a "reality beyond", to the domain of the aesthetic object where, by means of inspiration, the symbol of the emotional experience is formed.

"Psychic reality" is not synonymous with "belief", as is sometimes believed even by analysts. In this context, Money-Kyrle refers to the "two thousand year question" which divides people into "nominalists" and "realists"—realists being "descendants of Plato" (1978, p. 418). This division applies to analysts as much as to other groups. Bion, Meltzer, and all who are sensitive to the aesthetic development in psychoanalytic thinking, follow the poets in falling into the latter category. Nominalists talk *as if* there were an inner world, in which certain situations are *believed* to prevail. Realists are concerned with finding a true picture—a symbol—of the situation that actually exists, whether inside or outside the mind. Belief makes inquiry possible, provided it is not too rigidly adhered to;[1] but, as Bion's "Psycho-analyst" in the *Memoir* says, "I do not waste time believing facts or anything I *know*. I save my credulity for what I do *not* know", and adds, by way of example, "I *know* pregnant silences—I don't have to believe in them" (1991, pp. 445–446). Internal reality is no more a "belief" than external reality is merely a "shared reality", a cultural term which may apply equally to a communally agreed illusion or a communally agreed fact. A capacity for seeing truthfully is generated in the inner world and deployed equally towards internal and external reality. "The real world—meaning internal *and* external reality" (Meltzer, 1973, p. 96). As Money-Kyrle writes:

The condition for being able to form a true external world-model, including a true picture of people, is the possession of a true picture of the inner world. . . . We may or may not have correct knowledge of our inner worlds. That is, we may or may not have a true picture of our unconscious inner world. [1961, pp. 112, 74]

The activity that "*is* psychoanalysis" (Bion, 1970, p. 66) is designed to reveal this "true picture" of the inner world—on which knowledge of the external world is also based—by facilitating symbol formation and thinking. It is a private process between two people, but, as always, it is poets who have been most adept at evoking true pictures of the inner world on behalf of everyone, so are able to "give distinctness" (as Meltzer hoped) to key points of aesthetic conflict and catastrophic change. The pictures are idiosyncratic and individual, as they need to be, to be authentic, yet have a universal application.

The symbol*

When Bion spoke in *Transformations* of "the configuration which can be recognised as common to all developmental processes whether religious, aesthetic, scientific or psychoanalytical", and of its progression from the "void and formless infinite" to a "saturated" and "finite" formulation (1965, p. 170), he was seeking to impress the fact that there is a basic unit of integrated, mind-feeding knowledge. This is what has traditionally been termed a symbol, though not in precisely this way by Bion himself: for a while, he flirted with the term "ideogram", but realized it failed to convey sufficient complexity of levels and linkages and also was too limited to the visual sense.[2] At that period, he hoped to define this basic configuration for learning from experience in terms of geometry: point, line, circle, etc. Later, he sought other metaphors, but the underlying idea remained the same: a mental building-block whose sensuous receptors are not taken literally as the "thing itself" (as in Segal's [1957] "symbolic equation"), but, rather, represent abstract

---

*This section is based on "Coleridge: progressive being", in *The Chamber of Maiden Thought* (Williams & Waddell, 1991, pp. 95–108), and on "The aesthetic perspective in the work of Donald Meltzer" (Williams, 1998).

occurrences in the non-sensuous world of psychic reality. A symbol is the shape taken by a piece of ineffable knowledge when it becomes seeable, breathable, audible, ingestable. As Bion would have read in the *Upanishads*, "the unendurable and unattainable experience must be translated into symbols" (quoted in Williams, 2005b, p. 205). It has "finite existence" that points beyond itself to "forms of relatedness in an infinite universe" (Bion, 1965, p. 46); as Coleridge also said, it is not about things but about "the relations of things". It is something that takes shape, and that shapes the personality, rather than something that is shaped *by* the personality.

Symbol-making, explains Langer, is "an act essential to thought, and prior to it", and, as such, is "the keynote of all humanistic problems" (1942, pp. 41, 25). "The process of symbolic representation is the beginning of human mentality; 'mind' in a strict sense" (Langer, 1957, p. 100). Building on Whitehead's concept of "presentational immediacy" and Cassirer's of myth-making, she distinguishes between "symbols", which are expressive or self-expressive, and "signs", which are primarily referential. In pre-historical terms, primitive symbol-making emerged not for practical purposes, but for expressive ones: "to formulate experience as something imaginable" (*ibid.*). Symbols could, of course, take various forms, as in the earliest forms of art, and speech itself grew out of "song and dance" in a family context as it does with young children. Signs—linguistic or other—evolved for the purpose of transferring information and "storing up propositions" (Langer, 1942, p. 244), but a sign-language cannot represent our feelings and emotional dilemmas in a way that enables them to be observed and thought about—that is, expressively. Language is simply one of the manifestations of man's capacity for symbol-making; it is not the *cause* of his symbol-making, and this means that it can be used in two different ways: either referentially, as a sign-language in everyday discourse, or artistically, as in poetic evocation, which always has the aura of an idea "beyond" or beneath its surface meaning, known as its deep or musical grammar. Poetry, the most complex form of verbal symbolism, uses the same lexical signs as prose, but with increased dimensionality: it holds meaning rather than stating it. It feeds from the song-and-dance roots of original emotionality and points to abstract possibilities beyond our present comprehension. Through sense it can "discover the infinite in everything" (Blake).

Coleridge, who was instrumental in adopting the word "symbol" into common currency, differentiated two uses of metaphor as being either "symbol" or "allegory".[3] Blake did much the same, and their distinction, though it got a bit lost in subsequent years, provided the literary basis for the twentieth century philosophical revival of interest in symbol formation. Coleridge saw symbols as a function of "organic" form, which develops according to a "living principle" within itself, and allegory as a "mechanic" form which "superimposed" its meaning on a metaphor. He wrote:

> Now an Allegory is but a translation of abstract notions into a picture-language which is itself nothing but an abstraction from objects of the senses; . . . On the other hand a Symbol . . . is characterized by the translucence of the Eternal through and in the Temporal. It always partakes of the Reality which it renders intelligible; and while it enunciates the whole, abides itself as a living part in that Unity, of which it is the representative. [Coleridge, *The Statesman's Manual*; 1972, pp. 30–31]

The sign-language of allegory is intended to convince or convert rather than to express or evoke. It is well suited to moral exhortation—moral "lies", as Bion puts it (1970, p. 117) and as personified in the satanic figure of morality–Moriarty, in his *Memoir* (1991, p. 310). Even when not intended as a lie (unconsciously or not), it will fail to grasp the truth of a new situation that is pressing on the personality. It can manipulate old knowledge, but it cannot get new knowledge. Keats warned of the limitations of "palpable design" in poetry, and said his friend Dilke would "never come at a truth because he was always trying at it" (Keats, 1970a, p. 326). A shortcut that neglects the means in favour of the end is liable—Bion observes—to lead not to truth, but to the heap of old bones on the Siren's shore (Bion, 1985, p. 52). In Coleridge's theory, the route to symbol formation is through imagination rather than fancy, and imagination is a power of *perception* rather than of organization.

In order for life to enter the metaphor, story, or narrative, it is important to have no particular end in view (as Freud also said), and this is where a symbolic structure becomes essential: to give form without premeditated design. As Langer explains, a symbolic structure articulates not just individual feelings but the "life of feeling" itself, the principle that underlies their individuation. The symbol contains an aspect of spiritual truth that gives "translucence" to the thing it "renders intelligible", even if its meaning cannot be instantly fixed or quantified. It inhabits the Platonic–Aristotelian "receptacle" space (*chora*).[4] This has similarities with Winnicott's "transitional space" (1971) in that it is sufficiently flexible to allow the mind to digest and reorientate itself.[5] It is also equivalent to the space which Bion defines as scientific–artistic–religious, held between different vertices. Within such a space, features or elements can be selected from the disparate, chaotic, oceanic, and infinite, to give meaningful shape to the feeling-pattern of the moment, the source of pain or pleasure (or of both simultaneously). Bion points out that the capacity for genuine "suffering" applies equally to pleasure and pain (1970, p. 9). The emotions are traditionally intermixed by the poets.

In doing this, the art symbol achieves a "genuine semantic" of its own that goes "beyond the limits of discursive language" (Langer, 1942, p. 86). The meaning of symbols is implicit rather than explicit and this accounts for their untranslateability:

> Artistic symbols are untranslateable; their sense is bound to the particular form. [It is] implicit and cannot be explicated by interpretation . . . To understand the idea in a work of art is more like having a new experience than like entertaining a new proposition. [*ibid.*, pp. 260–263]

As Keats demonstrated with the Grecian Urn, a new experience cannot be converted into a message that can be pocketed and taken out of its context, and this means the Idea it contains cannot be "read" as a message, either. Bion said much the same when he said that with some books, just "reading" was not enough—you also have to have "an emotional experience of reading" (1985, p. 178). Treating a symbol as a symbol, rather than as a sign, demands this type of emotional response.

The supreme cognitive value of symbols, Langer explains, is that they can "transcend the past experience of their creator" (1953, p. 390). The great art symbols are not bound to their time and culture, which is why, as Bion says, they have "durability". They are not even bound to the personal knowledge or experience of the artist, whose creativity is exploratory, not omnipotent. The soul, said Coleridge, has a "reflex consciousness of its own continuousness", which enables it "to see or imagine mental states beyond its own present condition, hence to grope towards the 'terra incognita' of knowledge" (*Notebooks*, Vol. III, n. 3825). The poets' genius for creating such symbols of previously unknown mental states makes them, in Shelley's famous conclusion to his *Defence of Poetry*, the "unacknowledged legislators of the world" (written 1821; Shelley 1977, p. 508). As Bion says, they expressed what they could not possibly "know" because it had not yet happened; this made them the facilitators of aesthetic catastrophic change in a wider humanity. Yet, on a humbler level, the same principle applies to all authentic, autonomously created symbols in the life of an individual, such as dreams. Symbols may serve purely for internal communication or they may be for communicating with others; either way they have a "generative" quality that leads potentially to further symbol-making within the person or the wider culture. Coleridge writes, "Every living principle is actuated by an idea; and every idea is living, productive, partaketh of infinity, and (as Bacon has sublimely observed) containeth an endless power of semination (*The Statesman's Manual*, 1816; in Coleridge, 1972, pp. 23–24).

Byron defined poetry as bearing the rhythm of a "former world and a future", and the same is true of all symbols: they have the power to seed the next symbol in the story. As Langer says about rhythm, the underlying pulse of a musical symbol, "The essence of rhythm is the preparation of a new event by the ending of a previous one . . . Everything that prepares a future creates rhythm" (1953, p. 129).

The added dimension that accrues to a symbol and differentiates it from a sign is, therefore, this link with a vital principle of life, or, in psychoanalytic terms, this identification with the internal object. Money-Kyrle describes how a "function of the object" is always introjected alongside its "detoxifying answer" to the specific emotional problem, and this prepares the mind for the next stage in cognition (1978, p. 432). Coleridge implies the same thing when he says that a symbol contains within it not just a piece of information, but the principles of self-knowledge, that will then "become the mind itself [as] living and constituent parts of it" (letter to Gillman, 22 October 1826; 1956, Vol. VI, p. 630). Symbols are "consubstantial" with the truths they "conduct"; they do not just *refer* to reality, like signs, they *partake* of it, and thus contribute to the "growth of consciousness", which is inseparable from "self compre-hension" (letter to Clarkson, 13 October 1806; 1956, Vol. II, p. 1196). Plato's object, he said, was not to "establish any particular truth" but to "awaken the principle and method of self-development" (*The Friend*, 1818; 1969, p. 473); and the principle that underlies all prin-ciples is Socrates' "heaven-descended *know thyself*" (*Biographia Literaria*, 1816; 1997, p. 152): this is what Bion calls the "Sleeping Beauty", too often overlooked while rambling among the thickets of psychoanalytic jargon.

The distinction that prevails in the Platonic–Kantian tradition is that in the communion between self and object, sign systems stimulate action, whereas symbols are conducive to contemplation and articulate emotional experiences—making them first imagin-able and then "conceivable", thus engendering new experiences. As Shelley described the "two classes of mental action" in relation to poetry:

> Reason [the "principle of analysis"] is the enumeration of quanti-ties already known; imagination [the "principle of synthesis"] is the perception of the value of those quantities . . . Reason is to Imagina-tion as the instrument to the agent, as the body to the spirit, as the shadow to the substance. [*A Defence of Poetry*; 1977, p. 480]

A symbol may be considered the product of imagination, an attempt to commune with the not-known that, as Langer says, "lets us conceive its object", while a sign "causes us to deal with what it means" (Langer, 1942, p. 223). Signs are vehicles of instruction, whereas symbols are vehicles of inspiration.

Consequently, symbol formation entails non-narcissistic identi-fication processes. This is different from general discourse, which can employ a wide range of identifications, projective and introjec-tive. Even if the symbol depicts a narcissistic state, it will rest on a non-narcissistic identification which has enabled its meaning to become clear in the first place—"filtered", in Langer's expression. Meltzer says the concept of identification is missing in Langer's theory (1983, p. 99)—specifically, the range of mother–baby identi-fications, in which the musical deep grammar has to be learned from internalized speaking objects, in addition to the need for an outside object to draw forth the desire for vocalization (Meltzer,

1992, p. 51). He suggests we consider "vocalization" to be the actual symbolic form, with "verbalization its corresponding notational system" (1983, p. 111). In fact, Langer does cite the early anthropological studies that concluded that when a child has been for some reason deprived of human company during the playful, musical "lalling" stage of life, they can never after become fluent in language. Such children could learn the cerebral "referential" use of language (the deployment of signs) but never the poetic or symbolic—the music of communication. They had been deprived of the Platonic Idea of language.

Also, although it leaves room for much psychological filling-out, the concept of identification is implicit in Langer's focus on "having a new experience", "conceiving" the object of contemplation, and responding to the "underlying Idea" of an artwork. This is what the artist strives to capture through significant form, impelled by a sense of "moral obligation towards the Idea" (Langer, 1953, p. 121): "This central significance is what Flaubert called the Idea and its symbol is the commanding form that guides the artist's judgement" (p. 122). She explains that the art symbol has to be seen *in toto* first, and cannot be construed by its parts. This is equivalent to Bion's advocation of alignment with O, a state of imaginative apprehension that happens *before* the meaning of the experience can be introjected. Grasping the Idea is a response of the total mind, not merely the intellect, and generates a type of catastrophic change within the personality: thus, Langer cites a musician's description of how "definitely and rather suddenly . . . my personality is changed . . . I have grasped the musical idea" (p. 146). The Idea is the aesthetic object that the artist seeks to reflect through the art symbol, as in Milton's "idea of the beautiful" sought "through all the shapes and forms of things" (see above, p. xxiv, n. 12). The Muse is the internal "speaking object", and the play of feelings gathers at the caesura where minds or parts of the mind interact in quest of "terra incognita".

In the case of the analytic equivalent, the "idea of the beautiful" is the psychoanalytic process, whose "central feature" or "basic fundamental reality" generates symbols in response to the turbulence that occurs at the meeting of minds of the participants. As Bion puts it:

> The Platonic theory of Forms and the Christian dogma of the Incarnation imply absolute essence which I wish to postulate as a universal quality of phenomena such as "panic", "fear", "love" . . . I use O to represent this central feature of every situation that the psychoanalyst has to meet. With this he must be at one; with the evolution of this he must identify so that he can formulate it in an interpretation. [Bion, 1970, p. 89]

The Idea, or O, originates in the Platonic realm and is mediated by the aesthetic object such that it finds a Marvellian "mirror", or pattern of itself, in the domain of sense. The realm of symbol formation is, thus, the domain of the aesthetic object. Whether this be the psychoanalytic or the poetic process, or some other situation of learning from experience, it is, in each case, a response to the pressure of a reality beyond and outside the selfhood. Symbol formation incorporates, of necessity, the religious vertex. For, as Bion puts it, the individual becomes aware that thoughts are present in his mind through "religious awe", which may be given a variety of different names: incarnation, godhead, Krishna, mystic experience, inspiration, etc. But, whatever the name it happens to be called, "the source of emission of the received or evolved thoughts is felt as external, God-given" (Bion, 1992, pp. 304–305).

The aesthetic object—whether O or mediator with O—governs the tensions of the aesthetic conflict in relation to the three cognitive vertices of science, art, and religion, and holds them in balance while a symbol is being produced to contain the specific meaning of the emotional situation under scrutiny. A symbol, unlike a sign, contains an element of all these "contrary" tensions and this is how it comes into sensuous existence, through a correlation between vertices. It is a three-dimensional, not a two-dimensional, structure. The great art symbols provide a pattern for the formation of all personal, meaningful, autonomous symbols, and, thus, all mental growth. They illuminate our own continuous, mainly unconscious, everyday attempts to form symbols through which to think about our emotional experiences.

In the psychoanalytic situation, the boundaries of the container are "drawn by selective attention" providing a space of "privacy not secrecy, solipsism or isolation" (Meltzer, 1986, p. 67), a space demarcated in response to the aegis of the creative combined object. Having ideas means absorbing the Platonically pre-existing ones in a new or personal context. The crucial factor is identification with a principle of evolution; this is why it is not necessary for ideas to be new, provided they are genuine, experienced "on the pulses" (Keats). Whether or not they come with a "label" attached (Bion, 1997, p. 27), they become one's own, provided their "ancestors" are internally acknowledged. For the aesthetic realm of Ideas is "one's own home even if previously lived in by someone else" (Meltzer, 1986, p. 67). Thinking with one's ancestors means reading and acknowledging people who advance one's ideas rather than those who advance one's career.[6] Sometimes, these ancestors may not be formally attributable, or even known. Yet, they are known to exist; and if this is feelingly acknowledged, the necessary humility in the face of "awe" can be maintained, a "depressive" orientation which allows knowledge to be internalized.

So, this artistic aspect of psychoanalysis (that is, introjecting a function of the object) is what gives it the chance to be of enduring benefit to the patient and also, as Bion points out, to the analyst. It is an education in self-analysis, in internal conversations between objects. In a sign-language, this particular educational aspect is lacking, and, if it is employed in a single-vertex exclusive way, it will result in analyses that may be interminable but are not durable. Or, as Martha Harris writes in relation to some training analyses, a "learning about" situation may result in "successfully resist[ing] a real experience" and replacing it by a "collusion of mutual ideal-ization with [the] analyst" (1987b, pp. 329–330).[7] The "sleeping beauty" is still asleep, undiscovered amongst the brambles of jargon and two-dimensional interpretations. It has not infused its poetic spirit of "becoming" into the developmental process. In other words, it has not made links with the religious vertex of experience, the vertex that, as Bion says, relates to our capacity to deal with the Unknown.

In conclusion, therefore, the peculiar qualities of a symbol may be summarized as follows: first, it contains the meaning of the particular emotional conflict of the present time; second, it incorpo-rates a function of the internal object and so improves the capabili-ties of the mental apparatus; and third, it is "seminal" and contains a germ or foreshadow of the next logical phase in development to grow out of that particular piece of learning from experience. By contrast with a sign-language, a symbolic language depends on internal objects to govern the formation of the symbol and present the new idea to the infant mind. This underpins the therapeutic potential of the psychoanalytic process—as distinct from "cure", which is a goal (now generally outmoded) that belongs to the deployment of sign systems. Instead, the process as aesthetic object presents the idea in a symbol to both analyst and analysand.

The caesura

The "reality beyond" both partners—the new idea—is intimated by a generative experience at the place where contraries meet. These contraries may take many forms: love and hate, body and mind, sensuous and non-sensuous, active and passive, conscious and unconscious, artistic and scientific vertices, transference and countertransference, male and female, pre- and post-natal parts of the self. Probably, the place of aesthetic transformation involves a creative dialogue between all these contraries and more. In his paper on "The caesura", Bion concludes:

> Investigate the caesura; not the analyst; not the analysand; not the unconscious; not the conscious; not sanity; not insanity. But the caesura, the link, the synapse, the (countertrans)-ference; the transitive-intransitive mood. [Bion, 1977, p. 56][8]

He took the title of this paper from Freud's observation that "there is much more continuity between intra-uterine life and earliest infancy than the impressive caesura of the act of birth allows us to believe" (quoted in Bion, 1977, p. 37). Like all the developmental nodes of catastrophic change, the fact of birth (and its non-sensuous equivalent, the birth of ideas) is both a momentous transition and a logical extension of previous existence or knowledge; it is not always so dramatically manifest, but may often take place in tiny increments like "the nothing out of which something comes; the increment of a 'ghost of a departed increment'", as Bion's Psycho-Analyst puts it in the *Memoir*, discussing Berkeley's analysis of Newton's optics (1991, p. 315). His internal Group conclude it is "a tale told by an idiot, signifying nothing" (*Macbeth*, V.v.: 26–27). The vital "nothing" always occurs at a caesura where different *qualities* meet, clash, and interpenetrate.

Bion's "caesura" is the locus of the drama in poetry and dramatic literature, or indeed any art form, and I shall shortly give some examples. It is where, in Bion's language, emotional turbulence converts the "commensal" to the "symbiotic", where noumena—those emanations from the realms of Platonic ideas—"push forward" until they encounter a human mind, and "realization" or symbol formation takes place. Feelings are stimulated that provide a field for "action", that is, a psychic space where imagination can discover pain and proceed to seek for its meaning. Even the mud of Ypres may be such a field for generating meanings, a place where symbiosis and intersections with O may occur. To quote Tolstoy's description of the mental landscape before a field of battle, as yet untouched by contending forces, its boundaries quivering in anticipation of some strange transformation:

> One step beyond that line, which is like the bourne dividing the living from the dead, lies the Unknown of suffering and death. And what is there? Who is there? There beyond that field, beyond that tree, that roof gleaming in the sun? No one knows, but who does not long to know? You fear to cross that line, yet you long to cross it; and you know that sooner or later it will have to be crossed and you will find out what lies there on the other side of the line, just as you will inevitably have to learn what lies the other side of death. [Tolstoy, 1982, Vol. I, p. 162]*

Momentarily, time is suspended, and the battlefield becomes a field of "spiritual warfare" (Blake). Such a place, where contraries meet and are neither split apart nor smoothed over, is transitory, but not transitional in the sense of a temporary refuge from reality. On the contrary, it is imbued with tension and the danger of breakdown that realistically accompanies catastrophic change. It is, in fact, the tension that shapes the space, in response to premonitions of the Unknown reality. As Keats said, even the "spiritual Cottager" knows that beyond his "philosophical back garden" of feelings tidy and pleasant lie "the Andes and the Burning Mountains"—the "terra semi incognita of things unearthly" (letter to Rice, 24 March 1818, 1970a, p. 77). It points to the Beyond. The idea of death, and the impact of beauty, are always closely related and provide a similar cognitive stimulus.

---

*This discussion is based on "Holding the dream" (Williams, 1988b).

In this scintillating space of expectation, where roofs gleam in the sun, a new emotional event germinates. It is the threshold of new knowledge, the "undiscover'd country, from whose bourn / No traveller returns" (*Hamlet*, III.ix.: 79–80), the caesura between commensal worlds, which comes to vibrate with meaning as a "discovery" is heralded, and the idea of a mutually penetrating "common sense" (Bion) takes shape. The point comes later when Prince Andrei (a character mentioned in Bion's *Memoir*), watching the spinning bomb that would shatter his body, has a few seconds of eternity in which to imagine the implications of the caesura. Unlike Bion, with his escape from the tank (as described in the *Memoir*), the prince listens to the language of his Psyche not his Soma—and it takes too long: "Can this be death?" (1991, p. 963). He meditates intellectually rather than allowing his body to think for him, so comes to represent those who do not have the resilience to survive the bloody revolutions of the era to follow.

To take another example: a poem by Roland Harris on the subject of lovers meeting conveys the tension in time and space that identifies the caesura at the threshold of knowledge:

> First greeting's
>   true sign is
>   friction's meeting,
>   parts too apart
>   alighting in design,
>   as a bird breaks
>   into its image
>   in the tensioned lake;
>
> a sudden
>   foreknowledge
>   of death,
>   and the life between
>   unknown and the remembered
>   the winged meeting
>   rising skyward,
>   a windhover.
>
> Mind is a lone lake
>   in the high mountains,
>   with its pine and star;
>   and meeting should be there.

Ah! first meeting is
twi-pained of thirst
and after-thirst;
a little lake shut
in the mountain walls
of getting and forgetting . . .
[Harris, "Rendezvous"]

The friction and anxiety that tests the boundaries of the caesura is conveyed by the bird that "parts too [two] apart" and shatters its impeccable image in the "tensioned lake", the surface tension of the water being both mirror and anti-mirror, joining and separating. Then the "winged meeting" suggests the bird rising again, creating a new place for meeting, the metaphorical lake of the mind, held in place by the navigational pine and star. But this space also is transitory, like the "life between": held in place only by the double pain of before and after, the remembered and the unknown. It is the pressure of "Time's wingèd chariot" (Marvell) that shapes the symbol, and ultimately time brings the mind-lake back down to earth, to "London's dustiness, / Laved in a mountain pool" (Harris): as in Tolstoy, it leads on to the spinning bomb.

The emotional situation of the caesura (the threshold of symbol formation) can be seen to differ from the transitional space or play-space theory of creativity owing to its turbulence. Love, death, and beauty (aesthetic conflict) intrude and "alight in design"—in fact, redesign the state of mind. But there is another difference: the guiding aegis of the internal object, which requires a special type of dependence that Bion and Meltzer term psychoanalytic "faith". This, too, has been fully explored by self-analytic poets, in their relationship with their Muse.

Poetic inspiration*

The new idea arrives in the developing mind, as Coleridge said, in the form of a symbol. The *means* by which it arrives there is termed

---

*This section is based on "On the meaning of inspiration" (chapter 1 in Williams, 1982, pp. 1–21) and on "Inspiration: a psychoanalytic and aesthetic concept" (Williams, 1997).

by the poets "inspiration". It is a situation of aesthetic reciprocity, in which the idea or object created by the infant mind is returned to the creator, as it were, for authentication.

Poets in all fields have always feared the loss of inspiration, "drying up", more than they fear neglect, ridicule, or penury; more than anything, except perhaps torture and imprisonment, which is their reward in the most repressive societies. It is their function, through obeying the dictates of their internal Muse, to mediate on behalf of the rest of society and draw the culture forward towards more complex and thoughtful values. The personal reward for this is the clouded joy of being immersed in the "forms of truth and beauty", in the Platonic sense, as used by Hazlitt: "The lover of true fame seeks not the direct and gross homage paid to himself . . . but the indirect and pure homage paid to the eternal forms of truth and beauty as they are reflected in his mind" (Hazlitt, *On the living poets*, 1818; 2007, p. 211).

Or, as Milton said, "they also serve who only stand and wait" (Sonnet, "On his blindness"). To wait for inspiration is an honourable occupation for a poet, most delightfully described by Keats:

> Let us not therefore go hurrying about and collecting honey-bee like, buzzing here and there impatiently from a knowledge of what is to be arrived at; but let us open our leaves like a flower and be passive and receptive—budding patiently under the eye of Apollo and taking hints from every noble insect that favors us with a visit . . . [letter to Reynolds, 19 February 1818; 1970a, p. 66]

The condition of Negative Capability need not be one of ascetic self-denial; and Keats often describes his swings between a "fruitful indolence" and "energy" or "hammering", his mind at times "stuff'd like a cricket ball". There is an alternation in fact between "buzzing" and "budding", active and passive fertility.

Such swings are all part of the dialogue with the inspiring internal objects. They are different from the various types of withdrawal, omnipotence, self-delusion, etc., that masquerade as poetic power or achievement or even as modestly waiting-for-inspiration. There is a Claustrum (Meltzer, 1992)—or Claustra—in the field of poetry, as in any other. The poet who has lost contact with his source of inspiration may look "just like" a real poet in his social and professional life, and produce forms which look "just like" poetry (Bion's *trompe l'oeil* vision). False to their own Muse, they become the "mock lyrists, large self-worshippers" cursed by Keats:

> Though I breathe death with them it will be life
> To see them sprawl before me into graves.
> [*The Fall of Hyperion*, I: 209–210]

These are, of course, internal states, and only the individual poet can truly gauge his own condition, but this internal state ultimately *shows in the work*. A reconnection with inspiration, however, can lead the individual out of hell (the Bion–Blake realm of "non-existence") and back into the current of real life; as Meltzer says, the door to the Claustrum is "always open".

In Dante's words as he emerged from Hell through Purgatory:

> I'mi son un che, quando
> Amor mi spira, noto, e a quel modo
> ch'e' ditta dentro vo significando.
> [Dante, *Purgatorio*, xxiv: 52–54]

("I am one who, when Love breathes in me, take note, and in that manner which he dictates within me, go setting it down.") The context of this beautiful and precise definition is a leisurely technical discussion about the craft of making verse and the "new rhymes" of Dante's day. It sets Dante's art in its educational and historical perspective. But Dante the pilgrim is silent during the discussion (although it is, in a sense, speaking for one aspect of himself, his social and contemporary existence). So, when he finally speaks, his voice is all the more significant, and he uses it to define his poetic identity in a quite different sense: not by means of craftsmanship, but according to his relation with his Muse, "Love". The act of speaking out at this point is also a private moment of revelation in which the intimate link at the heart of his poetry is recognized. His inspiration is a personified power outside himself, and his own personal function is to "take note" (*not* to "create"), meaning to *pay attention*, and then finally to transcribe on to paper the precise form of the words which have been dictated to him. There is nothing about style and technique, nothing about invention or imagination—those belong to other facets of his activity as a poet.

Here, there is only inspiration, lucidly differentiated from those other faculties: "Amor mi spira".

The poet, then, *obeys his inspiration*, whatever qualms or objections he may have about the meaning of the words he is required to transcribe (and they may, for example, seem to him blasphemous, obscene, or humiliating). He writes down the words he hears spoken by his internal Muse, without cheating, rephrasing, softening, or disguising its unpleasantnesses. This is Milton's "unpremeditated verse" in *Paradise Lost* (IX: 24). Yet, "How vile, contemptible, ridiculous!" objected Milton's Samson, when the idea of "something extraordinary" that contradicted his sense of personal dignity found its way into his thoughts (*Samson Agonistes*, l. 1361). The essential test in inspiration is that the poet should not succumb to the temptation to change the form of the words that have presented themselves to his mind, for, in the aesthetic form of the words and their "before unapprehended relations" (Shelley, *Defence of Poetry*; 1977, p. 482) lies the inspired knowledge that society may at some future date comprehend.

When the inspired poet writes several drafts, these have the internal significance of listening better to the words of his Muse. In serving the Muse that speaks within him and that knows more than he does in his selfhood, he is serving mankind and its future, the children of the world. This is both his joy and his drudgery. And, when it is objected—as it always is—that the idea of "inspiration" makes a mockery of commonsense and provides an excuse for all sorts of perversion and aberration ("speaking by inspiration like a Bagpipe", as Hobbes joked ["Answer to Davenant"; 1908–1909, p. 59]), one can only reply (as the poets always do) that the reality of inspiration and the cynical exploitation of its appearance are two very different things. It is, nevertheless, a fact that the concept of inspiration is almost impossible to convey to people who have only a limited awareness of psychic reality.

Inspiration, as described by the poets, is thus a very specific mental process, not simply a mental quality or attribute like imagination; it is, in a sense, the opposite of an attribute, for it is not a possession of the self; it describes the process by which the mind is fed by its internal objects. Feeding, breathing, dreaming—these are the consistent, eternal metaphors used by the poets to set the scene for inspiration. Inspiration is hearing the still small voice amid the din of basic assumptions, that "savage clamour" that "drown[s] both harp and voice" (*Paradise Lost*, VII: 36–37); it is "seeing" when the "light of sense" (everyday perception) has "gone out" (Wordsworth, *The Prelude*, VI: 534–535).

> So much the rather thou celestial Light
> Shine inward, and the mind through all her powers
> Irradiate, there plant eyes . . . [*Paradise Lost*, III: 51–53]

Everyday, vital, sensuous functions of the body image the constant maintenance of the mind by "Spirits, no less than digestion or sleep" (Blake, *Jerusalem*; 1966, p. 621). The fibres, roots, and tendrils of what Keats calls "branched thoughts" ("Ode to Psyche") continuously inch forward under the influence of inspiration, which periodically requires greater leaps to be made, new branches initiated, at points of catastrophic change.

It is on the threshold of catastrophic change that the image of inspiration tends to appear most urgently and clearly in poetry. At such points, the poet needs to affirm his dependence on the Muse even though he feels he is "flying blind" and has relinquished his own judgement. As with Dante, "Amor mi spira", and he must forget about the "new rhymes". The context is always one in which the poet has done his utmost to collect all the knowledge and experience he has had so far, and then is required to relinquish *everything* before making what Kierkegaard calls a "leap in the dark". His previous knowledge is the springboard from which he leaps, but he leaves it behind. He could not make the leap without his talent and expertise, but it is the Muse who provides the "intimate impulse" (Milton) that carries him forward.

Plato's Cave, in *The Republic*, is the poetic prototype for all subsequent portrayals of the claustrophobic condition of the individual awaiting inspiration. Everyone remembers the shadows on the wall, the faint reflections of reality that seize the cave-dwellers' attention with such rigidity that it is as though their necks and heads were clamped in a vice, oblivious to the sun behind and beyond them. But it is not always remembered that the goal posited by Plato for his embryonic philosophers is not to escape forever into the world of eternal sunlight; this would be a false existence of its own, of no more use to the developing mind than remaining clamped in the Cave. In Plato's view:

> every human soul has by its very nature beheld true being—other-
> wise it would not have entered into the creature we call man—but
> it is not every soul that finds it easy to use its present experience
> as a means of recollecting the world of reality. [*Phaedrus*, 250; 1975,
> p. 56]

This innate knowledge is part of the human condition, and the
quest in life is to "recollect reality" (*anamnesis*), to make use of the
faculty of inner vision. All the same, the capacity for individuals to
do this is not innately equal. Souls who have "seen the most" in a
previous existence enter into human infants who are destined to
become seekers after wisdom and beauty, lovers, and poets. This
"divine power of knowing" is inspiration, the renewing of a link
between the infant mind and its internal parents. Each time this
happens, in Plato's myth, the mind's body ("the mind as a whole")
is seized by the shoulders and forcibly dragged upwards into the
sunlight ("the Good"), which results in a degree of confusion or
"unsighting"—the clearing away of previous assumptions. As Bion
says, the nearest description he can find for "O" is "passionate
love" (1991, p. 183).

But then—the part of the myth which is sometimes forgotten—
the mind is returned to its seat in the Cave in order to apply its new
vision. This involves another type of confusion: the mind may be
"unsighted" in two ways, Plato says: by the transition from darkness to light, and from light to darkness. And until this second
movement has been completed, inspiration has not taken place.
Inspiration is not the first movement—the escape from the Cave—
alone (an idealized projection). As Bion says, the "moment of illu-
mination is very brief" (1973–1974, Vol. I, p. 30). It is the entire
process of assimilating the knowledge, of allowing the infant mind
to be fed, and experiencing on the pulses the integration of that
knowledge, involving the realization of one's dependent and par-
tially sighted status. The poet knows his position is the humble one
of taking note of the Muse's dictates. Return to the Cave clinches
the depressive position. In the same way, Socrates, as mental
"midwife", ends his voyage of discovery of the principles of knowledge in the *Theaetetus* with the reaffirmation of his ignorance. As
Keats put it "we must discover whether a little more knowledge has
not made us more ignorant" (letter to Bailey, 25 May 1817; 1970a,

p. 98). The end of one journey (insight) is the beginning of the next catastrophic change. On this depressive stance depends the potential for future growth, for the process to continue.

Socrates said that only philosophy can rescue the soul from imprisonment. Emily Brontë gave a fine description of this type of philosophical rescue in her lines beginning "He comes with western winds". These lines (often printed as an independent poem) are embedded in a long and tedious narrative that forms part of her juvenile fantasy about the inhabitants of the imaginary realm "Gondal":

> He comes with western winds, with evening's wandering airs,
> With that clear dusk of heaven that brings the thickest stars,
> Winds take a pensive tone, and stars a tender fire,
> And visions rise and change which kill me with desire—
>
> Desire for nothing known in my maturer years
> When joy grew mad with awe at counting future tears;
> When, if my spirit's sky was full of flashes warm,
> I knew not whence they came, from sun or thunderstorm;
>
> But first a hush of peace, a soundless calm descends;
> The struggle of distress and fierce impatience ends;
> Mute music soothes my breast—unuttered harmony
> That I could never dream till earth was lost to me.
>
> Then dawns the Invisible, the Unseen its truth reveals;
> My outward sense is gone, my inward essence feels -
> Its wings are almost free, its home, its harbour found;
> Measuring the gulf it stoops and dares the final bound!
>
> Oh, dreadful is the check,—intense the agony
> When the ear begins to hear and the eye begins to see;
> When the pulse begins to throb, the brain to think again,
> The soul to feel the flesh and the flesh to feel the chain!
> [Brontë, 1941, p. 239]

In a commonplace view of poetry and inspiration, the poet's ambition is to escape from the prison of everyday existence through a flight of fancy. These lines, however, demonstrate a more realistic psychic event. The visitation of inspiration does not release the captive from the imprisonment of everyday routine, but instead reinforces it. What it does do is to transform its meaning. The process begins with aesthetic conflict, unintegrated "flashes" of conflicting emotions "from sun or thunderstorm", associated with not-knowing. The storm modulates into a period of calm, a momentary, transitional state in which the spirit like a fledgling bird finds "wings", supported and soothed by a nonsensuous "mute music".[9] The light of sense goes out, as in Wordsworth and Milton, to make way for a new way of seeing and feeling: "My outward sense is gone, my inward essence feels". The accuracy with which the poet "measures the gulf" is balanced against the desire to completely lose her identity and be absorbed by the object—the soul's "home, its harbour found".

Yet, the real test of the prisoner's capacity to receive inspiration occurs with the "check" described in the final stanza, "When the ear begins to hear and the eye begins to see". Instead of an escapist loss of identity, there is a structural change. "The soul feels the flesh and the flesh feels the chain": the rhyme "chain" replaces the expected "pain" and the climactic rhythm emphasizes the renewed conjunction of soul and body.[10] The soul's projection outwards is returned inwards with increased aesthetic impact and breathed new life into the body of the mind—"Amor mi spira". The soul is still in its world-body, but the world is no longer the Claustrum. Here, Brontë's Platonism differs from Wordsworth's in the "Immortality Ode", where he says farewell to the infant poetic spirit that has become swathed in "shades of the prison house". Brontë's poem is the opposite—a welcome; it is a springboard to writing her poetic novel, not an elegy to lost inspiration and the years that bring the philosophic mind. The Chain is the sensuous reality of the poem as well as the flesh of the speaker; symbols are a way of containing spirit in sense. Wordsworth adopted a philosophy of resignation; Brontë committed herself to a philosophy of passion, the sense-prison transformed into a Vale of Soulmaking. The Cave, the Chain: one person or state of mind may view the world as a prison of basic assumptions (a vale of tears), while another may view the same world as a workplace, according to his psychic reality. Escape from the first requires magic; release from the second requires merely a change of mind, as when Odysseus realizes that all he has to do to escape from Calypso's cave is to build a raft with his own hands.

Emily Brontë's poem demonstrates how the process of making the symbol is bound up with introjecting an aspect of the object (as Money-Kyrle said). The meeting with the internal object—the visitor that "comes with western winds"—has revitalized everyday existence in what Keats calls "our dull uninspired snail-paced lives", in the way that "ethereal Chemicals operat[e] on the Mass of neutral intellect".[11] The Keatsian vision, like the Brontëan, is one in which aspects of the "good", whether innate or imbibed from "men of Genius" or other aspirational objects, create a "ferment of existence—by which a Man is propell'd to act and strive and buffet with Circumstance" (letter to Bailey, 23 January 1818; 1970a, p. 53). Inspiration accounts for aesthetic integrity in a poet or solidity of character in an individual. It is the backbone of a person or a poem. The degree to which someone is able to place trust in his inspiration is what makes him a true "philosopher" in Plato's sense, "a solid reality among shadows" (*Meno*, 100; 1956, p. 157). He "feeds on thoughts, that voluntary move / Harmonious numbers", as Milton expressed it (*Paradise Lost*, III: 37–40). This aesthetic organization has solidity, not arrogance or rigidity, being the result of faithfulness to internal objects, not of a power struggle over one's contemporaries (those "shadow battles" despised by Plato). The poet–philosopher is "humble without inferiority" (Money-Kyrle, 1961, p. 69). Without this solid basis he cannot *become himself*, but remains a slave to the basic assumptions of his time, never developing his own identity.

There may be a difference in degree between the intense and agonized struggle with inspiration experienced by our great creative poets, and the need for growth through inspiration experienced by all of us. As Milton said of the prophets, divine inspiration may have been sweet, but the "irksomeness of that truth which they brought makes them everywhere call it a burden" (*The Reason of Church Government*; 1974, p. 50, "The reason of church government"). Poets everywhere stress the burden of the knowledge they carry and which is, in a sense, *beyond themselves*, and feel their shoulders strained to the limit, even to the point of madness (hence Keats's image of "fledging" the shoulders) (letter to Reynolds, 3 May 1818; 1970a, p. 92). But surely the rest of us have no need to strengthen ourselves for such an intense mental burden?

Bion considers this question in a letter in which he advises one of his children about their life choices. He cites the example of Milton's venturous journey into hell and back, which he says was

tough enough in all conscience, but made tougher by his knowledge of his own greatness and the burden that put on him. But
this is true even of ordinariness, if one can call a knowledge so
extra-ordinary as knowledge of one's ordinariness, "ordinary".
[1985, p. 179]

It is the reality of self-knowledge—of being ourselves and nobody
else—that is burdensome, and we all require inspiration—something extraordinary—to acquire it and sustain contact with it. People's lives (as distinct from just their occupations) express their
mentality in a way analogous to poets' works. The psychic condition of the individual is not a mere appendage that can be adjusted
with timely injections of culture or other forms of playing and holiday. The meaning—the psychic reality—of a person's world view
shows in their life. And, as Money-Kyrle reminds us:

> A man's good internal parents are felt to desire life as he does. So
> his own similar craving to be immortal in the persons of his real or
> symbolic children, that is, in his accomplishments, becomes also a
> duty to his super-ego which is felt to aid and support him in the
> task. . . . This, I suggest, is one of the ways by which a moral
> element may enter aesthetics. [1961, p. 129]

In this demonstration of a reciprocal affirmation of life between
self and object, the poets, with their aesthetic and meaningful
models of the essential aspect of human experience known as inspiration, can act for us like Bion's "thinking breast" or mother, who,
in her reverie, can mentally digest the fear of death and return
the concept of catastrophic change to the infant in a palatable and
hopeful form. Bion advises us to value the lessons of our "ancestors", whether or not we know who they were (1980, p. 97, 2005,
p. 23). He implies that we do know, unconsciously. Those *ante
Agamemnona multi*—the many unsung heroes of the poetic spirit—
can help us revive our "capacity for awe"; that is, for learning from
experience (1985, p. 241).[12] They model for us the very process of
assimilating the inspired knowledge which is the foundation for
mental growth. It is not easy to "read" them, but, if we can find
some means of access, they will help with our self-analysis as they
have helped others in the past.

Psychoanalytic faith

In a note that he calls a "reverie" about the baby's interior preoccupation, Meltzer writes about the "birth of meaning" in the infant
mind:

> It is not surprising if it comes out sounding like Genesis . . . It is not,
> in the beginning was the formless infinite, but the placenta as the
> primary feeding object. We might call this the experience of *surprise*
> . . . at an extraneous intelligence, the beginning of revealed religion.
> All the functions described are the fruits of identification with the
> extraneous intelligence. In the beginning object relations and
> identification are simultaneous. ["A reverie on the baby's interior
> preoccupation", c. 2002; published in a book in Spanish, 2008,
> unpublished in English]

The "extraneous intelligence" is what Roland Harris describes as
the "stranger" that bends and shapes the new mind (see below; also
Chapter Six, n. 14). The origins of knowledge are inextricable from
this "reflex consciousness" (Coleridge) that leads the infant mind
beyond its own boundaries. Bion uses the word "peculiar" to suggest that we need to step out of our familiar existential space.[13] He
consistently felt the religious vertex had been neglected by psychoanalysts, who, he said, "have been peculiarly blind to this topic of
religion" and focused only on sexuality. Ignoring the existence of
religion in the human mind, he says, is equivalent to ignoring the
existence of the alimentary canal in the human body. It is the religious vertex that supplies the necessary concern with the "future",
the meaning and end result of knowing the truth about one's condition: "How can a human being, with a human mentality and
character, not be interested in, or concerned with, the future?"
(Bion, 1973–1974, Vol. I, p. 15). "An act of faith has as its background something that is unconscious and unknown because it has
not happened" (Bion 1970, p. 35). It requires the internal poet to
catch the "shadow of the Future cast before" and, as in Shelley's
definition, "legislate" for the future. This is the "progressive being"
that in Coleridge's philosophy is founded on symbol formation,
which has its source not in the self, but in the fountain of faith or
the light of reason, a realm of infinite resource with which the self
is organically connected when it incorporates a "living part" of it
into the growing structure of the mind by means of a symbol.

Progressive being, or the capacity to imagine a future state, is, in turn, inseparable from the awareness of a realm of being outside the self that contains a "primary feeding object" whose initial post-natal impact, as Meltzer has elaborated, is that of an *aesthetic object* that arouses love, hate, and the desire for knowledge. Words that fitly convey this impact are "wonder" and "amazement"—words which suggest the suspension of the selfhood and its established outlook. Keats writes, "Poetry should be great and unobtrusive, a thing which enters into one's soul, and does not startle it or amaze it with itself but with its subject" (letter to Reynolds, 3 February 1818; 1970a, p. 61).

Meltzer says the word "amazed" is perfect for describing "the emotional experience before it has been worked on by alpha-function", and cites the Jewish Book of Law: "Stand close to the dying because when the soul sees the abyss it is amazed" (1983, p. 69). The growth of the baby mind on the verge of the abyss is entirely dependent on its relations with this amazing object from the first feed onwards, and the date of the first feed is gradually being pushed further back into watery, pre-natal realms in a way that previously only the poets dared to imagine: "those are pearls that were his eyes".

As Meltzer reminds us in his "reverie" about the baby, Bion is constantly invoking Milton's "void and formless infinite" as a realm which is both stimulating and yet so inchoate as to dampen aspiration ("dampened wing" is one of Milton's phrases). Milton felt he was led both "up" and "down" by the Muse, surviving the nameless dread of his "obscure sojourn" in the realms of darkness. Faith, in Bion's definition, is "a scientific state of mind" in which exploration and discovery become possible (1970, p. 32). At the beginning it is *both* the formless infinite and the primary feeding object. Speaking of the origins of both artist and scientist in the child mind, Meltzer emphasizes "the gradual aspect, the need to explore every permutation and combination of possible distortion before yielding to the truth" (1975, p. 220). Yielding to the truth means abandoning possessiveness and omnipotence, otherwise the artistic–scientific discovery cannot be made. This entails a sense of the personality being shaped by forces beyond its own capacity or control. As Rimbaud succinctly expressed it (1871), "It is wrong to say 'I think'; rather, I am thought". Or Roland Harris:

> Out of the waste of sky
> invincible arrows
> of beauty and danger,
> when the strong Stranger
> bends me, and trains his eye!
> [Harris, "Come wind, what shall I sing of?"]

"Thinking for oneself", in the aesthetic model of the mind, actually entails "thinking with the internal object" (Meltzer & Williams, 1988, p. 71); for "The integrated internal object learns in advance of the self and is almost certainly the fountainhead of creative thought and imagination" (Meltzer, 1992, p. 59). This is

> not simply a matter of containment or protection or comfort or pleasure and so on. It's a question of *an object that can perform* this particular function, that creates the symbols through which dreaming and thinking can proceed. [Meltzer, 1995a; also 1983, p. 38]

This is the "Stranger", as in so many myths in which gods are incarnated to guide or test humans. "Our minds are made up for ourselves by forces about which we know nothing", as Bion said (1980, p. 69). Or Blake: "we who dwell on Earth can do nothing of ourselves; everything is conducted by Spirits, no less than Digestion or Sleep" (*Jerusalem*; 1966, p. 621). The "work" is done by the "transference from internal objects, which enables us to seem to perform functions for the patient that are essential to the development of their thinking" (Meltzer, 1995a).

What, then, are the qualities needed in a developmental object? Faced with a "morass" of sense data, Bion questions who is going to put it in order and convert it into something aesthetic: "Who or what chooses or decides or acts as the authority in the person?" (1997, p. 51). Yet, this emphasis on the *reality* of the internal, symbol-making (aesthetic) object is an idea that is not "had" in very many accounts of creativity or personality development, either psychological or literary–philosophical.[14]

A problem is that the object that can perform such functions, and lead the personality through catastrophic change, is inevitably experienced as having an element of cruelty. There is a passage in *All My Sins* where Bion describes his "shock" at discovering a hitherto unsuspected "depth of cruelty" in himself (1985, p. 70). The context is his not responding to the calls of his baby daughter to pick her up, and in the absence of action on his part, she is "comforted" instead by the "maternal arms" of her nurse. By his non-action, he believed he had "lost his child", and this is generally accepted by readers at face value, despite the fact that it was clearly not the case, as shown by the same baby—now a toddler—running happily to greet him a couple of pages previously (p. 66).

However, if we look beyond the surface grammar of the incident, we can surmise Bion's inner response to the cruelty of an object beyond them both, which demands recognition of the near-insoluble "problem of existing" (p. 33). Bion had been crudely awakened to this problem more traumatically than many. He knew there is always a temptation to "rebel" against the dominance of this instinct to survive (1991, p. 609): despair, "self-murder", letting go—the ultimate form of negativity. "Why did she do this to me? Not quite audible was the question, "Why do you do this to her?" (Bion, 1985, p. 70) Bion wanted his daughter to survive, unlike her mother or his fellow-combatants. He felt "gripped in a vice" as if by the Great Cat Ra. The vice-like grip told him that the child needed to acquire tenacity, and he needed to acquire the courage to seek a new wife, which the whole episode made clearer to him. "Thought" was beginning to "invade [his] gratifying world" (p. 66), and this had ramifications also for his daughter's infant journey. It was appropriate for the nurse to pick the baby up, but perhaps not for her Daddy, her father–mother, in his enforced role of mediating her internal object. Bion, after all, had his own childhood experience of two types of mother, which perhaps enabled him to open up the vertices and establish binocular vision. No doubt, if Bion had been alone with the child in a single-vertex situation, Ra would have ensured he took on the role of a nurse, just as Athena impelled Odysseus to pick up baby Telemachos from the beach before he ploughed over him in his feigned madness. As it was, he responded analytically rather than parentally (as Meltzer would put it). And he was drawn to psychoanalysis, we remember, because he believed it offered the potential for mental "salvation". As Martha Harris points out:

> The infant that is in all of us probably requires in stress from time to time throughout life an external manifestation of that [maternal] presence. But holding is not the same as enclosure—the personality

is ossified by identification with closed minds and can be preserved alive only through developing and risking itself. [Harris, 1987c, p. 178]

In the same vein, Bion also speaks of the damage the analyst can do by omnipotently trying to "be helpful" (1991, p. 665), as distinct from enabling suffering—"pain-talk" (*ibid.*, p. 434). It is a subtler form of "therapeutic zeal" (Meltzer, 1967, p. 80), but equally an evasion of reality. Suffering is something reciprocally painful for the analyst; doing good may be subtly self-satisfying, depriving the potential operation of faith in both parties. This follows in fact from the recognition that, in aesthetic conflict, it is the present, not the absent, object that causes pain, owing to being unknown and unpossessable. In such a situation, the analyst needs to respond "analytically rather than parentally" (Meltzer, 1983, p. 9) and struggle to acquire an aesthetic attitude (Meltzer 1967, pp. 79, 84). Bion's idea of faith is not like the child swimming for the first time without water wings, confident of Daddy's support, but is more like "floating free in shark-infested waters" (Meltzer, 1978a, Vol. III, p. 99).

Thinking is painful, Bion thought, owing to the psychic restructuring of catastrophic change that is required of both analysand and analyst in their reciprocal identification with O. In the words of Kierkegaard, "Every movement of infinity occurs with passion, and no reflection can bring about a movement. That's the perpetual leap in life which explains the movement" (1985, p. 71, n.) A "suspension" of selfhood is required so the objects have freedom to "perform the movement", the movement of faith, the catastrophic leap. The true "knight of faith" is undetectable to outside eyes (*ibid.*, p. 67). By contrast, Kierkegaard was scathing about the "knights of resignation", who complacently adopted the eminently reasonable Hegelian system of ethics but withdrew from the passionate leap of love—not with despair or sorrow but with "resignation". This resignation becomes a mark of moral superiority and is worn "boldly" like a badge for all to admire. Such a knight indulges both memory and desire of a lost love, because it is easier to have lost it than to have pursued it. "He keeps this love young . . . From the moment he made the movement [of resignation] the princess is lost" (*ibid.*, p. 73). As in Bion's version of the story, there are endless circuitings around the Sleeping Beauty but no awakening, no alignment with O. As expressed by Roland Harris, those who listen to

The voices crying
"Beware beware
A false happiness
Is sadder than despair"—
Have the intense
Substitute for experience.
[Harris, "Faith and love"][15]

The aesthetic object—the princess—may easily be covered over by a *trompe l'oeil* "substitute for experience", in order to avoid the danger of a "false happiness". But, as Meltzer says, it can only be covered over, not destroyed (1986, p. 104). At a deep level, the mind contains knowledge that cannot be used. The personality's clinging to memory, desire, and resignation is a form of fossilization in K: an invented fairytale of a lost love that is forever young, a turning away from the uncertainties of the aesthetic conflict and its intolerable contraries.

The problem, says Bion, is: "How can we become strong enough to tolerate it?—a much more modest aim than trying to add something new to psychoanalysis" (1973–1974, Vol. I, p. 33). He recognized that it was intolerable to our monkey-like selves that we cannot be thought-producers, but merely thought-vehicles. This toleration—or "patience" as Bion sometimes calls it (weighting the word)—is not the same thing as disdaining whatever real experience the self has managed to acquire. On the contrary, the patient or analyst who has "no respect for what he already knows" (*ibid.*, p. 80) is floundering in the abyss, not floating free with the sharks. Faith is founded on hope generated by previous achievements, and observation "requires a model" as a basis (Meltzer & Williams, 1988, p. 203). But there is no escape from the fear and awe that, as Langer pointed out, accompany the symbol-making capacity each time it is reawakened. The psychoanalytic setting is, in fact, specifically designed to evoke it: "In every consulting room there ought to be two rather frightened people: the patient and the psychoanalyst. If they are not, one wonders why they are bothering to find out what everyone knows" (Bion, 1973–74, Vol. I, p. 13). The "fear of change", as Milton pointed out, "perplexes monarchs" and undermines the stability of even the most powerful mindsets (*Paradise Lost*, I: 598). Change is cruel—but then, as Bion says, it has vital links with primitive love (1991, p. 600). It is ambiguous what type of sea-change is undergone by Palinurus when he is torn from his smooth steering and submerged in the depths.

Meltzer addresses the question of whether or not it is appropriate to draw attention to phenomena that may well be experienced as cruel or overwhelming: "I cannot escape the often repeated accusations of the patients that I am doing something cruel, possibly lethal, and that I am intruding something into the patient that is potentially shattering" (quoted in Williams, 2005a, p. 436). What, then, distinguishes cruelty from sadism (cruelty for the pleasure in being cruel) or indeed from indifference, the cruelty of a failure of imagination, as in "war is cruel" and other blanket statements used to excuse the clumsiness of unacceptable violence? Meltzer says it is the intentionality discerned in the countertransference.[16] He points out that the lethal quality of this cruel truth directs itself equally at the analyst, who is participating in the thinking process, not merely directing it. This instigates in him, also, a "catastrophic change in my picture of myself". There is always the danger of this being, or appearing like, "self-mutilation" (Bion, 1980, p. 69).

Meltzer cites as illustration Kierkegaard's weaning metaphor from *Fear and Trembling* (1985), an interpretation of the otherwise incomprehensible cruelty of the story of Abraham and Isaac. In Kierkegaard's version, the story becomes a model for the kind of faith he felt he could never attain himself: faith that when one source of nourishment—one reason for living—is taken away, another, as yet unknown, may take its place. From this point of view, it appears that cruelty is the "contrary" rather than the "negation" of goodwill or benevolence, just as hate is a form of love, a feature of the vitality of the emotional links necessary to symbol formation. Meltzer also compares the forming of the symbol to the methods for netting wild birds:

> That seems to me a good metaphor for the way symbols are formed and the way they work: they capture these wild birds of meaning. If you say "oh, but there's something cruel in that", I'm inclined to agree that there's something cruel about the way in which it surrounds the emotional experiences and captures them. [1995a]

The cruelty has an aesthetic *raison d'etre*, rather than a philistine or destructive one. Indeed, the web or net or trap is a traditional poetic metaphor for symbol formation. An ancient Chinese definition of poetry, cited by Archibald MacLeish (1960), is "to capture heaven and earth in the cage of form". Another favourite metaphor is the hunt, as in *Sir Gawain*, *The Tempest*, or *King Lear*, or Keats's vision of "pouncing" upon "Beauty on the wing" in order to "gorge essential verse" (notes on Milton); or indeed Freud's view of himself as a "conquistador", or Bion's hunt for "that ferocious animal Absolute Truth" in the *Memoir*.

Mrs Klein, according to Meltzer, was impressed by the cruelly overwhelming nature of the combined object when she first discovered it—to the extent that she initially wondered whether it was healthful or psychotic in its implications. Its "monstrous" quality appears in Richard's dream:

> Richard's Adam and Eve dream, a primal scene dream, visualizes the parents and their genitals but he does not seem to be shocked with envy or overwhelmed with sexual excitement. In fact, seeing their genitals looking so huge like the monster he described, is unpleasant. This dream is an important prelude to the "Black Island" dream with its hopefulness about this destruction being reversible in psychic reality, that dead objects, dead babies can be brought back to life by goodwill towards the good, creative intercourse of the internal parents. [Meltzer, 1978a, Vol. II, pp. 114]

One should not assume, therefore, that cruelty is incompatible with growth-promotion. It is perhaps an essential feature of the religious vertex, with its requirement of faith in the internal object to carry the infant self into the next phase of existence. Meltzer said that Klein's "implicit" vision was that "mental life is essentially religious" (Meltzer, 2005c, p. xvi). The analyst is as much subjected to "fear of change" as the patient—but who or what is being cruel?

In his autobiographical books, Bion wonders about the Great Cat Ra raining shells on the hut in which he is cowering: is it cruelty or clumsiness, deliberate or casual? For cruelty is, in fact, a very precise psychological weapon, which does no physical damage but delineates the exact place in the mind where the meaning is trying to emerge. As John Donne wrote:

> Batter my heart, three-person'd God, for you
> As yet but knock, breathe, shine, and seek to mend.
>
> ["Holy Sonnets" no. 14]

"Stick to the fighting line" advised Bion (2005, p. 95). Even in an emotional storm "the troops will not run away, but will begin to stand fast" (1980, p. 78). The capacity to "stick" or "suffer" is crucial to symbol formation in the Bion–Meltzer model of thinking, in which each growth point entails a catastrophic change in the existing structure of the mind.

Perhaps the combined object appeared to Mrs Klein like Satan walking over the burning marl with the moon on his shoulder, as monstrous and ugly–beautiful as that vision was to Milton. Perhaps she observed through the telescope of augmented intuition the combined object moon-and-Satan, or Satan with his reciprocal tool of intuition, capable of illuminating that "other space, scientific space, religious space, aesthetic space", as Bion called it. Perhaps she too wondered, like Emily Brontë, did this thought come "from God or the Devil"? Was it a thought to steer by, knowing that the fleet was following, or an attack by a hostile god like Somnus? Perhaps the teeth and claws of the Great Cat Ra (Bion, 1991, p. 441) were directed very specifically towards Bion himself, sharpening his intuition. Perhaps that is how he survived the mindless massacres of the First World War, instead of being torn from his ship by Somnus like so many of the tank commanders and their crews. He realized he could not "be an egg-shell for ever" (Bion, 1973–1974, Vol. II, p. 15).

Once the immediate suspicion of cruelty has been weathered, however, there is relief for both patient and analyst. Allowing internal objects to think on one's behalf may initially appear cruel to the selfhood. For the patient:

> This would perhaps quite deserve the suspicion of cruelty if he were being nudged towards independent thought and judgement. But that is not what I think is happening. I think, and hope, he will find himself in the best of company, with the saints and angels of psychic reality, with his true teachers, with those aspects of his own personality which contain the aspects of genius that he can only aspire to. [Meltzer, 2005, p. 428]

Meanwhile, the analyst remembers that it is the process that is the guiding aesthetic object, and that his or her task is to follow the process, which lifts the personal load of the transference. In relation to one's peers, one may aim for independence of thought;

internally, in the domain of the aesthetic object, such a thing is an illusion. In order to develop our embryonic capacity for thinking, it is perhaps necessary to embrace the selective cruelty that can aesthetically organize our emotional constellations, and to distinguish it from the sado-masochistic obedience that governs our social and political nature. For the cruelty of symbol closure, outside and beyond our infantile self-image, may define the point at which the noumenon of truthfulness "intersects with the human intelligence" (Bion, 1973–1974, Vol. II, p. 30). The mind's gods are represented by the male–female qualities of the Kleinian "combined object", and the mind's growth takes place in relation not only to "the restoration of god the mother", but to "the evolution of god the ineffable" (Bion, 1970, p. 129).

Does all this help us to elaborate on some implications of the concept of the "depressive position"? Meltzer has described how the depressive position is initially characterized by release from persecution, but almost immediately bound by the weight of responsibility toward the trust placed in the individual by internal objects. It is concerned with "rescuing the lost children of the personality" (Meltzer, 1983, p. 98). As in Emily Brontë's poem, the mind in catastrophic change is not released fancy-free, but held in a chain-like vice of "iron hard and chill", which is, nonetheless, non-masochistically invigorating and integrates sense and spirit. As Shakespeare put it: "with a heart as willing / As bondage e'er of freedom" (Tempest, III.i: 88–89). Happiness is "development" (Meltzer, 1986, p. 10), a continuing process—hence, the Chain with its many links. Within the depressive position, he says, is "perhaps a limitless range for ethical evolution" (Meltzer, 1992, p. 138). There is no need to transcend this position; it is infinite in its potentialities.

Ethics means, essentially, concern for the mind's or world's children (or ideas) and their future existence. Bion explains how the pressing awareness of the burden of responsibility for the next phase in the quest is necessary to avoid the "calcification" of ideas, which otherwise begins almost immediately, as soon as a new idea has been "had" (Bion, 2005a, p. 11). This is the process of ethical evolution. This feature of the depressive position—the gaining of true knowledge—is experienced less as advantageous to the self than as doing good to the world and its children. Keats expresses this internal configuration: "I find that I can have no enjoyment in the World but continual drinking of Knowledge—I find there is no worthy pursuit but the idea of doing some good for the world" (letter to Taylor, 24 April 1818; 1970a, p. 88). It is the same as following "the principle of Beauty in all things", or as the soul "recollecting the world of reality". As Meltzer says:

> The formal and emotive configuration of [the artist's] works must be derived not only from the influence exerted upon him by his culture and fellow-artists, but also by the force of his *concern* with the present and future of the whole world. . . . In nature we can find reflected the beauty we already contain. But art helps us to regain what we have lost. [Meltzer & Williams, 1988, pp. 222, 225]

The beauty of art or poetry is offered not as consolation for the world's ills, but as a means of renewing contact with reality. It is a sign of the true poet or artist that they experience their work not as self-promotion, but as a gift to the world and their siblings, despite the inner turbulence this engenders, for, as Meltzer says:

> Every act of violence which [the artist] sees go unpunished and, above all, smugly unrepented, threatens his internal harmony because of the pain and rage stirred. Thus, concern for the outside world increases the temptation to renew the old splitting and projection of bad parts of the self. [*ibid.*, p. 222]

But any egotistical or crazy aspects belong to different, probably split-off parts of themselves, and can only detract from the quality of their work; the fact that this does not necessarily destroy the work altogether is testimony to the power of creativity and ideas "beyond the self". The intention of the artist's "sermonizing to siblings" is not merely to show what can be accomplished, but "to project into the siblings both the restored object [and] those capacities for the bearing of depressive pains which have been achieved by the artist in his own development" (p. 219).

The dependence and humility that characterizes the depressive position is not, therefore, directed towards other people, not even to mothers or psychoanalysts in their transference robes. It is a function of the religious vertex, and relates to the underlying principle of beauty and truth that is mediated through internal objects and the "conversations between" them (Meltzer). Keats said, in explanation to friends who were worried about the likely reception of something he had written, "I have not the slightest feel of humility towards the Public—or to anything in existence—but the eternal Being, the principle of Beauty, and the Memory of great Men" (letter to Reynolds, 9 April 1818; 1970a, p. 85). By "memory" he meant such internal conversations with figures of "Genius". Is it "too daring to fancy Shakespeare [his] Presider?" he wondered, at the start of his brief career (letter to Haydon, 10–11 May 1817; 1970a, p. 12). This is Money-Kyrle's "humble without inferiority": the quintessential depressive position, in relation to the internal deities who, through aesthetic conflict of love and awe, generate aspiration, humility, and a sense of privilege at the same time, resulting in creativity: a gift to these internal gods, like Milton's "humble Ode" presented to the Christ child in "On the Morning of Christ's Nativity", pre-empting the "star-led wizards" with their earthly gifts. A series of mediations takes place before the symbol is created—the poem, the flower—the child of love:

> In the conclusion
> Is the dedication
> Of what is worthy
> To the creator.
>
> I send back these songs
> For signature;
> To be corrected by
> The making eye.
>
> Were word there aught
> Worthy of thy report,
> One shine as if
> It were not mine,
>
> That I make over
> To her my lover,
> All that is worthy
> That I discover.
>
> Not as thy maker
> O divine loveliness!
> But as a walker
> Humbly in meadows,

Who seeing the flower
Growing so fair,
Would pluck it and place
It in her hair. [Harris, "In the conclusion"]

Notes

1. See, for example, Bion, 1991, p. 176. Rosemary "believes" she knows what Man is "up to", but is, nonetheless, able to change her mind.
2. Bion's "psychotic symbol" (1970, p. 65)—which he differentiates from "sign"—seems close to "symbolic equation" and a sub-category of Coleridge's "allegory". This is related to a Platonic–Aristotelian debate about the *eikon* and how it recalls the absent thing (see Ricoeur, 1977). See also Bion, 1967, p. 50.
3. Coleridge also coined, or introduced into modern usage (sometimes via the German philosophers), the words psychoanalysis, subconscious, subjective and objective, all crucial in laying the foundations for psychoanalytic philosophy.
4. An amorphous reality, capable of changing its shape in response to the pressure of ideas. "The things that enter and leave the receptacle are images of eternal realities (that is, imitations of the paradigms of the Ideas)" (Catan, 1990, p. 104).
5. There is also a difference, in that Bion's space is concerned with facing reality, rather than temporary refuge from reality. Winnicott's theory was that the baby "creates" the breast in the creative space; had he approached the same phenomenon (of the baby latching on to the breast) from a poetic–philosophical background rather than a paediatric–psychoanalytic one, he might have interpreted this in terms of the fulfilment of a Platonic preconception, as do Money-Kyrle and Bion.
6. Bion's advice to his son was to "only read the best, and acknowledge what you take" (Bion, 1985, p. 214).
7. Meltzer (1967) writes similarly of the "preformed transference", referring to the patient's preconceived idea of what an analysis ought to be like. Only dreams, with their authenticity, could break through this and allow a genuine transference relationship to form. But the preformed transference, which he said tends to be particularly stubborn in a training analysis, is liable to seduce both analyst and analysand into an illusory simulation of psychoanalysis.

8. By this point, Bion was using the term "countertransference" not (as he had earlier) to indicate the analyst's unprofessional projection, but, rather, the "marks" that the patient's emotional condition have made on himself and that need to be investigated scientifically.

9. See Williams (2008) for further exploration of the musical matrix in Emily Brontë.

10. Wordsworth writes of the "unrelenting agency" whose "logic . . . Did bind my feelings even as in a chain" (*The Prelude*, III: 166–167). Also, there is possibly a pun on French *chair*—the chain of desire.

11. Keats, lines from *Endymion* (IV: 25) quoted in a letter to Bailey, 22 November 1817; 1970a, p. 26).

12. Bion uses the phrase "ante Agamemnona multi" (from Horace) frequently in the *Memoir* as a type of refrain to the unsung heroes of his and our past, those whose memory is lost "for lack of a poet" (Bion, 1991, p. 120).

13. For example, he speaks of "the peculiar events of sleep", "peculiar people like Freud", in a "peculiar world" (Bion, 1997, p. 31), as if to dislodge a too-smooth condition of knowingness.

14. Meltzer wrote that "the problem has been long avoided as to whether the Muse is a formal figure of speech or a psychological reality" (Williams, 1982, book jacket).

15. There is a reference here to Coleridge's "Beware! beware! / His flashing eyes, his floating hair" (*Kubla Khan*).

16. Meltzer says, "How does one differentiate between showing it and acting out or acting in the counter-transference for that matter? I think the answer to that is really in the intention that you discern within yourself concerning the showing" (1995b).

CHAPTER FOUR

Sleeping beauty

I n her paper "Towards learning from experience in infancy and chidhood", Martha Harris stresses the limitations of the psychoanalytic understanding of the means by which qualities of the object become introjected into the structure of the personality:

> Introjection remains a mysterious process: how do involvement and reliance upon objects in the external world which are apprehended by the senses (and, as Wilfred Bion has pointed out, described in language which has been evolved to deal with external reality), become assimilated and transformed in the mind into what he calls "psychoanalytic objects" which can contribute to the growth of the personality: This is a process about which we have almost everything to learn. [1978; Harris, 1987c, p. 168]

However, one of the ways we can learn how it happens—even if not *why* it happens—is by observing how symbols are formed in art and poetry. Although Bion said that alpha-function was unobservable, it is possible to observe the evolution of poetic symbols through the close analysis of poetic diction. In this way, tracing the poet's "intensity [in] working out conceits" (as Keats put it)[1] we can find a congruence in our own mind between observer and observed.

Keats was one of the key contributors to the concept of the "aesthetic conflict", and to Bion's formulation of the "language of achievement" that rests on abandoning memory and desire. Keats's poetic philosophy was largely formulated before his best poetry was written. I want to focus here on the thinking process that evolves *through* his poetry, rather than his discourse *about* poetry: beginning by looking in detail at his "Ode to a Nightingale" and "Ode on a Grecian Urn". We can follow the poet closely through the transformations effected by alpha-function, as step by step the meaning of the emotional turbulence is located, developed, and refined, moving up through levels of the Grid "As once fair Angels on a ladder flew / From the green turf to Heaven" as Keats puts it. In addition, each of these poems expands our understanding of the complementary qualities of the three vertices of science, art, and religion. In the "Ode to a Nightingale" the artistic vertex is dominant: through *listening* to the underlying musical Idea, the poet makes contact with the unknown or unseeable inside the object—the invisible spirit of the Sleeping Beauty through "viewless wing". In the "Ode on a Grecian Urn", the scientific observation of the outside of the object is what shapes the poem, but it is modified by the intuition that somewhere is a voice that is inaudible to the "sensuous ear", yet still speaks by virtue of the shape of its silence.

The religious vertex in the group of spring Odes is perhaps most dominant in the revelatory nature of the "Ode to Psyche" (see Williams, 2005b, pp. 48–55), though it exists in them all in the form of the mystery and unpossessability of the aesthetic object. Further light can be shed on its complexity and ambivalence, however, by looking at Keats's struggles with two contrasting poems in the autumn of that year—the year of his great poetic achievement, when he was aware of his terminal illness. These are the ode "To Autumn" and *The Fall of Hyperion*, in which he reworks his abandoned Miltonic epic *Hyperion* into the form of a dream-poem.*

---

*The rest of this chapter is largely reprinted from "The principle of beauty in all things", in Williams, 1982, pp. 143–196.

The "Ode to a Nightingale"

Bion (quoting from a sonnet of Keats) spoke of allowing a strange thing called a thought to "swim into my ken" and the need to find a "box" to hold it in for the time being (1997, p. 29). This is the kind of attentive, naïve, imaginative ignorance appropriate to the aesthetic state of mind at the beginning of a thought process, corresponding to Freud's famous advocacy of an "evenly suspended attention". Such a voice or visitation from the unknown requires, first of all, a symbol in which it may be held or contained. This entails a "caesura" or meeting point between minds or vertices, a line on which the storm-clouds of an experience may gather and become mentally seeable, audible, tangible. "Where does that feeling of sadness originate?", as Bion asks.

The story of the "Nightingale" begins with the heavy thought-sickness that seems imposed on the poet by an apparently uncrossable divide between his and the Nightingale's mode of being:

> My heart aches, and a drowsy numbness pains
> My sense, as though of hemlock I had drunk
> Or emptied some dull opiate to the drains
> One minute past, and Lethe-wards had sunk.

The dense, emphatic, slow-moving words "My heart aches" are like a held note that anchors the entire poem in the sensuous reality of the drug-like thought-pain; they are prolonged by the heavy endstopped rhymes and assonance of "pains . . . dull . . . drunk . . . drains . . . sunk". The an-aesthetic draught of hemlock literally blocks off the breathing-in of sense. Yet, the poet's deathlike condition represents his response to the ethereal "light-winged" nature of the Nightingale, in complete antithesis:

> Tis not through envy of thy happy lot,
> But being too happy in thine happiness—
> That thou, light-winged Dryad of the trees,
> In some melodious plot
> Of beechen green, and shadows numberless,
> Singest of summer in full-throated ease.

The verse rhythm becomes light, quick, and smooth like the bird, whose imagined space of being—"some melodious plot"—

contrasts with the heavy sense-bound "heart aches"; *i* and *s* sounds draw out the sustained melody of the song and the emphatic word "Singest" establishes its power, which will sustain the progression of the poem throughout the following stanzas with all their crescendos, pauses, major and minor cadences, harmonic echoes, and metrical interplay of long and short lines. There is a sort of reciprocity between poet and object, but it is one of opposites and non-communication, a type of imprisonment. The Nightingale herself is the drug that binds the poet to his heavy "pained" state—"too happy in thine happiness".

However, the sound of the song, which the poet is, in a sense, transcribing, impels him to investigate further. In the ensuing transpositions he pursues various means of union with the Nightingale, advancing and retracting, always learning something about the nature of his identifications and their incompleteness or false notes, until, ultimately, it is the bird who moves away, leaving the poet still with his aching heart but one that is fed with meaning rather than blankly drugged. His first desire is to become part of the Nightingale's too-happy state, to "fade away" with her and leave his pain behind; he phantasizes an identification with her self-centred comfort and indulgence. This is metaphorized by invoking "the true, the blushful Hippocrene":

> With beaded bubbles winking at the brim,
>   And purple-stained mouth,
> That I might drink, and leave the world unseen,
>   And with thee fade away into the forest dim.
>
> Fade far away, dissolve, and quite forget
>   What thou among the leaves hast never known . . .

In his early poetry, Keats sometimes characterized himself as a greedy baby-poet "gorging wonders", drunk with the colours and sounds of verse. So he tries exchanging his hemlock-draught for wine, with its more heady bouquet. But this pathway, or mental feed, caricatures itself through the grotesque bacchic features of the "purple-stained mouth" and jostling consonants ("beaded-bubbles-brim"). The poet is jolted by his own diction back into a sharp contrast between the kind of poetry that is comforting, pleasurable, and escapist, and the actual emotional situation of real life:

> Here, where men sit and hear each other groan;
> Where palsy shakes a few sad, last gray hairs,
> Where youth grows pale, and spectre-thin, and dies;
> Where but to think is to be full of sorrow
> And leaden-eyed despairs;

The emphatic, repeated "Here—where—where—where—where" establishes the real world of everyday suffering. It contrasts with the repeated "fade away . . . fade far away" with its feminine rhymes, drawn-out assonance, and hypermetrically-inserted echoes. We see, of course, Keats's brother Tom in the youth who "grows pale and spectre-thin and dies". But the point is wider than that—the point is that anyone who thinks *at all* must be "full of sorrow": and that if poetry is just used as an escapist drug it can do nothing to alchemize this beaker of "leaden-eyed despairs" (echoing the opening "dullness"); it knows nothing about it—"what thou among the leaves hast never known". The Nightingale, therefore, becomes an object of hate. The poet's statement of pain here is the kind of necessary "initial attack" on the Muse's self-containment that has been described by Adrian Stokes;[2] only after this can "inequalities, tensions and distortions" become "integrated" and "made to work", to achieve a "harder-won integration" than simple object-otherness (Stokes, 1965, pp. 23, 16).

At this point, however, the bird's song seems to impinge on him again, urgently. The word "away", which had led to nothingness, now pulses to the fore and the poet sees a new way of using it. Instead of referring to a place of privilege and seclusion (and exclusion) it is used as a verb, to insist on recognition of the poet's need. Imbued with a new active energy, he makes an imaginative leap of union:

> Away! Away! For I will fly to thee,
> Not charioted by Bacchus and his pards,
> But on the viewless wings of Poesy,
> Though the dull brain perplexes and retards.

The "viewless wings of Poesy" echo words of Milton, and it is as though the poets of the past support him in his flight of imagination—"fledging" his powers, as Keats would describe it. Instantaneously, the Nightingale responds to his projection of desire:

> Already with thee! Tender is the night,
> And haply the Queen-Moon is on her throne,
> Clustered around by all her starry fays;
> But here there is no light,
> Save what from heaven is with the breezes blown,
> Through verdurous glooms and winding mossy ways.

It is a flight not of escapism, but of re-cognition, seeing anew that first aesthetic moment in the mother-goddess's court with its constellation of light in darkness. "Dullness" has been relegated to the brain, the faculty of conscious or discursive rationalization, and he discovers (or recognizes) the type of internal vision that the great poets have so often described. The short, direct statement, "But here there is no light", leads into the drawn-out cadences that qualify its meaning: in the long last line it is as though the moon's light has merged with the rhythm of the nightingale's song, and they fuse into an introjective pathway into the depths of the forest of the mind—intersecting with the human intelligence, as Bion would say—in its "embalmed darkness", a rich and sensuous intensification of natural process:

> I cannot see what flowers are at my feet,
> Nor what soft incense hangs upon the boughs . . .

This is the state Keats (again following Milton) calls "darkling", a word whose musical sound echoes the flitting and light wings of the Nightingale and conveys the enhanced listening capacity of the poet: "Darkling I listen". As Langer points out, listening is "the primary musical activity", and so it is also in poetry, once the poet has become firmly linked to the Muse. The strenuous passivity of the listening mode is upheld by the modulations of the song.

Before the meaning of this singing object can be properly absorbed, however, there is another journey of misconception to be explored and overcome: the temptation to "cease upon the midnight with no pain"—to "die" in the sense of an eternal, oceanic-type union with the object:

> To cease upon the midnight with no pain,
> While thou art pouring forth thy soul abroad
> In such an ecstasy.

This is to fix his blissful union with the Nightingale in a false kind of permanency, the pain-free death of complete incorporation, his living identity swallowed by the song. In the manuscript, Keats actually began to write something like "But requiem'd by thee although a sod". This would entail the illusion that the Nightingale existed for the purpose of singing the poet's requiem. But Keats, it seems, immediately changed his mind—or, rather, changed his way of hearing—so that the Muse's words were actually transcribed as:

> Still wouldst thou sing, and I have ears in vain—
> To thy high requiem become a sod.

Again it is the poem's music that conveys the meaning of this illusory phantasy: the outgoing sounds of "pour . . . abroad" are suddenly cut short by the rhyme with "sod"; the Nightingale's song itself appears to stop. Reciprocally, the poet realizes he would have "ears in vain": if he indulged in the pain-free death of eternal incorporation his talents would be useless, selfishly enshrined.

This leads to a complete change of perspective regarding his purpose in life and the purpose of his pain. He is strengthened, as Hazlitt said, by the eternal forms of truth and beauty that are reflected in his mind; it is for these, not for himself, that he seeks a type of eternal life. The poem modulates into a new key, major and majestic, as he understands and celebrates the transcendental sense in which the Nightingale is immortal and her song need never end:

> Thou wast not born for death, immortal bird!
> No hungry generations tread thee down;
> . . .
> The voice I hear this passing night was heard
> In ancient days by emperor and clown:
> Perhaps the self-same song that found a path
> Through the sad heart of Ruth when, sick for home,
> She stood in tears amid the alien corn.

The new ever-bountiful Muse cannot be "trod down" (an echo of "sod"); however needy, hungry, sick, or painridden the "hungry generations", their spiritual food is always potentially available. As Bion says, the thought does not need a thinker to exist, but for the thought to be of any use to these countless needy babies it has to enter in to the march of mortality, intersecting with the human intelligence, as here.

The poet who, in the "Ode to Psyche", focused on his personal garden—"some untrodden region of my mind"—now sees himself in a wider historical or legendary context, listening to a song—the spirit of poetry—that has been heard many times before, winding its way through the stanza like the breeze-blown light:

> The same that oft-times hath
> Charmed magic casements, opening on the foam
> Of perilous seas in fairy lands forlorn.

The original heartache is carried by the song through the heart of Ruth (pity), no longer divorced from the place "here where men sit and hear each other groan", but, rather, transposing and trans-muting its painfulness. The new thought ("alien corn") is foreign, and to a degree frightening, leading by sound-association to "peril" and "forlorn"; yet, at the same time, it provides a musical answer to that original "groan", the thought-sickness that needed to be symbolized.

The final stage in this transformation by alpha-function consists in the haunting separation of poet from Muse. This separation hinges on the word "forlorn":

> Forlorn! The very word is like a bell
> To toll me back from thee to my sole self!

Haunting, because the music of the final stanza resounds with echoes from the total experience, together with the ambiguity that accompanies the enigmatic nature of the aesthetic object. "Forlorn" is the word that requires the baby to grow up, and that completes the symbolic container for his new identity-shape. While the Nightingale disengages from the contrapuntal dialogue and returns to nature, the poet senses—with some disorientation—his newly-adjusted ego boundaries:

> Adieu, adieu! Thy plaintive anthem fades
> Past the near meadows, over the still stream,
> Up the hill-side; and now 'tis buried deep
> In the next valley-glades:

Was it a vision, or a waking dream?
Fled is that music . . . do I wake or sleep?

The bird has moved away, but the song has not disappeared—
except to the "sensual ear" (as Keats will put it in his next ode, "On
a Grecian Urn"). It still exists, unheard, "buried deep" in the "next
valley"—that is, the next "aching spot" of the human heart, ready
for the next encounter with the internal object, the next "melodious
plot".

The poem has been shaped by the artistic, musical vertex, in
response to the throbbing fluctuations of the bird's song, noting its
sound, weight, and rhythm. The scientific vertex of accurately
recording a natural phenomenon anchors the spiritual questioning
to the real external world, and, in the final modulation, the religious
vertex reorientates the Nightingale as internal object—the Sleeping
Beauty in the next valley-glade. For ultimately, it is ourselves for
whom the bird sings (not the bell tolls). When the poet is gone the
poem is still there. As readers, we are among the "hungry generations", and if we can respond to the tension of the three vertices and
their modelling of creative process, the poem can become "generative" in the way of all ideas (as Bion says: 1991, p. 572).

The "Ode on a Grecian Urn"

"In any object resides the unknowable, ultimate reality", writes
Bion (1970, p. 187). The Grecian Urn is such an object, partly in
itself, and partly by virtue of its activation by the poet with his
quest to understand its significance for humanity. Like the world
itself, it has the three-dimensional reality of external nature—something to be scientifically studied and questioned—and, at the same
time, it seems to contain the historical wisdom of a human civilization, the classical prototype for a happy life. It is a Sleeping Beauty
that has slept for centuries and acquired an aura of the eternal in its
sleep; our own lives appear insignificant by comparison. As
Shakespeare said, "our little life is rounded with a sleep", and the
function of the Urn—like the Nightingale—is to draw our consciousness into some kind of aesthetic harmony. The aim of the
poem is, thus, to establish what Bion calls an "intersection" of

phenomenon and noumenon. After the temptations of solipsism and possessiveness have been overcome, we find that the object is ultimately returned to its inviolate objectivity, again with a hint of expecting the "next baby", the next visitor who will found their imaginative venture into the interior on the external solidity of the object.

The poem is a dialogue with the mind of the sculptor, but not through psychobiography; the relevant processes are contained within the art form with its power to evoke something more abstract—not just feelings, as Langer says, but the "life of feeling". The Urn's material solidity proves the validity of its approach to the ethereal, but its internal mystery is yet unknown, since the link that both receives and describes has to be established through the poet's own symbol formation. Is it a container for charred remains or for spiritual essence? How can its spirit become accessible? The Urn is both complete and expectant, on the verge of maturity, of marriage with otherness, possibly the otherness of the poet's rhyme:

> Thou still unravished bride of quietness,
>> Thou foster-child of silence and slow time,
> Sylvan historian, who canst thus express
>> A flowery tale more sweetly than our rhyme . . .

The slow-moving sensuous concentration of the opening quatrain conveys the poet's cautious, meditative approach, as he takes in the silence of the object, something emphasized by the repeated "s" sounds, that wind about it and bring the passage of "slow time" into musical and visual focus (the ideas of being and becoming). We step into Plato's soul-space. The "rhyme" echoes the twistings of the "flowery tale". As the viewer moves around the object, as if to take in all its planes simultaneously, "slow time" is gradually speeded up as the poet begins to demand an answer to its mystery:

> What leaf-fringed legend haunts about thy shape
>> Of deities or mortals, or of both,
>>> In Tempe or the dales of Arcady?
>> What men or gods are these? What maidens loth?
> What mad pursuit? What struggle to escape?
>> What pipes and timbrels? What wild ecstasy?

The poet is building up his image and thus his knowledge of the surface of the object, conveying as he does so the loops and rhythmical swirls of its bas-relief. A "legend" is, by definition, something to be read, and this is a method of reading it. At the same time, however, the urgency of his demand to know the lines of the story has the effect of losing part of the meaning that lies inside it, within its concrete tracery. Instead of musical assonance we have the light but insistent hammer-taps of "What—what—what?"

So the poet–viewer modifies his approach. He now begins to explore the ineffable qualities of the Urn: those elements that are more than the sum or synthesis of its sculpted parts, leaves or figures (Langer reminds us, "no such elements exist outside it"). He modifies his own rhyme to pay homage to the ultra-sensuous:

> Heard melodies are sweet, but those unheard
> Are sweeter; therefore, ye soft pipes, play on,
> Not to the sensual ear, but, more endeared,
> Pipe to the spirit ditties of no tone . . .

There is a new music, not of consonants, but of vowels (playing on "ear", "I" and "on" sounds), modulating into the high "piping" that smooths itself flatly into "no tone", deadening its echo. It is a paradoxical answer to "play on", yet a kind of reciprocation that acknowledges the abstraction of an inner music that is by nature not accessible to the "sensual ear". The poet's rhyme, in sympathetic harmony, can echo in material terms this ineffable spiritual music (like Ariel's) just as it can evoke the visual qualities of the Urn's surface. It is a preconception of Eliot's "music too deep to be heard" (cited by Rhode, 1998, p. 259), the silent music of human consciousness, the deep grammar that underlies the Urn as art symbol. A preconception, because it is not fully realized as yet.

At this point, the poet responds with a new and passionate longing to the Urn's "incantation" (as Stokes terms the invitation to partake in the life of the object):

> Fair youth, beneath the trees, thou canst not leave
> Thy song, nor ever can those trees be bare;
> Bold Lover, never, never canst thou kiss,
> Though winning near the goal—yet, do not grieve:
> She cannot fade, though thou hast not thy bliss,
> For ever wilt thou love, and she be fair!

His observational perspective has changed, become close-up, as he desires to become part of the story and wrap his own identity within the leaf-fringed legend on its own terms of existence. In this momentarily merged or adhesive identification, he is himself the Lover outside the ravages of time, and, in scale, smaller than the Urn itself. It is the process Stokes calls "envelopment" or "enwrapping" within the borders of the object, under the boughs of the trees, with their suggestion of eyebrows:

> Ah, happy, happy boughs! That cannot shed
>   Your leaves, nor ever bid the Spring adieu;
> And, happy melodist, unwearied,
>   For ever piping songs for ever new;

However, the high point of bliss contains within it the seeds of its own limitations. Natural process and fulfilment has been stopped; the happy-happy brows (of two eyes) cannot shed leaf-tears—they are unable to sorrow; the piper as a model for the poet seems unable to listen—the word "unwearied" reminds us of the winding "ear" sounds of the previous stanza but with the added suggestion of un-eared. The repetitions of ever-ever and happy-happy become too insistent, like the hammer-glances earlier. The ideas of "ever" and "never" become interchangeable ("nor ever", "hast not . . . for ever", "nor ever bid", "for ever new"):

> More happy love! More happy, happy love!
>   For ever warm and still to be enjoyed,
>   For ever panting, and for ever young -
> All breathing human passion far above,
>   That leaves a heart high-sorrowful and cloyed,
>   A burning forehead, and a parching tongue.

By the end of this stanza, the poet finds himself separated from his illusion of being either the Urn's lover or piper. The Urn seems unable to contain his personal feelings and anxieties, being too "far above" his infant-like smallness, where quick "panting" leads to "burning" and "parching" rather than to internal feeding "for ever warm and still to be enjoyed". The Urn retires back to the Platonic realm of Ideas.

At this crucial point, where it seems all might be lost, and the object become his enemy by means of aloofness (the "hate" vertex), the poet is moved by a new inspiration. He has already walked right round the Urn and described the human drama within its leafy frieze. Yet, now he writes as though one section of the Urn's story or legend has only become visible to him at this very moment: in psychological terms, it has only just connected with his "attention" (Bion), his consciousness—only just become available for alpha-function. It is an example of what Stokes describes as a journey "beyond identification with realised structure", beyond the beautiful surface to the underlying artistic principles:

> Who are these coming to the sacrifice?
> To what green altar, O mysterious priest,
> Lead'st thou that heifer lowing at the skies,
> And all her silken flanks with garlands dressed?

He speaks with surprise. Yet, there is a certain inevitability that the "burning", starving infant of the previous line (La Belle Dame style) should be succeeded by the idea of "sacrifice". Something needs to be sacrificed to produce the garlands of poetry, the flowery tale. As in the Ode to Psyche, the poet now identifies with the priest rather than the piper or lover. At the same time, this is alleviated by the first colour in the poem, the green altar. The "s" sounds rediscover those of the poem's opening lines, and their evocation of the "bride of quietness"; yet, instead of the hush of silence, they evoke the swish of the procession, a frieze enlivened by present movement and by the swing of "altar . . . leads . . . lowing . . . garlands" ("l" sounds). It is different in quality from the frozen ecstasy of the lover's chase. The coming sacrifice is a new kind of marriage between opposing elements. With the "mysterious priest" comes an opening to the mystery of the Urn and its contents. We are now being led by neither love nor hate, but by the quest for knowledge. In tandem with the heifer lowing at the skies, the poet's vision intersects with the Urn's surface and opens it up to a sculpture-like scene that exists only in his imagination:

> What little town by river or sea-shore,
> Or mountain-built with peaceful citadel,
> Is emptied of this folk, this pious morn?
> And, little town, thy streets for evermore
> Will silent be; and not a soul to tell
> Why thou art desolate, can e'er return.

His sensuous vision is transcended; he has moved outside the leafy border with its sculpted solidity. Yet, the scene is all the more urgently present to his consciousness: "this folk, this pious morn", like "Here" in the "Nightingale", this makes an almost physical link with the world of present being: the imaginary townsfolk are ourselves. And the high sharp sounds of the earlier "piping" (an infant's voice) here gain mellowness, depth, and sonority: a more complex sensuousness than the drier musings of wordplay that knitted together the opening stanzas. In particular, the play on the words "leaves" takes on a new poignancy, with the idea of abandonment fully confronted at this green altar of eternity. A new rhyme is introduced: the long resounding "o" in "shore—morn—evermore" magnifies the reverberations within "can e'er return" (picking up "ever—never" from previous stanzas). These words acquire depth and elevation and longevity. They also pick up the "forlorn" bass-note of the end of the "Ode to a Nightingale" with its implications of tolling the passing-bell ("toll me back . . . to my sole self")—a bell which is also present here in "soul-tell-de-sollate", full of mournful echoes.

Like the equivalent moment of reversal in the "Nightingale" (Aristotle's *peripateia)*, this awareness of loss is the foundation for a new orientation of the poet towards the object, as suggested in the revolving vertices of morn–turn and town–urn, which end in "ret–urn". It differs from, yet reminds us of, the observer walking round the Urn at the beginning in order to read its "legend". Now there is a new identification with the Urn and a new sense of purpose for himself as poet. Reading the Urn is "a process that happens on our looking" (Stokes, 1965, p. 26). This scientific explorer will become the one to relay the story of the townful of souls to the rest of humanity. Like Ishmael, he is the soul who tells, and thereby relieves the siege of its desolation, the frozen-burning excess of "happy happy love" that could not feed the internal town. Having achieved this point of self-knowledge, the poet withdraws from his close intimacy with the Urn, which returns to its inviolate, self-sufficient state:

> O Attic shape! Fair attitude! With brede
>   Of marble men and maidens overwrought,
> With forest branches and the trodden weed;

> Thou, silent form, dost tease us out of thought
> As doth eternity: Cold Pastoral!
> When old age shall this generation waste,
> Thou shalt remain, in midst of other woe
> Than ours, a friend to man, to whom thou say'st,
> Beauty is truth, truth beauty,—that is all
> Ye know on earth, and all ye need to know.

In the powerful line "When old age shall this generation waste", with its surprising development "other woe / Than ours", the poet experiences his own transience, and transcends it. He realizes that the Urn demands different identificatory processes from him. As he puts it in an earlier poem, "All is cold beauty: pain is never done". The much-discussed pun-complex on "brede–breed" and "over-wrought" marks the poet resealing the boundaries between himself and the object with gently ironic *double entendre* emphasized by the repeated "r" consonants, almost a potter's finger-pressings ("brede–marble–wrought–trod–form"). The Urn crystallizes back into a sculpted artefact, not a living world—a "shape", an "atti-tude", a receptacle for the ashes of the human heart.

At the same time, echoing Hamlet's "thoughts beyond the reaches of our souls", the imaginative pathway through to the eter-nal realm of Ideas is held open—the intersection with O. Thus, "Out of thought / As doth eternity" echoes in sound and rhythm "ever-more / Will silent be". A scientific "reading" has been conducted, investigating the sensuous surface, while respecting the limitations of this approach, so ensuring this kind of knowledge is not too "thick" (Bion) for the unknown to penetrate. The real sleeping beauty of the urn consists in its silence, which has now become bounded by sound (the verse) and so echoes with potential mean-ing. The idea of silence has taken shape and become a container for the gaps in everyday sensuous knowledge that Bion refers to through his metaphors of the tennis net, or the sculpture that acts as a trap for light, etc. The poet has sculpted the "hole" in rational knowledge through which the non-sensuous religious–artistic vertex may enter.

With the affirmation of its eternal silence, famously, the Urn speaks; but not in the way that the Nightingale sings. The meaning is not in the message itself, despite its apparent summarizing of the Keatsian philosophy. It reads like a sculpted inscription, that requires touching into life before it becomes meaningful, as does the Urn itself as object. The statement, which out of context appears either trite or enigmatic, serves to remind us that we have to experience "on the pulses" if we want it to mean anything to us. Thus, the end brings us back to the beginning—to the eternal process of learning from the object through inspiration and internalization. This is the Urn's "friendship", accompanying the continual wasting-and-generating process of living. Starting with the object's external beauty, the poet has encountered its alienness, entered its world and become part of it, then moved beyond its realized structure to identify with "a process in train" (Stokes)—thereby incorporating something of its function, not just its story, as Money-Kyrle says of the aesthetic object. This results in his own separateness once more, yet, at the same time, in the creation of his own art symbol, the poem itself. The object is returned to its initial quietude, sealed even as it speaks.

With characteristic wry humour, Keats said he did not want to make his exit from life like that "of a frog in a frost". His "cold pastoral", sealing in personal form the rich, warm contents of the western founding civilization, is a gift of life not for himself but for the rest of us, ensuring that the silence of eternity would speak. Among the ashes of a mind remains, as Bion says, "a spark that could be blown into a flame at which others could warm their hands" (Bion, 1985, p. 31).

Moneta's mourn

Keats's series of great Odes were written in the spring of 1819, a few months after the death of his brother Tom from tuberculosis, and contemporaneously with his engagement to Fanny Brawne and his dawning suspicion, then certainty, that he had the same disease as Tom. The inspiration behind all the Odes was sparked into a flame by the religious vertex represented by the passionate, revelatory "Ode to Psyche", in which Keats for the first time truly discovered his poetic voice and Muse, and "let the warm Love in":

> A rosy sanctuary will I dress
> With the wreathed trellis of a working brain . . .

And there shall be for thee all soft delight
That shadowy thought can win,
A bright torch, and a casement ope at night,
To let the warm Love in! ["Ode to Psyche"]

In the autumn of that year, however, Keats—impelled by the pressure of mortality—tackled sharper and more sinister qualities in the religious vertex and its Muse. His struggle tells us something not only about his character and situation, but about the inherent cruelty of symbol formation and the terror with which the infant self has to deal even in ordinary "catastrophic" circumstances. It is, says Bion, present at the beginning of every new experience; and in the "desperate situation" of a terminal illness there is still a place for "truth" in the sense of self-knowledge, and the *trompe l'oeil* pseudo-symbol is less satisfactory than ever (1980, pp. 126–127).

In this process, first, the religious vertex is gradually withdrawn from, during the two final Odes in the spring sequence: "Ode on Melancholy" and "Ode on Indolence". "Melancholy" is a joyous but monstrous Muse who "lives with Beauty—Beauty that must die", affirming that there is no escape from the aesthetic conflict: Joy's "grape [must] burst against [the] palate fine". In reaction to this, the poet gently seeks a temporary respite from the inner "shadows", who make emotionality too vivid, in "Indolence":

The open casement pressed a new-leaved vine,
Let in the budding warmth and throstle's lay;
O Shadows, 'twas a time to bid farewell!
["Ode on Indolence"]

The window opened for "warm Love" has now lost the metaphorical significance of the "Ode to Psyche", and becomes factual natural description. And this vertex, avoiding linking up with the religious aspect that stirs emotion, is pursued further, in a sense to a *reduction ad absurdum*, in the ode "To Autumn".

"To Autumn" is, in one sense, one of Keats's finest poems, yet, in another sense, almost sinister in its implications that the spirit has gone out of nature, leaving only a suffocating sensuousness that is blind and deaf to the infant-poet's need for reciprocation. For the primary difference in structure between "To Autumn" and the spring Odes on which it is modelled is the absence of a visionary world, or other dimension differing in quality from ordinary sensuous perception, with which there is a dialogue—an exploration of knowledge. The language of the poem is not really "natural", but artificial in its deliberate avoidance of all abstract or interpretative vocabulary. This quality of restriction is reinforced each time that the poem recalls the earlier Odes, which it does at key points, particularly the "Grecian Urn". The first quatrain is like that of the "Urn" in sound, in personification, and in visual layout:

> Season of mists and mellow fruitfulness,
> Close bosom-friend of the maturing sun,
> Conspiring with him how to load and bless
> With fruit the vines that round the thatch-eaves run.
>
> ["To Autumn"]

"Season . . . mists . . . -ness . . . close bosom . . . sun . . . conspiring . . . bless . . . vines" echoes "still unravished bride . . . quietness . . . foster . . . silence . . . slow time". The "unravished bride" has become a "close bosom friend" of a maturing sun, and the vines running round the thatch-eaves are a version of the leafy border fringing the "legend".

But from this point, "To Autumn" proceeds with its story in an opposite manner. Instead of opening out the fringed picture into the land of "no tone", the series of images are confined and locked in their original space, but stuffed with more material, like the Coachman's face saying "eat eat eat".[3] The trees are mossed and bent to the ground, the fruit is filled "with ripeness to the core", whose sound is reiterated in "set budding more / And still more, later flowers". Sound and rhythm and the heavy monosyllabic verbs ("load . . . bless . . . bend . . . fill all fruit . . . swell . . . plump") all convey the heaping on of substance. Fruitfulness becomes surfeit and excess:

> Until they think warm days will never cease
> For summer has o'er-brimmed their clammy cells.

The process of intensifying is analogous to the "happy happy", "ever ever" passage at the centre of the "Grecian Urn", except that it is more claustrophobic because restricted entirely to the world of sense, so that there is no movement either way between material and imagination. The clammy cells and mossed apple trees are like those "happy happy boughs / That cannot shed / [their] leaves, nor ever bid the spring adieu", except that the adjective in the "Urn" refers to lovers as they pivot between the imaginary and the mortal, whereas in "Autumn" there is only one reality filling the whole of the picture, and no chance of movement. In "Autumn", Keats indulges briefly the idea that nature alone can suffice, that man can live "by bread alone", like the Coachman, and still be a poet, still sing like a robin. The most minute attention is paid to the experience of the senses (touch in the first stanza, sight in the second, and hearing in the third), but there is no place for gods, dreams, or the inner world. Sense experience takes over, not as a vehicle for mental reality, but as a blocking agent; the landscape of "Autumn" is not a "thoroughfare for thoughts".

The succession of pictures in stanza 2 is far more solid and sculptural than anything in the "Grecian Urn", and portrays personified Autumn, the moving force behind this sensuous existence and therefore on one level the Muse—or substitute Muse—of the poem:

> Who hath not seen thee oft amid thy store:
> Sometimes whoever seeks abroad may find
> Thee sitting careless on a granary floor,
> Thy hair soft-lifted by the winnowing wind;

In this stanza, all outward movements ("seeks abroad", hair "soft-lifted"), are caught in mid-passage and brought back to earth, given a specific location in space; this is the nearest Keats's technique ever gets to *ut pictura poesis*. Some aspects of Autumn recall Moneta in *The Fall of Hyperion*, with the sense of artificially suspended time; except that Moneta's tragic knowledge, contained within the "teeming" hollows of her brain, is antithetical to that of the "careless" Autumn, who seems to have no knowledge of the process she personifies, but whose sense orifices are blocked like the "clammy cells" as she is drowsed into insensitivity, "sound asleep". Her "laden head" is weighed down, not with thought, but with sensuous superfluity. The picture of Autumn in particular suggests Ceres, the mother of harvest, whose search for her lost daughter had such special significance for Keats (and Milton), except that in the figure who "with patient look . . . watchest the last oozings hours by hours", one sees Ceres *without* "all that pain" (underlined by Keats in his copy of *Paradise Lost*). The mother–infant reciprocity is lost. The Muse who brings the poetic harvest in "Autumn" is specifically deprived of those qualities which made the Ceres legend meaningful, and deliberately restricted to the role of a neutral personification of a season, rather than that of a presiding goddess. She is not just motionless, but emotionless: she "watches", but she does not "care".

The third stanza begins with a poignant reference to a lost music, suggesting perhaps the spring Odes, and the Proserpine side of the Ceres myth—that lost child of spring:

> Where are the songs of spring? Aye, where are they?
> Think not of them, thou hast thy music too . . .

The question, which seems to venture outside the season's bounds, is immediately withdrawn; instead of being absorbed and integrated, like the movements between realms of experience in the Odes, it is gently denied: "Think not". The poet of "Autumn" wishes to keep within bounds, not learn any more—he knows too much already, and already feels his body "too small" to accommodate the "restless" searchings of his mind (letter to Fanny Brawne, March 1820; 1970a, p. 367). And the questioner, who had shown signs of mourning for a lost spring, is offered instead a variant of the pathetic fallacy:

> Then in a wailful choir the small gnats mourn
> Among the river sallows, borne aloft
> Or sinking as the light wind lives or dies . . .

The "mourning" sound made by gnats stems not from their foreknowledge of death (or mental pain), but is merely a coincidental function of meaningless currents of air. The observer is advised, implicitly, to accept nature's knowledge and to separate the aesthetic from the emotional; he should relinquish his memory of lost music (the music of loss), and regard it as mere appearance, as simply one of the sensuous variations of nature's full orchestra: the bleating of the lambs, the singing of the crickets, the whistling of the robin, the twittering of the swallows. Mourning, like Autumn's "watchfulness", is a freakful trick of the emotions with which humans unnecessarily torture themselves—on closer inspection, it is an illusion.

The final line of the poem, "And gathering swallows twitter in the skies", has an air of foreboding as the landscape closes in from above and the skies darken, and recalls the mysterious ritual in the "Grecian Urn" in which humanity prepares itself for the sacrifice at the altar of a heifer "lowing at the skies". But here, the skies are divested of their supernatural associations; man's question about the passing of song is ignored, and Autumn seems deaf to his plea for understanding as he is marketed at the altar of eternity. "Autumn" presents a landscape in which many creatures sing, but none has "a soul to tell / Why thou art desolate".

As with Shakespeare and all the great poets, the music of a poem is precisely where the meaning lies. The Keatsian music seems to intensify at the moment of loss, as if trying in vain to awaken the gaze of the Muse from her "careless" (uncaring) preoccupation. By the end of 1819 he has the technical virtuosity to do so, but she does not respond. She is attentive, but not to him, and not to the "hungry generations" who cry for spiritual food. She is not cruel, just uninterested in their plight. She is preoccupied with the world of sensuous existence, with fulfilment of the natural cycle in which living and dying play an equal role. The claustrophobia of sense impressions that weigh so heavily on poetic sensibility is not alleviated by any break, hole, or roughness (in Bion's language) that could allow for an intersection with O. It is the world of art and science without the religious vertex—like Keats's nightmare vision of America, the land which he once saw as poetic and pioneering, but, owing to his brother George's difficulties, came to see as a callous and "monstrous region . . . unowned of any weedy-haired gods" where "great unerring Nature once seems wrong" (ode "To Fanny").

The nature-religion of "To Autumn" was very different from the complex religious vertex that was being played out in *Hyperion*, the Miltonic epic on which Keats was working simultaneously. In this poem, the love–hate relationship with a Muse who seemed literally to be killing him focused on his ambivalence towards Milton, the poet who seemed at times to deny him access to his own Muse and assert his own personality instead. "I have but lately stood on my guard against Milton", he wrote. "Life to him would be death to me" (letter to G. and G. Keats, 21–27 September 1819; 1970a, p. 325). A part of him felt that his efforts to acquire Miltonic style were suffocating not just his prosody but his very life—on the lines described by Bion as how the "accepted rules for a poem might stifle rather than protect the growing germ of thought" (Bion, 1985, p. 55). Yet, at the same time, Keats saw his relation with Milton (now on a par with Shakespeare) as providing—in spiritual terms— the only possible way out of the sensuous claustrophobia of the Autumn-goddess:

> Shakespeare and the *Paradise Lost* every day become greater wonders to me—I look upon fine phrases like a Lover . . . My own being which I know to be becomes of more consequence to me than the crowds of Shadows in the shape of Man and women that inhabit a kingdom. The Soul is a world of itself and has enough to do in its own home. [letters to Bailey, 14 August 1819, and Reynolds, 24 August 1819; 1970a, pp. 277, 281–282]

It is in *Hyperion*, rather than "Autumn", that Keats houses his soul in its own home. He only stopped the process of revising the poem when he stopped writing poetry altogether (as he did during the last year of his life). So long as he was writing, he continued to face in his poetry the aesthetic conflict inseparable from "my own being which I know to be"; and strove to achieve a type of poetic immortality—a spirit beyond sense—by virtue of fanning the spark of sincerity and confronting the truth with all its terrors.

However, he abandoned the original version of *Hyperion*, with its restrictive shell of rules and "Miltonic inversions", and reconstructed the poem in the form of a dream that tells of the origins of human mentality and the pitfalls of delusion liable to entrap the aspiring poet on his life's journey. He was seeking different qualities in his Miltonic muse—the exploratory Milton who could face the terrors of the "vast and formless infinite" rather than the dogmatic Milton who preached truth to others and said "let this be your balm". The very subject of the poem is the making or unmaking of the poet. It begins with a mysterious and fluid background whose shadowy forms suggest primitive mental processes:

Fanatics have their dreams, wherewith they weave
A paradise for a sect, the savage too
Guesses at Heaven; pity these have not
Traced upon vellum or wild Indian leaf
The shadows of melodious utterance.

[*The Fall of Hyperion* I: 1–6]

The high tone and rigid structure of the epic style in *Hyperion* has been replaced by a new, flexible use of language, which can accommodate both decorative turns of phrase ("wherewith they weave") and almost shorthand colloquialism ("pity these have not"), giving an effect of words falling into position at the moment of thought with no endeavour to force them into a particular style or genre. In a graceful, melodious movement, the tapestry of dreams (what Keats earlier called the "tapestry empyrean") is momentarily brought into focus as it seems to be imprinted or "traced" on the veins of the wild Indian leaf, and then fades back into utterance which has not, in fact, been captured in formal art.[4] If a new poet is to be woven in the following poem, it will not be from a style already formulated, but from the ancient materials of the unfathomed unconscious, as with "emperor and clown" in the "Nightingale". In recording such a dream its quality is changed:

But bare of laurel they live, dream, and die;
For Poesy alone can tell her dreams,
With the fine spell of words alone can save
Imagination from the sable charm
And dumb enchantment.

Poetry is not merely a technical instrument at the service of the poet; it has the power, through evolving symbols, to save the imagination from a kind of death, in "dumb enchantment".

After "guessing at heaven", the imagination needs to "tell its dreams", to find reciprocation in form:

Who alive can say
"Thou art no poet; may'st not tell thy dreams"?
Since every man whose soul is not a clod
Hath visions, and would speak, if he had loved
And been well nurtured in his mother tongue.

> Whether the dream now purposed to rehearse
> Be poet's or fanatic's will be known
> When this warm scribe my hand is in its grave.
> *[The Fall of Hyperion* I: 11–18]

With this extraordinary surreal depiction of his own life-in-death (in the sound of "warm–grave") he stakes his commitment to the next stage in symbol-making. In *The Fall of Hyperion* there is not one climactic dying-into-life, but a series of experiences of death at each new stage in awareness, and with each step "thou hast dated on / Thy doom". Every gain in knowledge seems to shatter the poet's very existence, as in the clinically vivid description of the approach of death whose "palsied chill" ascends to "those streams that pulse beside the throat". The overpowering quality of this succession of catastrophic changes which make him "die and live again" before the "fated hour" of actual death is the curse of those "to whom the miseries of the world / Are misery, and will not let them rest" (I: 148–149). Those who "have no thought to come" to the Muse's sanctuary and are content to restrict their imagination to the natural world portrayed in "Autumn" do not "venom their days" in this way.

As the poem progresses (and it was written in pieces, over many months) Keats veers between hope—"flying to heaven"—and self-doubt, and tries to take a grim solace in the possibility that he is being punished for the quality of his dreams. Perhaps they are not poetic after all. When he asks the Muse directly what kind of creature he is, she replies:

> "Art thou not of the dreamer tribe?
> The poet and the dreamer are distinct,
> Diverse, sheer opposite, antipodes." [I: 198–200]

After a period of fruitless self-castigation, however, Keats ceases to demand a definition of his own activity and purpose, and instead asks the Muse to tell him a story. It is the story of the fall of the Titans, as in the first *Hyperion*. Now that he is no longer responsible for the forthcoming images, the poem begins to move again: "tell me where I am, / Whose altar this. . . What image this" (I: 211–212). Almost immediately the focus changes from Keats to "sad Moneta" herself and the depressive pain associated with an intensifying of aesthetic conflict, called forth by the veiled mysteries of her intolerable knowledge. These are contained within the misty, white curtains of her veils, whose "fragrant curtains" have from the beginning filled him with "terror", and constituted a partly protective barrier between them, consonant with "my mind's film".

Then, Moneta draws the veil. "Moneta's mourn" is very different from the "wailful choir" of "Autumn"'s gnats, whose mourning is an illusion of the breeze, a spiritless Aeolian harp. Even though she "softens" her "sphered words" as nearly as possible to those of a "mother" (I: 250), he cannot avoid seeing the truth that they convey:

> But for her eyes I should have fled away.
> They held me back, with a benignant light,
> Soft-mitigated by divinest lids ...
> So at the view of sad Moneta's brow
> I ached to see what things the hollow brain
> Behind enwombed; what high tragedy
> In the dark secret chambers of her skull
> Was acting, that could give so dread a stress
> To her cold lips, and fill with such a light
> Her planetary eyes; and touch her voice
> With such a sorrow. [I: 275–282]

The language is extraordinary and—though based on Milton's and on Shakespeare's "hollow crown"—utterly original, shadowing forth the implications of the Muse as memory, Milton (poetic forebear), adviser (from *monere*), moonlight, mother, and mourner. The poet "strain[s] out [his] eyes" as before, writing the "Ode to Psyche", he "strain[ed] at particles of light". Moneta's brow is a landscape, stretching surrealistically; the dusk vale is suddenly flooded from the light source of Moneta's eyes, as the transition is made from ordinary vision to things invisible to mortal sight.

Moneta is Keats's final Sleeping Beauty, seen by the haunting light of her own "planetary eyes". With her voice of sorrow, she is the antithesis to care-less Ceres (who is not even named as a goddess). Keats listens to the story standing by Moneta "like a stunt bramble by a solemn pine" (I: 293), like a child by its mother, saying he felt his body "too weak to support me to the height", and "I will not sing in a cage".[5] He finally relinquishes the story of his life as a poet, on the threshold of yet another catastrophic change, learning to "see as a god sees". From the Chamber of Maiden Thought he has "gone on thinking",[6] stepping over the thresholds to explore the "dark passages", ultimately to find himself in the antechamber of a dream where he dares ask for no further stories:

> Onward from the antechamber of this dream
> Where even at the open doors awhile
> I must delay, and glean my memory
> Of her high phrase—perhaps no further dare. [I: 466–468]

Nonetheless, he steps over the threshold into Canto II, just far enough to write a final farewell to the music of inspiration, in which the sound of the Muse's voice is distilled from leaves in the wind, spun out from meaningless natural process into a tapestry empyrean:

> "Mortal, that thou may'st understand aright,
> I humanize my sayings to thine ear,
> Making comparisons of earthly things;
> Or thou might'st better listen to the wind,
> Whose language is to thee a barren noise,
> Though it blows legend-laden through the trees." [II: 1–6]

Poignantly, Keats quotes these lines to his friend Woodhouse for the sound of "legend-laden". The image echoes Dante's description of the fading of inspiration "in the wind on the light leaves", retracing the "shadows of melodious utterance", and prefigures Keats's own desire for the epitaph "Here lies one whose name was writ in water". The poet standing at the open doors, like Shakespeare recording his experience of inspiration returning to the elements, provides a truer farewell to Keats's tragically curtailed life than does the solely sensuous orchestration of "To Autumn". The world of sense is not enough; it requires an internal mediator to interpret the legend-laden winds in words of poetry, that is, words of meaningful emotionality, however painful their truth may be.

　　Keats, in his final great poetic symbol, thus makes a kind of peace with the cruel "principle of beauty in all things" that he said had been his guiding aegis, recognizing that its musical spirit speaks for a reality beyond himself, though, for a short period, he has tuned in to its "humanized" language and transcribed its sayings in a reciprocal form—the "language of achievement". As Borges put it in relation to the "music" of the "Ode to a Nightingale", "Then the moment comes and he knows who he is . . . I have been feeling it ever since" (Borges, 2000, p. 99). In facing once again the emotionality of the religious vertex, Keats models the kind of symbol formation that shows us who we are.

Notes

1. Letter to Reynolds, 22 November 1817; 1970a, p. 40.
2. For a synopsis of some key features of Adrian Stokes' aesthetic philosophy, see Chapter Six of this book.
3. In a letter written in the same month as the poem, Keats describes the figure of a coachman who epitomized for him sensuous non-spirituality: "The Coachman's face says eat eat, eat . . . Perhaps I eat to persuade myself I am somebody . . . O that I had so sweet a Breast to sing as the Coachman hath! I'd give a penny for his whistle . . ." (letter to Woodhouse, 21 September 1819; 1970a, p. 293).
4. Keats had been reading Dante, and this passage echoes Dante's description at the end of *Paradiso* of the "light leaves" which momentarily held, and then released, the oracle of the Sibyl.
5. Letters of 24 August 1819 to Reynolds (p. 282), and March 1920 to Fanny Brawne (p. 365); Keats, 1970a.
6. Letter to Reynolds, 3 May 1818; Keats, 1970a, p. 95.

CHAPTER FIVE

Moving beauty

B ion and Meltzer were both, especially in their later years, concerned about the "durability" of the psychoanalytic spirit in the midst of the "clamour of gang warfare" and the economic pressures of a conformist society. The true psychoanalytic spirit, if it can be found among the brambles, is the one that should live for "hundreds of years" and reaches right back to the archaic origins of mind, and is only accessible through the countertransference dream of an art form. In the Bion–Meltzer view, psychoanalysis—that single stripe on the coat of the Tiger—existed in the world for centuries as a sleeping idea awaiting discovery by Freud, who "gave it form" (Meltzer, 1978a, Vol. III, p. 2). It was finding form that enabled him to think the underlying thought of psychoanalytic process. The Platonic artist–lover–scientist seeks for the idea of the beautiful "through all the shapes and forms of things". And, as Keats showed us, the light-winged spirit of the Nightingale moves from one form to another and sings in the next valley-glade.

With this in mind, the aim of this penultimate chapter is to open the language of the countertransference to the opportunities of another aesthetic dimension. This chapter is about life-drawing, or, rather, a particular type of life-drawing which involves combining the aesthetic features of dance, music, and the human body in its underlying Idea of an aesthetic object.[1] The aesthetic object does not stand still, but is in process of evolution, and life-drawing—an art which is temporal as well as spatial—enables us to relate directly to this quality and observe its impact. The occupation of drawing the moving body—a physically strenuous one for all concerned—may seem far removed from the contemplative mode of analyst and analysand, whose technique of communication discourages even ordinary means of eye contact. Nonetheless, this very distance between art forms may help to enhance observational skills in relation to hidden movements, hidden music, hidden balance, and responsiveness to the process of symbol formation that is happening between two distinct minds.

In *Transformations* (1965), Bion made an initial attempt to include his key new concept of "turbulence" in an aesthetic formulation. He based this on Monet's poppy-field and trees reflected in a lake. However, it was hindered by his mechanical language of "invariance" and looking for "invariants", which reduced the object to a two-dimensional Gestalt, and the interaction of observer–observed to a single-vertex pseudo-science. An invariant is a sign, not a symbol containing the essence of a Platonic Idea. The discussion does not come to life, and his own love of impressionist painting fails to convey itself.[2] However, in later works he returns often to Leonardo's skill in portraying "turbulence" through his depictions of hair and water, and meditates on their holding or symbolic capacity. As Roland Harris more beautifully describes it, in his vision of swans "struggling to rise from the long, dark water":

> As men from knowledge strive to mysteries;
>   Then yield; recall the soft returning surge
> When water receives them once more, and in dusk they burn
>   On the smooth lake in phantom, silver fires.
>
>   [Harris, "Swans"]

Turbulence is not an interference with some impeccable "invariant" quality of the "thing itself". Turbulence is what enables us to recognize reality, both external and internal, even if only momentarily before we sink back into the lake, or Plato's Cave. It is the first requirement in elevating a sign-language into a symbolic one, knowledge into mystery. Something exists that we do not know, and, as Bion's P.A. says, "Mystery is real life; real life is the concern of real analysis" (1991, p. 307). Yet, we would not have become aware of this indicator of mystery without the conjunction of at least two minds or vertices in a resonating or watery field of some kind:

> We may not so easily see this turbulence in the world that we call the mind. If we can, then it becomes possible to believe that there is such a thing as a human personality in the world of reality . . . [Bion, 1973–1974, Vol. I, pp. 41–42]

Turbulence is precisely what is presented by the human figure in space, even the apparently static figure, disturbing the surrounding air. In the life-studio it is a turbulence that demands a response, of a nature both sensuous (expressed through body-movements) and abstract, since it is concerned with the underlying idea or musical spirit, the Sleeping Beauty of the pose.

In the consulting room, playing is gradually superseded for the child by drawing as the main genre for symbol-seeking. Drawing is one of those activities that are free from the complications of verbal obscurity, and goes back to the beginning, to the childhood of our race. Perhaps, by focusing on the drawing process, we can arrive at some general considerations as to how we might invite in to our work this breath of life that derives only from the health of our internal objects, rather than making mechanical marks as a result of being too competent. Life-drawing provides another analogue for the countertransference orientation in which, rather than resting content with our limited knowledge, we can find a mode of striving to mysteries. "Modern art", said Kandinsky (cited in Hulks, 2001, p. 99) "can be born only when signs become symbols"—a statement about art in general with which all aestheticians who understand that distinction would agree. In the medium of life-drawing, how do signs become symbols, and how can we use it or be used by it to discover our own symbolic identity?

Beneficence in space: on life-drawing*

My own longstanding but somewhat jaded interest in life-drawing was rejuvenated during a period when, for several years, I attended life classes run by Meriel Hoare, in a tiny village in Hampshire. Her methodology was that of her own teacher, Cecil Collins, well known as an innovator in this field, and the classes were attended mainly by artists who wanted to "loosen up" in a way that would feed back into their other work by putting them back in touch with their creativity. The focus was not on the finished product, but on the process of making contact with the creative springs which lie outside one's own control. In this type of life-drawing, it should always be the model who discovers the pose—he or she should not be posed. (Some professional models, initially, are uncomfortable with this; they would prefer to be a passive tool of the artist or group, or to take up preconceived poses.) Instead, the model concentrates on searching for a pose, and is stopped by the artist when it is found. Music is an essential emollient in this process— for the model primarily, but also for the people drawing. Probably it is not *listened to* in the strictly aesthetic sense, that is, for the sake of the music itself. Its function is to mobilize what Stokes (1965) calls the "incantation", the invitation to partake in a dynamic situation in which lines of tension are established between model and drawer, to be embodied in lines and marks on the paper. Without the incantation of identificatory processes, there is no sense of self-exploration; this is what guides beyond to process, rather than stopping at the self-sufficient object, although it is simultaneously aware of the object's otherness.

The literal music enables the flow of a more idiosyncratic, non-sensuous music, as in Keats's "Grecian Urn". "What is the dance?" asks Langer:

---

*This was given as a talk at a conference on the theme "Drawn from Experience" in September 2004 at Oxford and later published in Portuguese ("A descoberta da identidade simbolica atraves do desenho de Modelo Vivo" [Discovering symbolic identity through life-drawing], *Revista de Psicanalise da Sociedade Psicanalitica de Porto Alegre, 11*, 2004). A version was published in 2008 as "The role of incantation: life drawing as an analogue to psychoanalytic process", *The Psychoanalytic Review, 95*(3): 463–472.

... an apparition. It springs from what the dancers do, yet it is something else. In watching a dance, you do not see what is physically before you—people running around or twisting their bodies; what you see is a display of interacting forces ... single in its motion. [Langer, 1957, p. 10]

The lines traced by the model in space are a type of abstract dance, which the drawer strives to match with lines on paper. It is this abstract apparition with which the drawer strives to identify, invited by the music, to dance in response with hands and fingers on the paper. The model's curve, and the drawer's line, both express the underlying Idea, the aesthetic essence of the scene. Stokes's (1963) phrase for this is "widely symbolic". Indeed, the drawn line itself is a type of artificial abstraction; lines do not exist in nature, yet a drawn line has the power to translate three dimensions into two dimensions, owing to its intense magnetic qualities: the "line of the Almighty", as it was termed by Blake (1966, p. 583). All the conflicts relating to boundaries (the dance between inside and outside, between body and space) congregate along the line; it pulls together and it separates simultaneously.

It is not a dance in the academic sense of having any preconceived choreography; it can indeed be a dance that is very still and quiet, almost static. But once a level of abstract communication has been reached between model and drawer, the dance of hands becomes *symbolic*: "Once the work is seen purely as a form, its symbolic character—its logical resemblance to the dynamic forms of life—is self-evident ... organic form seems to be directly contained in it" (Langer, 1957, p. 30).

Francis Sparshott explains the Aristotelian view that dance is about human states of mind, but these do not necessarily coincide with the dancer's personal state (Sparshott, 2004, p. 282); the personal presence is necessary to make the "practical wisdom of the body" visible and thereby allow it to make its own statements. "How can we tell the dancer from the dance?", as Yeats put it ("Among School Children"). In this genre, Soma is able to commune with Psyche, and past and future are gathered into the present at the temporal caesura that Eliot calls the "still point of the turning world":

At the still point of the turning world. Neither flesh nor fleshless;
Neither from nor towards; at the still point, there the dance is . . .
. . . and there is only the dance. [Eliot, 1944, "Burnt Norton"]

The invocation of the life-dancer means that the *meaning* of the
dance extends beyond the physical figure into the space between,
like Tolstoy's battleground. This Idea guides the drawer's hands
and brush or pen in a way analogous to (though not identical with)
composer and performer in music.

Any mark on pristine white paper is initially experienced as a
scar. This is not because life-drawing *is* inherently aggressive in the
Kleinian paranoid–schizoid sense, but because of the anxiety that it
might be. The tension of that possibility looms. Stokes speaks of the
need for an initial "attack" to dynamize the tensions and "make
them work". Until this happens there is no movement, the symbol
remains aloof and does not speak to the viewer or the drawer; the
final "reparation . . . is dependent on this initial attack" (Stokes,
1965, p. 23). But aggression, in itself, has no place in art, not even in
the initial stages. The type of communicative attack of which Stokes
speaks is more like the infant clamouring for attention, or like jump-
ing into the sea to explore its rocks and whirlpools, as Keats
described his entry into the world of poetry. It activates the "incantation" that the artist feels to emanate from the model, and roughens
the paper surface with expectation. The initial attack is really a statement of commitment to the search for the symbolic resolution of the
impact of the aesthetic object. Like the art viewer, the artist has trouble with the "greedy, prehensile, and controlling act of vision"
(Stokes, 1961, p. 14), that is, with omnipotent phantasies. The work
to be done between artist and model requires that a "pulse in
common" be found, a oneness as well as an otherness. This, then,
can lead to the "answering image of a reconstituted and independent good object" (*ibid.*, p. 20). Like Keats's Urn, it begins by being a
"still unravished bride of quietness", and ends "a friend to man".

In his early work, *Smooth and Rough*, Stokes finds a language for
stone whose tactile qualities could also be applied to life-drawing:

Much crude rock stands rearranged: now in the form of apertures,
of suffusion at the sides of apertures, the bites, the tears, the pinches
are miraculously identified with the recipient passages of the body,
with sense organs, with features . . . [Stokes, 1951, p. 56]

The rough treatment of smooth paper is a response to the "invitation in art", infant-like but not intrusive, as in the original Kleinian theory—just, literally, "rough", on the lower rungs of the Grid. The intactness or symbolic quality of the image is a function not only of its contained rounded existence, but also of the degree to which it invites processes of identification from the viewer—its incantatory function. In Bion's metaphor, the underlying idea lodges not in superficial smooth complacency, but in the "rough" places of the mind which are not so well-groomed by the ego: "psyche-lodgement" (Bion, 1991, p. 265). Stokes's concept of "intactness" of the object similarly relates to an ideal of beauty that is different from flawless perfection; it is the result of a relation that can survive aggression and turbulence and the tensions of the aesthetic conflict. The incantatory process interacts with the flatness of the paper to evoke a feeling of many-layered existence. Our achieved "contemplation" involves seeing the work of art "as an image not only of an independent and completed object but of the ego's integration" (Stokes, 1965, p. 19). The independent object relates to the "carving" aspect of our contemplation. By "carving", he meant refraining from manipulation and instead allowing the image to emerge or form itself, like Michelangelo's description of releasing the form within the stone, or the poets' description of inspiration. For the true symbol is not man-made; it appears from within, always with an element of the unexpected. This strenuous passivity is "hard won", but ultimately results in "beneficence in space" (Stokes, 1963, p. 69), the point at which artist and viewer, dancer and drawer, are in harmony with the dance of the emergent Idea.

Kenneth Clark, in his classic study *The Nude* (1956), traced the history of the representation of the nude not in Aristotelian terms of imitation, but in Platonic terms of humanity's search for the ideal, for an abstraction that comes to be embodied in the "human form divine" (to borrow Milton's phrase). Clark saw this as being most fully realized in the art of ancient Greece, which combined the celestial (Apollonian) and the sensuous or timeless (Dionysiac) to achieve a "finality of form" which would "control the observations of artists for centuries to come". These two approaches, like those of carving and modelling, combined culturally to form the classical ideal. The Dionysiac is moving, ecstatic, intense (also associated with Hermes and his shape-changing); the Apollonian is balanced, static, contemplative. Clark describes the function of loosely hanging drapery in the nudes of ancient Greece, particularly the female nude:

> Clinging drapery, following a plane or a contour, emphasises the stretch or twist of the body; floating drapery makes visible the line of movement through which it has just passed. Thus the aesthetic limitation of the nude body in action, that it is enclosed within an immediate present, is overcome. Drapery, by suggesting lines of force, indicates for each action a past and a possible future. [*ibid.*, pp. 169–171]

This clarifies the significance of the life-drawing "dance" to music. Clark describes the Dionysiac, or dancing, nude figures in "a pool of movement in which their bodies seem to swim" in their effort to merge with a spiritual world (p. 267). We can see how these lines of drapery are equivalent to the swirls of expressionism or to the background "possibility" marks that are drawn by the artist initially feeling his way with a drawing, marks in which the final image is embedded and contained. Such possibility marks, like the classical drapery, while representing the artist's insistence on being let in to the object's existence, do at the same time establish the nude's objective existence in time and space. The poise of a figure, whether still or moving, whether relaxed or trying to hold a difficult pose, should indicate the body's mergence with the spirit world, its potential dissolution, and, at the same time, affirms contact with the space outside it, its physicality. This is what links the Dionysiac with the inviolate balanced stillness of the Apollonian nude. These different types of nude, with their apparently different guiding divinities, are really complementary aspects of the dual approach of "modelling" and "carving" that Stokes (1963) came to see as interdependent (rather than antagonistic or mutually exclusive). Thus, the dual approach of the artist or art viewer is, in fact, a response to formal qualities inherent in the object—the work of art, or the model who is representing the Nude. Beneficence in space is achieved by means of poignancy in space—questioning, trouble, uncertainty. Ultimately both the self and the "other" are enriched, separately, via their intermixing, a form of transference–countertransference.

The problem faced by each individual artist in any life-drawing session is that of how to establish contact with the "human form divine". In other words, how to achieve a drawing that is not merely accurate but that *has life*. During a life-drawing session, it is the near-tangible sense of space surrounding the model that helps to set up carving and modelling tensions for the drawers. The opportunity to mirror this space is represented by the sheet of paper on the table. The space collapses during coffee breaks, or when people come late into the room. In the life-room, nobody talks. In order to evolve the Nude from the naked—that is, to achieve symbolic form—the model's body becomes an object of contemplation, free from any of the excitement or embarrassment or sexual feeling associated with nakedness in other situations. Immediately, the person who is the model takes on an ideal role, modelling the Nude—that aesthetic abstraction—weighted with its awesome cultural history. It is, in a sense, a role beyond themselves, like the actor on the stage. The drawer stands in awe before the model who is to take on this role for them.

The "ideal" quality cannot be packaged in a quantitative sense, in the way that post-Grecians tried to academicize and improve on physical proportions. Clark's study focuses literally on the physical proportions of the classical ideal. He also describes the stages of decadence which led to losing the spirit and, thereby, the physical fulfilment of the classical ideal: Roman grandiosity and medieval coyness. The ideal was resurrected by the Renaissance in association with Platonism, only to follow an equivalent pattern of deterioration into the dullness and pornography of the Victorian over-smooth finish, which then required to be broken up by Cubism and deconstructed by constructivism, etc. However, it may be doubted whether the reduction of the body to cubes and cylinders is really an abstracting or essentializing process, as Stokes suggests. Rather, it seems to be an aspect of the pseudo-scientific craving for respectability that bedevilled the arts throughout the twentieth century. The Helen of the *Iliad*, we remember, is known by her movements, not her features. Her face launched a thousand ships, but we have no idea what she looked like. This does not mean that physical characteristics are ignored or generalized; on the contrary, the individuality of this particular model's body and personality shows in the pose. But it is a different quality—the mysterious quality of natural poise—that enables the model to make contact with the spiritual world beyond themselves, through the interface of body-planes and surrounding space.

Life-drawers and teachers have an armoury of techniques designed to relax the fear of aggression and to discourage the smooth manipulations that arise from the need to remain in control. Thus, the "scar" anxiety can be overcome by covering the paper with faint scars, which can then be selected and accentuated constructively (by a mixture of erasing and drawing) to begin forming the image. Or one can create background texture by other means: charcoal all-over tones, ink washes, etc. Wax scumbles washed over with a light tone imitate the texture of a limestone wall; Rembrandt's nudes have this feeling of emergence from the cave. Any of these methods will create the sense of a fertile ground, which is more than a background—rather, a field of possibilities similar to the carver's marble. Frequently, this background is created by a series of quick attempts at drawing the image, a multiplicity of possible lines. Then drawing becomes a matter of choosing, matching, accentuating. The lines which are not chosen remain an integral part of the drawing: they are not erased in favour of the "right" lines; they support the final lines and represent the ground of their emergence, like Milton when he discovered a way to see "things invisible" by tracing over the vision he had lost, and seeing the unconscious meaning via the gaps in the conscious or already-known. It is well known how an artist's "mistakes" enliven a drawing; this does not apply to all wrong lines, only to those that are part of the initial exploration of space and tensions surrounding the model. A common technique is to draw in series, either the same pose from slightly different angles or a slightly different pose, each on top of the previous one. A true symbol contains the history of its own begetting, and the artist's phantasy is not of imposing form and order, but rather of discovering a congruence, following the contours, matching the image to his own inner voice.

In psychological terms, we could say that the life-studio is a microcosm of the world and the drawers are using the opportunity to develop their "world model" through mapping out experimental lines of tension. Money-Kyrle's exposition of how we "construct" our world model through the mutuality of internal and external reality is as follows:

> What we call the world is in fact a thought-model, a kind of map, of what we believe to be the possibilities of experience—"true"

where it corresponds with these possibilities, "false" where it does not, and "incomplete" where it fails to give any information about what is to be expected. We can paint it, as it were, of any colour, or embroider it in the margin as we will, and to this extent it is an arbitrary construction. But if it is to be true, it can only have one "shape"—that which fits the facts of observation. [1961, p. 62]

Here, drawing is used as an analogy for the kind of corrective cognitive experience that we expect from the transference–countertransference, in both its carving aspect (its essential or core "shape") and its modelling aspect—colouring and embroidery. As distinct from photographic representation, it becomes possible for the drawers to produce entirely different drawings, which may, nonetheless, all be "true" to "the facts of observation".

In life-drawing, then, the search for beneficence in space is a "carving" goal done by "modelling" means: the twisting and turning of a mark-making instrument, with its variations in pressure, direction, fluidity (literally, in the spreading of tones through a medium such as water). There are many techniques designed to help deflect the natural omnipotence of the modelling medium and let the inner life take over. You can draw without looking at the paper, or in a masking-out medium that can be revealed afterwards by a wash. The Chinese categorize five positions for holding the brush, graded from tight to loose. Long-handled instruments may be used, or delicate ones such as goose-quills, which also relax the hand's control, its long-established muscular dominance. The hand is complex in its capabilities; what is needed is a return to pre-history, when no movements are automatic and there is no learnt or cultural prejudice towards one type of mark over another.

In the caves of Lascaux, prehistoric man sometimes used the pre-existing contours of the limestone rock to help bring out form in a natural bas-relief, a fusion of carving and modelling. Bion said these sculptures represent "a collaboration between a human character, personality, and the forces of nature; the earth bulges out in a certain place and the artist uses that as part of his sculpture" (2005, p. 50). This bulging earth, with its painted contours, constitutes an early diaphragm or meeting-point between man and his anthropomorphic objects. Picasso said nobody would ever be able to draw as well as these cavemen. These deer and bison are, in a sense, the

first life-drawings. Their sympathetic relation to the rock epito-
mizes the coming-into-being qualities which should always
surround and define the Nude as an artistic genre. Before divinity
became incarnate in the human body, and before man saw himself
as ruling the world, he perhaps saw the divine as incarnate in the
animal body with its power and beauty and food-providing qualities. By comparison, he saw himself—on the same walls—as a tiny
stick-like creature. Man is a mere sign, an indicator; the bison is a
symbol of God on earth—a whole object in the Kleinian sense, an
expressive art symbol in Susanne Langer's sense. It exists, forever
emerging from its limestone wall with beneficence in space.

"All art is of the body", wrote Stokes in *Reflections on the Nude*
(1967, p. 40). In the Kleinian view, which, in many ways, is a restate-
ment of neoclassical or Romantic philosophy of the imagination,
the world of external nature represents the internal mother, and
works of art are organized representations of the internal mother
(Stokes, 1963); indeed, art "bears witness to intact objects even
when the subject-matter is disintegration. Whatever the form of
transcript, the original conservation or restoration is of the mother's
body" (Stokes 1967, p. 37). The Nude (most evidently the female
nude) is a specific or concentrated instance of this. Indeed, writes
Stokes, "The human body thus conceived is a promise of sanity"
(1967, p. 4). All the more, then, are representations of the body in its
direct nakedness likely to have an especially poignant significance.
Probably the drawer in the life-room, surrounded by others equally
tense with preoccupation, has some affinities with the sincere
worshipper in a house of religion. The type of "loosening up" that
goes on has nothing to do with freedom or relaxation. The artist is
aware that he or she is paying obeisance to this manifestation of the
idea of the aesthetic object. The atmosphere created in the life-room
by whoever is conducting the activity is crucial, like the "music" of
the countertransference. This is why the Nude, as an art form, has
always attracted historical associations of the processes involved in
making contact with internal objects or deities at an age-old shrine
of civilization, following in the footsteps of the priest-artists of
Lascaux.

It is well known that even a single mark already evokes an
image in the eye of the beholder. Two marks can convey the essence

of a whole figure. This links Meltzer's use of the metaphor of the deer's-tails in "making precise the function of observation" in the countertransference (see Chapter Six). One or two flicks of a white tail in the darkness are enough to generate a congruent dream in the mind of the analyst. He has also compared the psychoanalyst to a violinist, an athlete, and a racehorse (1967, p. 93), just as Bion compares the analyst to poet, artist, and musician. These comparisons are not intended to glamourize the analytic process, but to place its particular craftsmanship within a wider artistic context, in empathy with which it may refine its own model and, thereby, expand what is observable and tell-able in the analytic situation. The life-drawer, like the analyst, is even in daylight in a state of nocturnal vigilance, looking for the flash of part-object movements, the abstract essence of the dream-dance. Drawing the moving figure, with both hands in order to disable the ego's control, and identifying with the sequence rather than the finished product, is probably the ultimate incantatory response. And always, somewhere amid the wild wood of marks with its tangled thickets of lines, a genuine symbol exists: a pattern of flashing tails. For, in the psychoanalytic dance, the aesthetic object is the psychoanalytic process itself, and both the players respond to the music of the transference–countertransference. The Sleeping Beauty awakes. "How can we tell the dancer from the dance?"

Notes

1. Kina Meurle-Hallberg, in Sweden, from a basis in physiotherapy and psychotherapy, has studied the role of movement in the psychoanalytic relationship.

2. Bion and Meltzer shared a love of art, including a particular admiration for impressionist landscape painting. Bion painted; Meltzer was well read in aesthetics.

CHAPTER SIX

Psychoanalysis as an art form*

The aim of this chapter is to make more distinct the sense in which psychoanalysis may be considered an art form, as Bion and Meltzer always hoped. They believed that identifying analogies with existing art forms would benefit the practice of its own relatively new method: "a new method as old as religion and art . . . but more poorly implemented than the arts which have developed their craft for several millennia" (Meltzer, 1994b, p. 474). The future of psychoanalysis, said Meltzer, rests on "the method and the process it engenders" (1986, p. 210), and our improved understanding of the process as an "aesthetic object" (p. 209) leads to a new conception of the psychoanalytic method as an art form in which two minds together read this aesthetic object, and each gain in self-knowledge.

An aesthetic model of psychoanalysis, which is in line with artistic and poetic ideas of creativity, presupposes a more complex and dramatic field of operation than the models of single-vertex science or softhumanism (subjective relativism). The domain of

---

*A version of parts of this chapter was first published as "Psychoanalysis as an art form", *British Journal of Psychotherapy*, 25(3), 2009: 381–392.

modern psychoanalysis, Bion says, is "much wider than that known to classical analysis" (1973–1974, Vol. I, p. 39). It is based on tolerating contrary emotions of love and hate, establishing tensions between different cognitive perspectives, and seeking for congruences. These emotional and cognitive tensions create a scientific–aesthetic–religious space (Bion) that "scintillates with potentiated meaning" (Meltzer, 1983, p. 148). This is the space in which symbols are formed which contain the meaning of emotional experiences—Bion's "facts of feeling".

When Bion asks "what sort of artists can we be?" (1980, p. 73), and when Meltzer says "there can be no arguing, only evocation" (Meltzer & Williams, 1988, p. xi), they are each highlighting the importance of symbol formation in the complex artistic sense that was superbly exemplified by Keats in his twin Odes. The essential features of an art form are a symbolic structure that can hold a meaning otherwise inexpressible, and a capacity to arouse empathy or identification in the reader or viewer. These correspond to the two reasons Meltzer thought psychoanalysis would survive: first, because it helped with symbol formation, and second, because of the transference–countertransference interaction that constituted a new method for doing so. The intuited "realizations" of which Bion speaks (1970, p. 7) are not words, nor can they immediately be put into words, even though psychoanalysis is pre-eminently a verbal medium; this is the heart of the problem—how to use words symbolically rather than just as a sign-language.

Langer's investigation of the nature of symbols focused on the art symbol, as something whose organic unity had to be intuited as a single indivisible whole, however finely "articulated" the elements of its composition (1953, p. 369). She quoted Croce on intuition as a special act of perception, through which content is turned into form (ibid., p. 375). The symbols of the psychoanalytic session may appear different in formal quality from art symbols. Nonetheless, here, as in art, the primary necessity is to "formulate experience as something imaginable in the first place" (Langer, 1957, p. 100). The specific dream of the session needs to emerge from dream-life by virtue of the artist–analyst's observation in line with O (psychic distance), just as the traditional artist is characterized not by the effusion of his own feelings (subjective relativism), but by his intuitive capacity to recognize forms "symbolic of feeling"—that is, representing "not just feelings, but *the life of feeling*" (Langer, 1953, p. 372). These are what Bion calls "realizations" (1970, p. 7).

Meltzer says it is the dream that "comes to the rescue" of the analyst's predicament regarding poverty of expression, and sets symbol formation in motion (1997a, p. 176). The goal of observation and description is thereby focused, but no less difficult. First, says Bion, "we have to look—and most people don't—and while look-ing, recognize the meaning which lies beyond" (2005a, pp. 64–65). "The foundation of Truthfulness lies in the quality of observation" (Meltzer & Williams, 1988, p. 203). But which comes first, the observing or the describing? he asks (Meltzer, 1994c, p. 504). He cites Ella Sharpe on the "poetic diction" of the dream, and says the analyst's task is to find some way of "matching" it (1983, p. 136); for dreams constitute the "most passionate and creative level" of mental functioning (p. 159).

With the aim of illustrating and elaborating on these essentially aesthetic problems, I shall now consider firstly, the nature of dreams as the first observable step in symbol-formation; secondly, the symbolic congruence between two minds or parts of the mind that is needed to observe and contain the dream; and thirdly, the more abstract level of a dialogue between internal "objects in common" that relates the symbol to "the meaning that lies beyond".

The stuff of dreams

The ancient equivalence between art and dreams goes back as least as far as recorded history, and, by inference, back to the beginnings of mankind. The language of dreams "shapes the substance if not the essence of art" (Meltzer, 1992, p. 74). In both art and psycho-analysis, the mind is shaped by its dreams, even though an artwork pursues the process of dreaming to a higher level of abstraction and communicability. As Shakespeare puts it:

> We are such stuff
> As dreams are made on, and our little life
> Is rounded with a sleep . . . [*The Tempest*, IV.i.: 156]

The peculiar value of a dream, and the dream-level of an artwork, is that it cannot be invented by the self; it is a gift from the gods—

or a curse. Blake's "daughters of Beulah" (imagination) feed the sleepers with their "fairy hands"; but is it the "milk of Paradise" (Coleridge) or the sinister "manna dew" of Keats's Belle Dame? Dreams are the psyche's attempt—with a varying level of aesthetic achievement—to symbolize its present emotional conflicts in order to reorientate itself toward external and internal reality.

Artists working in all media are likely to say their work is "a dream", whether based on remembered dreams or worked-through as a type of dream in itself. As Borges expressed it:

> I write a story believing in it not as a mere history but as one believes in a dream or an idea . . . I try to be loyal to the dream and not the circumstances . . . I forget about my personal circumstances . . . I merely try to convey what the dream is. [Borges, 2000, pp. 114, 115, 119]

Art forms, as Langer said, both articulate and engender emotional experience. The dream is the originating symbol in any medium and the basis of "presentational form". Both the dream and the art-symbol have a presentational logic that differs from positivist logic, though the art-dream differs from the personal or private dream owing to its inbuilt "sense of moral obligation towards the Idea" (Langer, 1953, p. 121)—the sense of vocation that Meltzer termed "sermons to siblings" (Meltzer & Williams, 1988, p. 222). In the words of the sculptor Anthony Caro, "The artist surrenders to art's authority in an unpossessive and unselfish way" (2003, p. 205). The dream-idea governs the formation of the symbol, and he endeavours to identify with its evolution. He follows the dream, not the surface story of his desires or intentions.

Artists are also likely to object that art is not *just* a dream: implying that being dismissed as a dream overlooks the formal structure of the art symbol, and the work—both mental and physical—involved in its creation. Probably the type of psychoanalytic interpretation that, as Bion says, "victimises" art (1991, p. 588), has contributed in the past to many artists' impulse to disengage. Indeed, Francesca Bion tells us that Bion's projected anthology of poetry for psychoanalysts was specifically not intended for the purpose of encouraging "virtuosity in giving so-called 'psychoanalytic' interpretations" (1985, p. 241). Owing to the remaining echoes of Freudian psychopathography on the one hand, and the modern tendency to devalue the psychic reality of art on the other, the pre-eminence of art as a model for psychic investigation has been neglected in mainstream psychoanalytic exegesis.[1]

The artist labours to realize the dream in communicable form for the outside world, while the private dreamer has no such obligation. Yet, the quality of the generating dream behind the art symbol may itself be a crucial factor in demanding that the artist express it for the world to see. Dreams, according to Byron, are the place where "mind" is to be found in its most concentrated form:

> Attend for the moment to the action of Mind. It is in perpetual activity . . . independent of body: in dreams for instance incoherently and madly, I grant you: but it still is *Mind*, and much more Mind than when we are awake. [*Detached Thoughts*, no. 96]

Despite (or because of) the wildness of his own dreams, Byron grasped the metaphysical problem that we should take an interest in the life of dreams as a substantial phenomenon in itself. For him, dreams were proof of the immortality of the soul, and there is "more Mind" in them than in everyday consciousness, even when this mind appears to be a "sad jar of atoms" (as he described his own restless state). These atoms are the sense data of intuition. Our interest should be aroused not just by their jostling association, but by the nature of the strange, immaterial stuff of which they are made, as in Emily Brontë's description of "dreams that have run through and through me, and changed the colour of my mind" (Brontë, 1972, p. 72). Dreams are "peculiar events", says Bion (1997, p. 28), and he stresses the strangeness, the peculiarity, the aura of the unknown that trails around them.

"The dream is my landscape", said Meltzer (unpublished letter). He and Bion both adopted Freud's formulation of consciousness as an "organ for the perception of psychic qualities", to be steered around with a view to locating the turbulence that becomes manifest in conditions of "evenly suspended attention". The landscape of the mind comes to life when a dream shadow passes over it, when two minds meet. Starting from our "abyss" of ignorance, Bion suggests we "give our imagination an airing" so it has "the chance to develop into something scientific", and follow Robert Frost's road through the woods to seek out "the spirit of man . . . lurking somewhere [along] that path of thought or being" (1997, p. 29). This is the active aspect of thinking: directing attention on to shadowy thoughts which already exist and are moving in the forest of the unconscious mind waiting to be discovered. Meltzer describes this as

> waiting in the dark for the deer, grazing at night, seen by their flashing white tails . . . on the alert for movement of the quarry, part-object minimal movements that with patience can be seen to form a pattern of incipient meaning "cast before". This catching of the incipient meaning cast before is a function of receptive imagination—open to the possible, unconcerned with probability. [Meltzer, 2005b, p. 182]

The meaning has to be imaginatively discovered, peering through holes in the darkness of existing knowledge, "open to the possible", and allowing these tiny flecks of light to form into a shadowy pattern. Keats calls it "straining at particles of light in the midst of a great darkness" (letter to the George Keatses, February–May 1819; 1970a, p. 230). Bion evokes "possibility clouds" rather than "probability clouds" (1965, p. 117). Emily Dickinson similarly distinguishes the poetic or creative space from the prosaic one of the already-known, plausible, probable:

> I dwell in Possibility—
> A fairer house than Prose—
> More numerous of Windows—
> Superior—for doors . . . [1955, no. 657]

As with Dickinson's windows, or Meltzer's deer's-tails, Bion sees himself as making "boxes" in which to catch beta-elements—tiny potential thought particles—"in case that strange creature should exist and should it swim into my ken".[2]

Again, Shakespeare in *Pericles* evokes how dream thought steers its way through fluid spaces of air and water:

> Think his pilot thought
> So with his steerage shall your thoughts grow on . . .
> Like motes and shadows see them move awhile. [IV.iv.: 17–21]

The thought-pilot is Freud's organ of attention, steering across the mind-sea's turbulence, focusing on the shadowy shapes that flicker across its surface as dreams are generated and seminal thoughts are "grown on". Roland Harris, building on Shakespeare's metaphor, elaborates on the rhythmic overlappings of this flood of consciousness in his poem "The Sea":

> There are voices in the morning
> By the lonely estuary,
> Voices softer than silence calling,
> Or whispy tones of ghosts that haunt
> Falling, in Autumn leaves, the dark stairway.
>
> The exiled flood comes humbly there,
> As son to mother, kissing her feet,
> Sadly returning to the patient shore . . .
>
> Words are confined, as land to maps.
> But marshy wits and dull must find
> In heaving waves, as poets shapes
> Of terror and delight in motes,
> Symbols of power moving to no known end.
>
> [Harris, unpublished]

In this estuary landscape, the mind's dream motes and shadows (Bion's alpha-elements) wash over the caesura between sea and shore, mother and son, like heaving waves with a sense of silently returning. In the process they accrue emotional aspects of "terror and delight" (aesthetic conflict), on the journey to becoming Wordsworthian "types and symbols of Eternity, / Of first, and last, and midst, and without end" (The Prelude, VI: 571–572). Similarly Prospero's exiled (split off) compatriots return to his island-mind and, reciprocally:

> Their understanding
> Begins to swell; and the approaching tide
> Will shortly fill the reasonable shore
> That now lies foul and muddy. (The Tempest, V.i.: 79–82]

All these extracts are dreams-in-the-making, and illustrate the underlying dream of the poetic tradition, in which words and their music are perennially reconstituted into new symbols that retain the sounds and colours of their ancestry.

It is easier to understand the importance of dreams in governing our attitude to reality if we take on board the implications of
Meltzer's concept of "dream-life", in which individual dreams are
only the tip of the iceberg. Dreaming is co-extensive with Melanie
Klein's "unconscious phantasy", and continuously generates the
meaning which we then apply to our view of the world. In this
sense, dreams are not separate entities, but weave into one another
as the story of our inner life. As Bion said, dreams do not need to
be related to solar time of waking and sleeping; they are occurring
all the time (1991, p. 674). Whether or not we notice them depends
on whether the personality is turned outward or inward (Meltzer,
1994b, p. 473). An early type of artistic dream is the "buccal theatre"
(Meltzer, 1986, p. 179)[3], which is a good demonstration of how inner
and external reality act in unison and do not pull the mind in opposite directions, as is so often assumed.

Far from being undifferentiated, as in the older view of the
unconscious as a system, the dream-life that is "sampled periodically" by means of psychoanalytic (or self-analytic) observation
consists of

> a number of formal structures . . . drawn up into juxtapositions to
> create a space scintillating with potentiated meaning. Sometimes
> words and visual forms are seen to interact . . . At other times
> spaces are being created as containers of meaning. At other times
> the movements from one type of space to another, and the
> emotional difficulties of making such moves, are made apparent.
> [Meltzer, 1983, p. 148]

Such a stream-of-unconsciousness allows for the fact that not
all dreams necessarily have an aesthetic character in themselves.
Nonetheless, if mental movements, spaces, linkages, and closures
are to have any aesthetic quality, it will have its foundations here,
in dream-life. For dreams are how we deal with our aesthetic experience (ibid., p. 29); they embody our absorption of—or locate our
turning away from—the beauty of the world and its manifestations.

Dreams inevitably vary in their vividness and in their complexity, structure, and impact: from poetic condensation to repetitive
day-residue. The ancient Greeks grouped dreams into those that
came through the gates of horn or the gates of ivory, differentiating

them as being either prophetic or misleading. Dreams may be impoverished or derivative, as with "scavenging" types of learning,[4] or they may simply be poorly evolved, depending on the individual or their state of mind at that moment. The "thought" that the dream heralds may be at a primitive stage. Even so, by its very nature, "the dream is the *evolution* of O where O has evolved sufficiently to be represented by sensuous experience" (Bion, 1970, p. 70). As an alternative to the gates of horn or ivory, dreams could therefore be categorized according to how developed their aesthetic quality may be. The greater the poetic quality of the dream, the more integrated the scintillation between the various different senses and the more poetic it becomes, in the sense of fusing the visual and verbal also with the musical. Arne Nordheim, the composer, wrote of *The Tempest* that "Caliban has eyes and ears for the stuff dreams are made of. He gazes from his ugly, half-buried body up to the stars and his soul conjures up resounding visions" (Nordheim, 2006). He "guesses at Heaven" as Keats would say (*The Fall of Hyperion* I: 4). Caliban is the foetus-like sleeper who opens out the spectrum between primitive and abstract, sensuous and non-sensuous, dream and waking, for the foetus, Bion suggests, is "neither conscious nor unconscious" (1997, p. 50). "If somites could write", he declares in his *Memoir of the Future*, "the book would be 'On the Interpretation of Reality', and the theories would all be what we call dreams" (Bion, 1991, p. 470).

This half-buried aspect of the mind is always in danger of being over-regulated by the tyrannical or patriarchal aspects of a Prospero who is still struggling to accept that the island-mind is his dream, not his kingdom. Roland Harris's poem "The Statesman and the Snake" illustrates this perennial dichotomy:

> Beware, snake, of this
> Forthright gentleman!
> Turn away
> To your ferny lair; he
> Is content unknowing to
> Fashion it for you
> Out of the glare
> And you unknowing to dream
> His dream for him?

Could you, you would
Hate, as he despises,
Important beautiful adder,
Under his heel
Writhing; he walks erect
Very masculine,
His thought goes erect,
As bee to foxglove
Buzzing boldly
In as straight a line as may be -
There is no delicate inflorescence
He will not pierce:
Does he, like the bee,
Serve the flower?

He serves right and power. . . .
His frank and genial foot
Will crush you.

You will not feel him permeate
Gently with otherness your tonality . . .

Give no cause to suspect
Your inattention
To his sufficiently correct interpretation.
He will spy
Danger in you
With his frank and fearless eye.
He will turn
Every stone
To slay you
In the forest
By your lair
Alone,
Glistening in the warm sun,
Lying along the warm rocks
Listening with your inward ear
To a sound half-heard
Only within your brain. [Harris, unpublished]

The drumbeat of the short lines conveys the aggressive tread of the
boot, and contrasts with the long-drawn-out, feminine rhyme

"Glistening–listening", evoking the music of the snake's hiss and the curvaceous linkage of its vertebrae. The statesman–snake antagonism, pictured, as by many authors, as a conscious–unconscious scenario, portrays the dangers of the benevolent dictator, the single-vertex scientist of the magic staff and book who maintains power by splitting Ariel from Caliban, soul from body, music from sense. Such a statesman figure in the mind suppresses to his peril the powers of the chthonic unconscious in its "ferny lair", embodying the somatic roots of horizontal psychic stability.

The somatic, linked snake is the sleeping beauty, the underlying Idea, the dream-generator. The story of the statesman is that of the real dream censor: the "interpretative" mind ("sufficiently correct" surely?) that regards psychoanalysis as a purely discursive form, ignoring the duty to conduct it as a presentational form in which symbols evolve in response to the "inward ear" and "sounds half-heard within the brain". As Bion says, our instinctive reaction to the New Idea is either "kill it" or "find out about it" (1973–1974, Vol. I, p. 47). Instead we should respect the "lowly glandular origins of thought" since this is the way to a "language that penetrates"—a new "common sense" (1991, pp. 440, 512).

What about the terrifying or ugly dream, the dream that we might prefer to crush, rather than allow its "otherness" to "permeate"? If dreams are the "royal road to the unconscious", as Freud said, then Bion adds that these realms "have an awe-inspiring quality" and invite us "down to descend" (Bion, 1985, p. 241). He remembers the "terrifying dreams" on the walls of Lascaux and the caves of Elephanta (2005a, p. 49). These are primal dreams about the creativity of the combined object, taking the archetypal forms of hunting and sex. Their impact is bound up with love, hate, and awe, as in the aesthetic conflict. Byron gives an account of wakening from such a dream:

> I awoke from a dream!—well! and have not others dreamed?—
> Such a dream!—but she did not overtake me . . . I could not wake—
> and—and—heigho! . . . And am I to be shaken by shadows? . . .
> Since I rose, I've been in considerable bodily pain also. [*Journal*,
> 23 November 1813; 1974–80, Vol. III, p. 216]

Yet these disturbing qualities or somatic reverberations do not in themselves make the dream unaesthetic: often the contrary is the case. Haunting dreams—whether terrifying, blissful or just strange—epitomize the religious or spiritual vertex. Truth itself, as Bion said, can be "ugly and frightening" (Bion, 1977, p. 32), so it is to be expected that its representation in dreams can be too, just as "built-in ugliness" is a necessary feature of transformations in beauty (Bion, 1991, p. 145). A bear may be a bush, as Shakespeare said; meaning also, a bush may be a bear.

Meltzer further suggests that the very "vividness" of dreams makes them subject to be taken "pornographically" and acted out (Meltzer, 1983, p. 160), as perhaps were Byron's, through his continual restlessness. "She did not overtake me", as Byron said of his vivid dream, ambivalent as to whether his poetic female pursuer was seducer or mother, devil or deity. If "all work is sexual in its meaning" (Meltzer, 1973, p. 130),[5] then so are all dreams—they shake us with shadows. The alternative to a pornographic reading that results in action is to read the dream aesthetically, absorbing the impact of the object. "Action", in this context, may refer equally to verbal formulations; it is a psychological rather than a literal movement, and is the opposite of symbol formation. An interpretation constitutes an action if it colludes with a pornographic (excitable) rather than a contemplative mode of viewing the dream.

Another aspect of symbolic congruence which may appear confusing is indicated in Meltzer's discussion of the sense of passionate conviction that can be displayed by people like Melanie Klein or Esther Bick, which could be misunderstood as dogmatism (Meltzer, 1997a, p. 177). Working symbolically is very vivid, which means, also, enjoyable and interesting. It has the "appearance of life" that—as Bion bemoaned—so many psychoanalytic papers seem to lack. Yet, this may be construed as a tyrannical need to convince, and Meltzer describes how Klein or Bick might change their mind the very next day and offer a quite different interpretation to the bewildered analysand or supervisee. When asked why, they would reply, "New evidence". Conviction, owing to its realistic quality, may be construed as action, but is not necessarily intended as such: it may be an expression of the analyst's current dream of the aesthetic object.

The nature of presentational form is that it is both more primitive in its roots and more sophisticated in its implications than discursive form. As with Caliban and the snake, it is the primitive, monstrous, fish-like aspect of the mind that is most sensitive to the aesthetic and spiritual—the sea-songs of Ariel. The violinist Stephane Grapelli said that when improvising he feels like "someone half sleeping . . . great improvisers are like priests; they are thinking only of their god" (cited in Sapen, 2008, p. 247). When music enters into the dream, it gathers inevitability, as with Emily Brontë's "When the ear begins to hear and the eye begins to see". As Bernstein said, music is nothing without this sense of "inevitability", the underlying pulse of a movement that cannot be resisted (1969, p. 30). The musical Idea has "commanding form" (Langer), and, once it has been sensed, its authority takes precedence like Coleridge's "shaping spirit" of imagination. It is probably musical spirit rather than kaleidoscopic gestalt that cruelly insists on symbol closure and forces the infant self to ingest the meaning of the experience.

Within the "quiet chrysalis of dream-life" (Meltzer, 1983, p. 177), respectful of the snake in its ferny lair, we may all become the stuff that dreams are made on: that is, psychic material on which internal gods may work, subject to the "shaping spirit of imagination" (Coleridge). In this sense, people are made by their dreams— Shakespeare does mean "on" as well as "of". So the aim of the psychoanalytic process could be said to improve the quality of the patient's dreaming, not simply through interpreting dreams (a discursive form), but through re-dreaming them (a presentational or symbolic form). When Shakespeare concludes that "Our little lives are rounded by a sleep", he does not merely mean "terminated", but "rounded" in the sense of aesthetically completed and contained, which means that it reverberates beyond itself, leading to a "brave new world". Each step in growth is a "little life" and its end is really a new beginning, a "stepping of the Imagination towards a Truth" (Keats, 1970a), as is the essential nature of the depressive position. In presentational form, the scientific–artistic and the therapeutic aspects fuse and unite under O to simultaneously explore the mysteries of the mind and "rescue the lost children of a patient's personality" (Meltzer, 1973, p. 98). Shakespeare's farewell to dreaming in *The Tempest* is not disillusion, but a poignant affirmation of human mentality and a model for future generations. For as Keats maintained in *The Fall of Hyperion*, the world can be saved by the dreams of its children.

Symbolic congruence

The analyst's unconscious (and conscious) intentionality is the key to whether psychoanalysis is being used solely as a sign-language or as a symbolic one: Bion's "language of achievement" (1970, p. 2). It is possible to imagine a hypothetical scenario where the same words might be said, but with a different underlying meaning. Martha Harris speaks of the "enabling" interpretation, as distinct from the correct one, meaning, the interpretation that enables the patient to proceed with the next stage in their thinking (Negri & Harris, 2007, p. xiv).[6] Whether psychoanalytic interpretation is enabling or dogmatic (end-stopping) is something not visible to anybody but the analyst, who has to look inward for "the intention that he discerns within himself" (Meltzer, 1995b). An enabling interpretation is founded on symbolic congruence with the patient's dream—something that stems from the empathy or "imagining-into" (Keats) of which poets provide such prime examples.

Unlike poetry, dreams are not primarily for communication, writes Meltzer, but for "problem-solving" (Meltzer, 1983, pp. 13, 51–70). Initially, the analyst's impression is probably one of confusion:

> Our first striving is towards order, for the material impinges on us as analysts in just as confusing and "meaningless" a way as it does on the waking dreamer himself—probably more so. But this striving is not to put order into the chaos of the dream, for that has its own order. Rather we seek to put order into the confusion in our own minds . . . [pp. 136–137]

The initial impact is one of not-knowing, to the degree that Bion describes the analyst as repeatedly in the position of a newborn infant. How, then, can a process of putting order into our own confusion proceed, and how can it avoid the temptation to become statesman to one's own "snakiness" and act-in the countertransference with heavy tread?

The answer lies in seeking symbolic congruence with the aesthetic object. In this, as Bion often points out, the most "powerful assistance" the analyst will ever find is provided by the patient, his partner in the investigation (Bion, 1997, p. 35). He compares the search for knowledge between two minds (or parts of the mind) to Picasso painting on both sides of a piece of glass (1991, p. 465). The countertransference dream needs to match the "poetic diction" (the deep grammar) of the related dream in order to make it "enabling". Forming the symbol of the session is a result of "the fitting of the analyst's attention to the patient's co-operativeness" (Meltzer, 1986, p. 208), a process which he calls "counter-dreaming". A dream has to be *read* as well as *had* to discover the ethical implications; and reading the dream is different from just interpreting its content within the terms of a given psychoanalytic theory. Dreams are not just puzzles to be decoded, nor can they be explained away by historical trauma or its partner, wish-fulfilment.

"Countertransference is everything in psychoanalysis", said Meltzer; "The historical idea that you must not communicate the countertransference is an illusion. You are communicating it in the music of your voice all the time" (in Oelsner & Oelsner, 2005, p. 458). Bion, for a long while, in the wake of earlier psychoanalytic debates, maintained that the countertransference is by definition unconscious and therefore unknowable, so "using" it belonged to the dualism of repression-acting out.[7] But in the light of his later, more aesthetic philosophy, he saw a different use for the term and spoke of it as the analyst's prime tool for making observations (see, for example, 1977, p. 56).[8] In the "gross darkness" of a new situation, the first thing the analyst can see for sure are the "marks" which a particular emotional situation have made on himself (Bion, 1997, p. 38). In the *Memoir*, he describes the hunt for truth in terms of tracking a never-capturable "ferocious animal" known as "Absolute Truth" (1991, p. 5). Observing such tracks is the basis of the psychoanalytic hunt for meaning. The countertransference constitutes valuable evidence that "a psychoanalytic situation exists and has reality". This is different from trying to talk *about* the countertransference (Bion, 1991, p. 515). As Meltzer says in *The Psychoanalytical Process*, it is the "ambush" of "countertransference *activities*" (my italics) that constitutes a failure of psychoanalytic faith (1967, p. 92). Verbal action in the countertransference is a type of seduction or tyranny, probably taking the form of pseudo-know-ledge or moralistic interpretation. The countertransference *dream* is another matter; it is, in fact, the *only* way to read the aesthetic object of the psychoanalytic process.

Keats compares the process of dream-thinking to that of a spider weaving its web from the inside outwards, becoming gradually more complex and spatially adventurous:

> Almost any Man may like the Spider spin from his own inwards his own airy Citadel—the points of leaves and twigs on which the Spider begins her work are few and she fills the Air with a beautiful circuiting; man should be content with as few points to tip with the fine Webb of his Soul and weave a tapestry empyrean—full of Symbols for his spiritual eye, of softness for his spiritual touch, of space for his wandering, of distinctness for his Luxury. [Letter to Reynolds, 19 February 1818; 1970a, p. 66]

The Spider, like the Sleeping Beauty at the core of the mind, gener-ates "symbols for the spiritual eye", in a contained network of infi-nite possibility. Keats further develops his spider's web into a meeting of minds:

> Minds would leave each other in contrary directions, traverse each other in Numberless points, and at last greet each other at the Journeys end—an old Man and a child would talk together and the old Man be led on his Path, and the child left thinking . . . [*ibid.*, p. 66]

The dream now becomes the countertransference dream between different parts of the self who "talk together" to their mutual advancement, traversing at numberless points, leaving the inner child "thinking". Responsive to the tension of the spider at the core, the child learns *how* to think. It is a meeting that occurs not only in psychoanalysis, but in other aesthetic encounters in life that stimu-late a new way of looking.

Looking, reading, and listening, are complex processes that, like psychoanalysis, entail abandoning the intellectual "possessions" of memory and desire for total absorption in the feeling-present (Bion, 1970, p. 43). A particular type of attention is required to allow the "underlying Idea" of the emotional situation to manifest itself, and there has to be a mental space sufficiently flexible and receptive to apprehend the idea. It is no wonder "reading" is one of those terms that Bion adjures us to consider more carefully, like "experience" or "thinking" or "knowing", in order to restore its value:

> It is as well to be reminded by the poet Herman Melville that there are many ways of reading books, but very few of reading them properly—that is, with awe. How much the same is it true of reading people. [Bion, 1985, p. 241]

How do we "read" books, people, paintings, music, "with awe"— that is, with the aid of internal objects? In the following paragraphs I would like to draw some parallels with the activity of the aesthetic critic, taking the approach of the Kleinian art critic Adrian Stokes by way of an example.*

Stokes regarded our own search for comprehension of an artwork as tracing the artist's own search for aesthetic completion of the artwork: we follow its emotional contours like Keats with the "Grecian Urn", absorbed by its invitation yet finally returning it to its composed objectivity. The transient features of the attachment to the object never disappear but stay forever encapsulated in brush-strokes, colours, chisel-marks etc., and it is this quality of mental exploration that invites our identification. Observing the integration of artistic elements, we respond to the "incantation" of the aesthetic object, and find ourselves "in touch with a process that seems to be happening on our looking, a process to which we are joined as if to an alternation of part-objects" (1965, p. 26). He described this projective–introjective dialogue as "envelopment and incorporation". Like Bion and Meltzer, Stokes emphasizes the "non-pathological splitting" necessary to create a three-dimensional response to the aesthetic object in its rounded wholeness. The projective movements are communicative, questing ones, not omnipotent ones designed to control the object.

---

*This section is based on "Holding the dream" (Williams, 1988b) and on "'Knowing' the mystery: against reductionism" (Williams, 1986) in which the mode of "symbolic congruence" is distinguished from those of "linguistic behaviourism" and "softhumanism".

We can observe this process of the critic tracing the artist's *mental* movements in a passage such as this:

> It remains to speak of the tension, the counterpoint, the bringing together of storm with sun, disaster with beauty, melancholy with protected ease . . . More significant, however, even here (as deep-laid symbol) the high, lit, sail-tops, ghostly against a sky that falls in curtains of rain, cleave to the rainbow's half-circle triangularly, in contrast with foreground water, wastes rich in light flanked by darker mounds of sea, that topple over towards the spectator yet seem at the back to climb up to the boats and to the falling sky. The meeting of these movements occurs near the centre of the canvas from where one has the sense of extracting the heart of so vertiginous, so desert, yet so various a scene, in terms of the rose-red jib on the nearer sailing boat: at either side verticals incline outwards and thereby stress that centre. Awareness of a centre in great space will favour a *rencontre* of contrary factors in whatever sense. [Stokes, 1963, p. 76]

Here, the critic's achievement is to follow the artist in the abstract or essential sense of finding a pulse in common, and thinking *with* the aesthetic object. This is possible because he has immersed himself in the artist's struggle to achieve formal integrity, and has evolved a descriptive language of his own to meet the corresponding struggle of his own relationship. Making contact with the deep-laid symbol of form, and fastening himself on to the drama between warring forces that traverse "great space," he ultimately comes like the artist to the awareness of a "centre"—here the rose-red jib at the heart of a "various" scene, like the boat which "cements" the world. As with the tangential forces of the Keatsian spider's web, the lines of tension direct inwards and the governing centre radiates outwards. Instead of the frightening feeling of loss of identity and of objects in the normal pictorial sense, which alienated Turner's first viewers, the viewer here, through a "containing" mode of criticism, has his self held and reinforced even in the midst of Turner's fiery whirlpools, in the midst of awesome "great space", like Milton in the "formless infinite". He is both inside and outside the picture; space and light "envelop them and us"; "wastes rich in light . . . topple towards the spectator" then climb upwards again, governed by the heart of the picture imaged in the red jib, which is at the same time experienced as the viewer's heart or his umbilical or nipple-link with the art symbol.

In Stokes's conclusion: "Accepting his sublimity, and entertaining thus a merging experience, the spectator shrinks as a complete or separate entity but regains himself as he absorbs the stable self-inclusiveness of the art object" (*ibid*. p. 78). This drama of identifications is what the aesthetic critic can exemplify for the viewer; being drawn inside the art-object in such a way that its and his own independent integrity is established. In this way, not only does the final shape of the work of art become known, but also the developmental thrust of its author's mind become introjected. This is the experience of "beneficence in space" (p. 69)—space for a life-formative event in the mind of the observer.

We see how the creative mentality is contained within the contours of the artwork, in its sensuous beauty, and is accessed through latching on to its formal structure and setting up a projective-introjective dialogue, "a process that seems to happen on our looking . . . to which we are joined as if to an alternation of part-objects" (Stokes, 1965, p. 26). This differs from the subjective relativism that separates creative process from the thing created. The aesthetic approach of symbolic congruence demands a disciplined emotional response to the art object; it is where the Platonic spirit interdigitates with the Aristotelian emphasis on a work's structural integrity in the finite world of being. In the sophisticated aesthetics of the Kantian–Coleridgean tradition, thinking is not applied to it, but, rather, drawn out of it. It is not "superinduced", but a principle emerging from within, as Coleridge explains:

> The difference between Fabrication and Generation [is that] the latter is ab intra, *evolved;* the other ab extra, *impressed*—the latter is representative always of something not itself . . . but the former [of] its own cause within itself. [*Notebooks;* 1957, Vol. II, no. 2086]

We think *with the work*, rather than *about* it, aligning ourselves with its O. To cite a contemporary theorist, "the art itself informs modes of thinking": "The structural ordering of language . . . determines the ordering of thoughts in the reader . . . its value aesthetic and cognitive lies in the power to create complex structures of thought in our minds (Lamarque, 2004, p. 335).

The life of thoughts is embodied, like the sleeping beauty, in the "stable self-inclusiveness of the art object", ever ready to be re-awoken. As Bion said of reading Kant, he was not claiming to interpret Kant's intentions but rather, "I am using *his* 'concepts' to match with *my* 'intuitions' because in this way I can bring together a concept and an intuition, making it possible to feel that *I* know what *I* mean" (Bion, 1991, p. 194). This type of symbolic congruence is analogous to the analytic countertransference.

As Langer, Stokes, Money-Kyrle, and others have pointed out, the emotional experience of artist and art viewer is essentially the same—the difference being "primarily that of degree" (Stokes, 1961, p. 13). Reading through symbolic congruence makes for a "new experience every time", writes Borges; indeed, "art happens every time we read a poem" (Borges 2000, p. 6). The objective and the subjective, said Coleridge, are "in necessary antithesis":

> All knowledge rests on the coincidence of an object with a subject
> ... During the act of knowledge itself, the objective and subjective
> are so instantly united, that we cannot determine to which of the
> two the priority belongs. [*Biographia Literaria*; 1997, p. 152][9]

Despite the perennial debate in academic aesthetics, therefore, there is no contradiction in the fact that the aesthetic qualities are objectively inherent in the artwork, and yet can only be drawn out through a subjective response—provided it is a truthful one. As Pater put it, "in aesthetic criticism the first step towards seeing one's subject as it really is, is to know one's own impression as it really is" (1893; Pater, 2005, p. 1). Aesthetic judgment has an "internal communicative structure . . . a dialogue is thus enacted within the viewer's awareness of the work" (Podro, 2003, p. 65). An acknowledged personal response is more accurate in relation to both subject and object: "more faithful to the particular and specific features of a work of art and phenomenologically truer to the depth and range of our psychological response" (Maclagan, 2001, p. 117). As Bion says, "Non-artistic methods of communication are less accurate than those used by artists" (1991, p. 110). For the inheritors of the classical-romantic mindview, therefore, self-scrutiny in response to the aesthetic object is a prerequisite for adjusting scientifically to reality both internal and external.[10]

As Bion says, we "marvel at the product of a mind like [Shakespeare's]" (1997, p. 42). It is the *product* that is marvellous; the mind of the man we name Shakespeare was the vehicle for a truth that had become lodged in him in a way reaching far beyond his everyday consciousness. Yet, Bion reminds us, most people depend on the actors to interpret a Shakespeare play for them and bring it to life. The same is often true of music and poetry: we may require a mediator to perform or demonstrate its evocativeness before it can become a dream of our own. The life is within the object, but it does not automatically speak out, as Keats showed with the Urn. The art-object is neither a plaything for private omnipotent fantasy nor a secret whose knowledge can be unearthed by means of some clever hermeneutics. It is a mystery, not a riddle, and this is what makes it enabling and dream-generative. Academic analysis encourages the riddle model and searches for answers or diagnosis by means of discursive sign systems; listening for the inner music or poetry encourages the mystery model, and depends on the projective–introjective, inquiring–receptive mode of symbolic congruence—in other words it has to be an art form in itself. And both these modes—the discursive and the symbolic—have their corresponding equivalents in psychoanalytic practice.

Bion and Meltzer increasingly emphasized the "musical deep grammar" of the psychoanalytic dialogue, together with the negative capability required to heighten sensitivity to its communications. Together with technique, this constitutes psychoanalytic craftsmanship or method, and leads to the "language of achievement" (Bion, 1970, p. 125). Reading the deep grammar entails taking into account matters such as intuition, posture, nuance, and resonance, "temperature and distance" (Meltzer, 1994d), the balance between "routine and inspired interpretation" (Meltzer, 1994e). Bion says his "increased readiness to perceive non-verbal quality" resulted in the analytic situation becoming more "lifelike" (1977, p. 17). Interpretation, instead of being a two-dimensional framework of statements, can be used in a more flexible and complex way, so that symbols may arise from the spiritual core of the emotional phenomenon itself. Meltzer speaks of initial or background "ruminative interpretations", whose function is to "facilitate emergence" of the material rather than to pin down its significance. Beyond this, and extending the inquiry, is (he continues) the "poetic function" which "finds the metaphoric means of describing the inner world through the forms of the external world" (Meltzer, 1994d, p. 377).

"I wonder what I do when attempting to draw an analysand's attention to a pattern", asks Bion (1991, p. 227). The pattern is the symbol that is emerging between the two minds of the participants. In order for the symbol of the session to take shape, the patient's dream and the analyst's counter-dream need to work in reciprocity. Among the artistic analogues that may be sought for this, is the "duet" of melodist and contrabass in jazz, which has been described by Daniel Sapen. Sapen writes that jazz players "collectively dream new structures . . . which maintain and elaborate the piece's structure" while following emotional contours in a resonant space. The transference–countertransference may be seen as "a meeting of rhythms seeking or resisting a groove" (Sapen, 2008, p. 302).[11] In this context, Bion describes his own experience with Mrs Klein in terms of a slight failure of fit, as if they were not always on precisely the same wavelength:

> She tried to pass on to me her interpretations of the material of which her senses made her aware. But to become efficacious her methods were dependent on my receptivity . . . There must be someone or something willing to receive. [Bion, 1985, p. 68]

He is not attributing blame to either partner, but pointing to a lack of congruence at the time which was later repaired through internal re-dreaming, in a way that ultimately helped him to formulate a reverberating tension between different vertices as "O" or "passionate love".

The poet John Donne calls this search for internal musical resonance "tuning the Instrument" of the mind:

> Since I am coming to that Holy room
>   Where, with thy Quire of Saints for evermore,
> I shall be made thy Music; as I come
>   I tune the Instrument here at the door,
>   And what I must do then, think here before.
>   [Donne, "Hymn to God in my sickness"]

Ostensibly about death, these lines are actually about life and the thinking-room in which body and soul are tuned in line with O and transformed into its music. They describe the analogous process of "abandoning" oneself to psychoanalysis:[12] "If analysts can abandon themselves to analysis in the psychoanalytic sessions, they are in a position when recollecting the experience in tranquillity to discern their experience as part of a greater whole" (Bion, 1992, p. 285). This, he says, is when the analytic pair begin to "participate in the evolution of the analysis" (*ibid.*, p. 287). It is a type of "passionate love" that instigates the process of "becoming". The mind becomes the instrument of the aesthetic process of "counterdreaming": "How does [the analyst] know what he is talking about? He doesn't—he is "counter-dreaming"; he has, in fact, abandoned "thinking" (science) for intuition (art, poetry): the verbal tradition of Homer" (Meltzer, 2005b, p. 182).

In fact, as Meltzer says elsewhere, this poetic match between the domain and the instrument for investigation makes psychoanalysis "the perfect science" (1983, p. 164), and, as Bion says, it is what enables the discovery of further "configurations revealing yet other and deeper groups of the theory" (Bion, 1992, p. 285). The analyst has not really abandoned thinking; he has abandoned one type of thinking for another: abandonment to the psychoanalytic process.

Objects in common

Bion often reminds us that the dream the patient brings is not the dream he had the previous night: when he had that dream he was in a different place and was a different person. As an analyst, he says, he is well trained in interpreting dreams: the only problem is, "what was the dream?" (2005b, p. 46). The dream has already been transformed by the time it is related, not just because it has taken on verbal form, but because in doing so its meaning will have been either refined or clouded over—it will have taken a step either up or down the Grid of thinking. This is in line with philosophical investigations regarding the nature of memory (see, for example, Ricoeur, 2004). So, the relevant psychoanalytic dream is the one that is engendered during the session and that relates to its fundamental reality, its sleeping beauty. The model of the psychoanalytic process has moved from "interpreting" dreams to "reading" them to "dreaming" them in a state of awe, as in other art forms.[13]

The artist intuitively recognizes forms symbolic of feeling, and symbols come into being as a result of communication between minds. These are the vertices or co-ordinates that hold the experience for observation, as noumenon approaches phenomenon. Only when the underlying idea presses on the interface between two vertices—the caesura, or synapse (Bion)—are tensions set up that demarcate the emotional conflict. These then await potential resolution by the aesthetic object—the process. Bion says that "in an analytic situation there is the analyst, a patient, and a third party who is watching—always" (2005b, p. 19). He emphasizes the need to "identify" with this third party, which is another way of saying they need to align themselves with O, the underlying idea or basic reality of the situation, by means of a "willing suspension of disbelief" (Coleridge). Whether or not one takes O to stand for "object" or, more abstractly, for the Platonic realm of ideas, it is always the internal object who is the advance receptor for this knowledge. Meltzer says that the analytic work is done "by the transference from internal objects which enables us to seem to perform functions for the patient that are essential to the development of their thinking" (cited in Williams, 2005a, pp. 437–438). He says the analytic pair aim at a "congruence" in their phantasy (Meltzer, 1983, p. 46), so that—as he often put it in later years—there can be a "conversation between their internal objects". What sort of conversation is this?

When seeking to describe this third dimension of identification with an observer who is in some way beyond either analyst or analysand, the musical parallel is frequently sought to aid formulation. We should allow Wordsworth's "music of humanity" (*Tintern Abbey*) into the consulting room, says Bion—or at least "a little bit of it" (2005a, p. 74). The musical dimension of any art form is often the key to the way it communicates its "ineffable" meaning, the Sleeping Beauty of its spirit. As Walter Pater famously said, "All art aspires to the condition of music" (Pater, 2005, p. 90). In music, says Langer, it is the "musical matrix" that articulates all the different elements of the harmony and counterpoint, to realize its underlying idea. Bion asks, how can we make contact with this sleeping beauty or the oracle at Delphi: "Is that voice in any way audible?" (Bion, 1977, p. 37). Yet, in psychoanalysis, the verbal "talking cure" and the visual nature of dreams have overshadowed its musical resonances. If we learn to observe and appreciate this hidden music, we will become better symbol-makers and less reliant on sign systems.

Engaging objects in common is very much a function of the *music* of the transference–countertransference, and it is the objects who actually conduct this music. To illustrate the kind of consonsance that may be hoped for:

> For friendship there must be a like reaction;
> A consonance, let's say, in the perception of beauty;
> Two hearts vibrate when the lute-player passes;
> And also, difference, which the stranger gives us,
> A separate strength for the hand to offer.
> Then, far apart, to the strange note sounded,
> Friends stir in memory like tuned strings.
> [Harris, "A note with *The Silent Traveller*", unpublished]

It may be well along in a psychoanalysis before the relationship between two minds can be experienced as anything like a "friendship"; nonetheless, this is the goal towards which both partners know they are striving, drawn by a "stranger" beyond themselves: it is the awe-O, a "strange note" which tunes the vertices of two minds towards the lost knowledge of the Platonic good.[14]

In this reciprocity, or "consonance", lie the conditions for rectifying misconceptions and errors that block our eyes and ears to this music of humanity. Bion calls it getting in touch with "this other invisible self" (1997, pp. 121, 123) or "at-one-ment"—"two minds becoming one" (p. 121). These minds may also be those of artist and art reader, or (in the case of creative artists) two parts of the mind, such as the self and the internal object that speaks through an artwork. For there is always an element of countertransference in this apparent unifying, the experience of a reciprocating tension, which traditionally has been most frequently expressed in the genre of love poetry. In Donne's famous metaphysical conceit (itself not a novel one):

> Our two souls therefore, which are one,
>   Though I must go, endure not yet
> A breach, but an expansion,
>   Like gold to airy thinness beat.

If they be two, they are two so
As stiff twin compasses are two,
Thy soul the fixt foot, makes no show
To move, but doth, if th'other do.
["A Valediction forbidding mourning"]

The psychoanalytic love affair is with the method (Meltzer & Williams, 1988, p. 23), but it rests on the twin feet of the compass, and reaches its most congruent realization during the weaning process, which is a form of mutual mourning, a "valediction".

In the "natural history" of the psychoanalytic process, says Meltzer (1967), the search for objects in common begins by noting and discarding the patient's "preformed transference", that is, the preconceptions about the process brought by the patient, a version of Bion's "memory and desire" or Coleridge's "fancy", as distinct from "imagination". This constitutes a daydream (sometimes a tyrannical one) that stands in the way of the authenticity of the transference communication and of true imagination. Langer describes how, in the "daydream" type of easy listening to music, the listener is carried along by their own *petit roman*, leaving "no musical insight, no new feeling, and actually nothing heard" (Langer, 1953, p. 167). This is not a problem of understanding, in the sense of knowing-about; for the strictly *musical* elements are something "which any child can hear", and are to be distinguished from the "logical analysis of technical points". Child and adult are equally capable of either daydreaming, or of the kind of attentive listening that is "thinking music" and that develops the personality. The "primary musical activity", says Langer, is listening (*ibid.*, p. 148), so the quality of listening is indicative of the quality of learning. "Thinking music" means that composer, performer, and audience all listen to an underlying idea that is beyond themselves, "stirring in memory like tuned strings" (Harris). Here, "memory" suggests the psychic distance that is attained as a result of the aesthetic conflict being "filtered": thus, Langer says, the audience experiences "not joy or sorrow but the poignancy of either and both" (Langer, 1942, pp 222–223). This results in harmony—Bion's "at-one-ment".

The insights of psychoanalysis, says Bion, occur in "psychoanalytic talk", not in "talking about psychoanalysis". Yet, too often, the real conflict is "silent" as a result of too much knowledge (Bion, 1963, p. 55). "Psychoanalytic talk" is the psychoanalytic music. It is founded on a "polyvalent" rather than a "monovalent" state of mind (Bion, 1977, p. 25), reaching out for notes and chords with which to link and identify. Neither Bion nor Meltzer profess any particular musical talent (indeed, they both disavow any in the usual sense), yet they both regard the stirring music of the transference as of prime importance, and are aware that there is much yet to be investigated here if we had the tools for doing so. In his paper "Temperature and distance" (1976; 1994d), Meltzer enumerates some of the significant factors employed in the analyst's speaking voice to "modulate" emotionality—such as tone, rhythm, key, volume, and timbre (p. 377). Elsewhere he speaks of the "harmonic response" of the countertransference (1983, p. 164) and says that its "music" is "absolutely what the patient hears; what he hears of the meaning through interpretation is quite secondary" (in Oelsner & Oelsner, 2005, p. 458). The "duet" engaged in with the patient has "its own rhythm and cadence, like the chanter or the bagpipe" (Meltzer, 2005b, p. 181), while Bion, in his attempt to make vivid the kind of fruitful ignorance that new knowledge can penetrate, provides a musical memory of his own:

> The nearest I can get to it is probably the sort of thing the musicians know about and have developed very successfully. I remember seeing some kind of animal in a zoo when I was very small: it was rattling its horns on the bars of the enclosure. The peculiar thing about this creature was that it kept on entirely rhythmically . . .
> [1997, p. 31]

The "very perceptive grown-up" who accompanied him in this "peculiar" little adventure agreed that here was "an established rhythm that could be written down". The interstices of this container are filled with a primeval music. They are the holes in existing knowledge through which the spiritual can find a path. It has affinities with the familiar soul-in-body metaphor, and also calls up the image of a baby in a cot (we remember that Bion was fascinated by his younger sister's capacity for screaming). Like rhythm and metre in verse, is it constraint or imprisonment? For, as Bion notes elsewhere, the "accepted rules" for a poem may either stifle or protect the "growing germ" of its inner life (1985, p. 55). Bion concludes his recollections here by noting, "I am still stirred by these rhythmical communications". Perhaps the "highly perceptive grown-up" who accompanied him to the "psychoanalytic zoo" (as he calls it in the *Memoir*) was Bion's first internal analyst—that is, an early contributor to his combined object. As Meltzer says, the dreamer is the thinker: the analyst merely the comprehender of his thought.

Sometimes, the music of the meaning may consist simply in its "monotonous reiteration" (Bion, 1980, p. 45). Nothing could be less pleasurable to the outside ear, yet the analyst searching for the meaning may find it here. The underlying Idea of the communication may consist in this very repetitiveness—it may be the sound of sincerity.[15] Bion complained that in his own teaching he felt he had to make up through quantity (repeating himself) what he could not convey through poetic quality. Again, he gives an example of an incoherent stammerer who, like a one-man band, produced a "pattern of sound . . . from different parts of his anatomy" each with "a personality, like a real person, and each . . . ambitious to make use of your phonation" (1977, p. 18). In this case, the deep grammar, or underlying poetic spirit, has taken on something of the quality of a performance. It is a prelude, perhaps, to what he calls the "Bedlam" of his internal dialogue with the stammerer within, in the *Memoir*: the poet struggling to get out and achieve "disciplined debate". He compared the *Memoir*, indeed, to a musical composition written without the key signature (1991, p. ix). A whole orchestra of internal object relations underlies the music of the psychoanalytic process.

Where there is music, however, there is also "anti-music", or a category of the anti-poetic: as in the barkings of a Hitler, composed of beta-elements that lie "outside the spectrum of thought" (1977, p. 23), or "the clamour of gang warfare" that issues from external groups—Milton's "savage clamour that drowned both harp and voice" (*Paradise Lost*, VII: 36). As Bion questions, in the context of trying to make sense of his first wife's death in childbirth, was there some type of anti-music in the invisible pressure-waves that surrounded this event?

How would a sensitive conductor feel if God or Fate or the Devil condemned him to an eternity of eliciting a harmonious response from a tone-deaf, malicious, instrumentally armed orchestra? [Bion, 1985, p. 62]

This type of anti-music, imaged by poets as the "poetry-killer" (see Williams, 1982), in which the musical instruments have become a gun-battery, differs from the meaningful repetitiveness described above. It is different also from the failure of adjustment that Bion described in reflecting on his time with Mrs Klein. A patient may bring a musical instrument instead of a gun—such as a "scream" (1977, p. 44); or, in a more sophisticated way, use the power of their instrument to attempt to subvert the psychoanalytic process, like the pianist who could not respect the "discipline" of the analyst's minimum conditions (1997, p. 45). These did not include literally listening to piano music; this would simply constitute an evasion of the proper verbal medium that, as Meltzer says, acts as a "forcing house"—in the horticultural sense—for the growth of symbols (1986, p. 81). Even an accomplished musician may use their talent to block their ears to the different music of the psychoanalytic process, which, as Keats would say, is properly a "ditty of no tone", or Harris, "a sound half-heard / Only within your brain". In neo-Platonic terms, it is the inaudible music of the spheres. Well-played music can still be a cloudy or "excrementitious covering" of lies, as Blake put it—a projection needing to be withdrawn. The analyst may be seduced into a genre error by borrowing the clothing of other art forms in order to evade the stress of the art of psycho-analysis; there are many possibilities of misconception. But once the clamour of anti-poetry with its intrusive projections has died down, "As my ears became used to the silence, little sounds became easier to hear" (Bion 1977, p. 22).

A note on terminology

Bion says, "A real poet is able to use language that is penetrating and durable. I would like to use language that did the same" (Bion, 1980, p. 60). He and Meltzer frequently lament the inadequacy of discursive language to convey the psychoanalytic music—at least, in clinical papers. But, in the private clinical setting, how can a language evolve that is sufficiently evocative to reach beyond what the analyst already knows, and join the poets in attaining a

cognitive value that "transcends the interpretant's past experience"? (Langer, 1953, p. 390).

On the countertransference alert for quarry, watching with
"nocturnal vigilance", the night phone rings:

> Phone's bell
>   showers ice
>   cold drops
>   over
>   darkness.
>
> Gasping
>   from night's
>   pool it
>   shakes out
>   night in
>   our eyes.
>
> Someone answers:
>   like rain
>   in gusts
>   intel-
>   ligence
>   of pain
>   spits, flits
>   across
>   ether:
>   is known.
>
> So, in the night of day
>   rarely, rarely,
>   beauty
>   startles
>   and we obey
> [Harris, "The Night Phone", from *Pictures in a Hospital*]

Psychoanalysis, like art, begins with locating the point of pain, the
turbulence. Beauty—like pain—"startles" with its "intelligence",
flitting through the ether into the domain of sense, as in "amazement"[16] or Bion's intersection of noumenon and phenomenon. It
rings like the jarring, split burrings of a bell in a wartime hospital.[17]

Once it has penetrated consciousness (the "night of day") our response has the inevitability of a perfect cadence: "and we obey". The idea has been *had*. Yet, "in turning ourselves into receptors", says Bion, "we are taking a big risk":

> From what we know of the universe we live in some of the information may be most unwelcome; the sound or signal we receive may not be of the kind that we want to interpret, to diagnose, to try to pierce through to this "thing" behind. [1980, p. 60]

This is why psychoanalysis needs to acquire a poetic equivalent to the way that Shakespeare, for example, "strings together ordinary words in a way that starts things vibrating inside countless generations of people. Why? How is it done?" (*ibid.*). This is the language of achievement, penetrating and durable.

Bion does not mean that analysts need literally to speak or write poetry, but, rather, that they need to keep listening for the psychoanalytic music or poetry, for its commanding form or underlying idea; it is the quality of this experience that the poets help to define. The first step towards a language of achievement is to *pay attention* to the way we use words. Bion repeatedly warns us that we should not use words as if they were the "things themselves" that, in fact, they merely denote, and that we need to find ways of restoring meaning to worn-out words such as "basic" and "fundamental"—as in "fundamental reality". We need to ask: does this way of using words "resemble life", as does Vermeer's little street? In the aesthetic view of psychoanalysis, the analyst "constructs a story" (Bion, 1973–1974, Vol. I, p. 32) by means of his countertransference dream, in such a way that beyond this is glimpsed the evolution of the psychoanalytic method as aesthetic object.[18]

Many key words have lost value owing to usage: faith, belief, imagination, inspiration, transcendence, love, hate, thought, feeling, meaning, reality—all can be devalued either by too much casual use or by over-dissection, worried to death. But simply replacing one word with another does not make a formulation more precise, and attacking a word in order to get more meaning out of it or into it is rarely illuminating. Up to a point, it is possible to use words with both an everyday and a special, intensive meaning, according to the context of the occasion—as in Bion's loaded phrase, "learning from experience". We accept this naturally in discourse, and it does not, of itself, pose a problem. Indeed, as Bion said, blaming the difficulty of putting feelings into words can be an evasion of the minimum conditions necessary for functioning. It depends, as always, on the inner intentionality, and the degree to which words are functioning symbolically or just as sign systems. For, in principle, "Anything that can be said can be said clearly, poetically" (Meltzer, 2005a, p. 422).

One of Bion's attempts to solve the problem of "banality" (as he put it) was his use of desaturated, mathematical symbols instead of faded, saturated words. But this proved to have its own disadvantages, perhaps most notably in stimulating a riddling mentality in his audience; it tended to encourage the attitude that the aesthetic object was a secret to be decoded, rather than Hamlet's "heart of mystery". Another solution is to invent neologisms, yoking together syllables, puns, and part-words. And some neologisms, of course, have acquired "durability", a term which Bion associates with aesthetic evaluation. Words like "aesthetic" and "symbol" were neologisms in their day, and their classical roots gave them elegance. Bion approvingly quotes Klein saying that "psychoanalysis" was an ugly word "but available" (1980, p. 59).[19] The same applies to Klein's own ugly terms "depressive position", "paranoid–schizoid", and "object", which could well have been replaced by "humility", "arrogance", and "deity", had not those already been saturated to such a degree that nobody would have taken any notice of them in their new psychoanalytic context. However, they too have acquired durability as a result of their usefulness, and as Borges says, we have to use the ugly mythology of our time—words like "subliminal" and "subconscious" instead of "the muses or the Holy Ghost" (Borges, 1969, p. 10). Or as Bion puts it, "I was supposed to be dealing with the psyche. Not the soul exactly—that was the job of the Chaplain's Department—just the psyche if you know what I mean (because I don't)" (1985, p. 47).

The other solution, however, to the problem of terminology, favoured by Bion and Meltzer (see 1983, p. 102), was not to invent neologisms but to try to restore meaning to our beautiful existing words, to use them in a meaningful way. Certainly, Bion restored a Socratean aura to the word "ignorance", as the starting-point for any journey towards knowledge that is based on the "facts of

All receiving all;
Is identical
Imagination.
[Harris, prologue to "Sonnetinas", unpublished]

Such words have an "active principle in them", a needle-point that divides and unites. "Identical" is answered by "Imagination", moving beyond analogy to the drama of identification. The phone rings and is answered; beauty startles and we obey. The key to durability is reciprocity. In order to achieve a language that expresses the music of psychoanalytic talk, it is necessary to seek a harmonic response between internal objects, an identity of imagi-nation—the "passionate love" that Bion equates with alignment with O. Otherwise, analysis will not be durable; it will erode with oncoming emotional storms.

Notes

1. In an attempt to remedy this, Meltzer believed for a period that perhaps the primary social function of psychoanalysis was literally to analyse artists so that their art could help repair not just their own internal world, but also that of external society (1973, p. 96). This goal, however, was modified as his confidence grew in the nature of psychoanalysis as an art form in itself (*ibid.*, p. 149).

2. Referring to Keats' sonnet on Chapman's Homer (Bion, 1997, p. 29). Bion's beta-elements are (if noticed and worked on by alpha-function) potential precursors to alpha-elements, which are the building blocks of symbol formation.

3. Formulated by Meltzer in response to a clinical presentation by Maria Rhode.

4. See "A model of the child in the family in the community" (Meltzer & Harris, 1994), which expounds six types of "autonomous" learning: through introjective identification, through projective identification, through adhesive identification, learning by scavenging, and delu-sional learning, all of which contrast with learning *about* the world, which has its source in the motives of the teacher (pp. 393–394).

5. Meltzer extrapolates from Freud's original insight.

6. Romana Negri cites from an interview conducted by R. Parlani:

[Martha Harris] believed the Kleinian idea of "correct" interpretation had a certain omnipotent content, as if the patient was to be "stamped" with the right interpretation. Instead, she searched . . . for the "enabling interpretation". By "enabling" she meant that which aids the patient to express more clearly their emotional state in a way that leaves space open for further experience. The "right" interpretation closes off the experience.

7. Bion and Meltzer differ on the possibilities of alpha-function and the countertransference (both unconscious operations) being observed; see Bion, 1973–1974, Vol. II, p. 88, and Meltzer, 1995b, where he writes:

Bion thought that alpha function was not observable. Its existence could be construed from its consequences but its workings were not observable. I don't think that was necessarily correct and I think that myth formations are part of the method by which alpha function operates.

There are unconscious means of observing unconscious functions.

8. Bion also thought the term had, over time, gradually undergone a change in meaning.

9. Coleridge was here adapting Schelling's *Transcendental Philosophy*, which said that knowledge of Reality can only be attained when subjective and objective, conscious and unconscious, internal and external, reciprocally unite.

10. This is in line with the critical thinking of I. A. Richards in the first part of the twentieth century and the American "New Critics" of the 1960s, working in the Coleridgean tradition of "Such is the life, such the form". This tradition was subsequently neglected for several decades in favour of a fashion for behaviourist linguistics and mechanical modes of superimposed interpretation, which also swamped the parallel twentieth-century movement of "reader-response". However, partly owing to the new bonds forming with psychoanalytic practice (not just psychoanalytic theory), it can be seen that the Richardsonian method of focusing on the work's poetic diction, and the complementary need to focus on the reader's self-awareness, are not alternatives, but, in fact, interdigitate constructively.

11. Sapen considers, among others, Rycroft's suggestion for an auditory model of the psyche, and cites Knoblauch on "resonant minding" in the analytic situation.

12. There are echoes in Bion's wordplay on "abandon" of his puzzlement as a child over the phrase "an abandoned woman", with reference to his mother's fruit-covered hats and, thus, fertility (see Bion, 1982, p. 15).

13. Grotstein emphasizes Bion's continued exhortations to "dream the session". This is perhaps first verbalized theoretically in *Attention and Interpretation*, with Bion's more tentative observation that "the dream and the psycho-analyst's working material both share dream-like quality" (1970, p. 71).

14. The "stranger" suggests both an internal deity or muse, "strange" to the everyday self, and, the sense in which Coleridge uses the term in his poem "Frost at Midnight", where the "fluttering stranger" refers to the last flickerings of a fire on the grate, such a "stranger" traditionally portends the arrival of an absent friend, and Coleridge muses on how it "makes a toy of Thought" (ll. 23–26). Coleridge's poem turns into a meditation on the future of his son—the baby "cradled by my side"— and hopes that he will discover "The lovely shapes and sounds intelligible / Of that eternal language" of God-in-Nature.

15. In relation to the repetitiveness of the latency child, Martha Harris writes that cultivating Coleridge's "willing suspension of disbelief" can support the analyst's capacity for observation of signs of life that may underlie the "apparently interminable unchanging sessions . . . drawing similar geometric patterns" (Harris, 1987b, p. 332).

16. "Poetry . . . does not startle or amaze with itself but with its subject" (Keats, letter to Reynolds, 3 February 1818; 1970a, p. 61).

17. Despite the painful quality of the sound, it is essentially the same as the throbbing song of Keats's Nightingale that "pains the sense".

18. Just as Freud's discovery of the transference initially appeared to him a hindrance liable to undermine the entire psychoanalytic process, yet later became its linch-pin, so has his anxiety about the way his case histories always read like stories without "the stamp of science", come to be seen in a different light. Telling stories enables truthfulness and is, therefore, more scientific, not less.

19. A word coined, in fact, by Coleridge in 1805 ("psycho-analytical").

20. Keats, letter to G. and G. Keats, February–May 1819 and 17–27 September 1819 (1970a, pp. 230, 236).

My Kleinian ancestors

> As Horace said, Vixere Victoria ante Agamemnona multi,
> and yet the poet had not turned up; so the recording tape
> was a blank! They disappeared into the shade—unwept! For
> want of a poet. What a joke!
>
> (Bion, 1991, p. 120)

In dedicating this book to "my ancestors", I mean primarily the poets and other teachers or parent-figures who have become incorporated into my own internal objects. This is the sense in which Bion means it when he uses the refrain *"ante Agamemnona multi"*.[1] Such figures are remembered through internal transformations by the individual's poetic faculty, so the poet has to "turn up". At the same time, however, for anyone who has got this far in the book (including myself), there may be a certain interest and relevance in saying something specifically about my debt to some of those people—in particular my family—who have a now historical existence in the field of Kleinian psychoanalysis and from whom I learnt whatever I know about it. Needless to say, there is a significant overlap between the two types of ancestor, but they can be observed from different vertices.

To write authentically about psychoanalysis it is necessary to have had a real analysis, of the sort that (as Bion said) can be measured by its "durability" rather than its duration; to write authentically about poetry or art it is necessary to have had the emotional experience—what Bion calls "reading with awe"—as well as to have acquired the craft of reading or practising it. This book—as will have become very apparent—cannot claim to constitute even a glancing survey of the literature and research in all the related fields. It is idiosyncratic and narrow-ranging. It is not written *as* an autobiography, but, nonetheless, it has something of this quality, and follows the path of my previous books in trying to describe and locate the poetic spirit that underlies its subject: the nature of the self's relation to its inspiring objects. I have always been interested in internal ancestry, seeking to document something that is essentially ineffable: the spirit of evolution that finds its way through "mediators" in the Vale of Soulmaking. As Virginia Woolf wrote in her autobiographical *Sketch of the Past*:

> Virginia Stephen was not born on the 25th January 1882, but was born many thousands of years ago; and had from the very first to encounter instincts already acquired by thousands of ancestresses in the past. [Woolf, 2002, p. 82]

The enduring process of self-analysis is one that taps into innate internal relationships that lie at the heart of symbol formation and that date back—as Meltzer said—to at least the last glaciation and the time "when man first saw the world 'as' beautiful".

I have quoted passages from the writings of Bion and Meltzer that illustrate and illuminate my personal experience of participating in the art form that is the psychoanalytic process, and of the countertransference dream in reading literature. Meltzer (later my stepfather) was my own analyst from the age of seven to eighteen; Bion my father's during the last two years of his life. Roland (R. J.) Harris (1919–1969) was a poet and teacher who started the schools counselling course at the Tavistock Clinic together with his wife Martha (Mattie) Harris, a psychoanalyst and also head of the child psychotherapy training at the Tavistock. During his years of secondary-school teaching, Harris wrote many books for schools: plays, stories for slow readers, textbooks, including one on the reading and writing of poetry (1986).[2] His PhD thesis, still widely used among educationalists, consisted of practical research into the benefits—or otherwise—of the teaching of formal grammar. He worked for the Schools Council, and was instrumental in getting the school-leaving age raised to sixteen. Subsequently, he left schoolteaching and joined a university department (Brunel) to teach psycholinguistics. After his premature death in 1969, the Roland Harris Educational Trust was established, which published as the Clunie Press (now the Harris Meltzer Trust). My father became an analysand of Bion's—according to my mother—not for therapeutic but for philosophical reasons. It was probably she who arranged this match; she was herself a devoted supervisee of Bion's, and in the late 1970s, when Bion was still resident in California, invited him to give some lectures at the Tavistock. She and Meltzer (both then working partly in Oxford) were sadly disappointed when hopes of working with him again when he resettled near Oxford ceased with his sudden death in 1980 (see F. Bion, 1995). The Clunie Press published a book of Bion's lectures in New York and Sao Paulo (1980), the third volume of his *Memoir of the Future* (*The Dawn of Oblivion*) and its *Key*.

My mother believed that my father had a bearing on Bion's turning to fictional modes of expression in his later years. When I showed her the first draft of my essay on the *Memoir of the Future*, she remarked that "Roland must have had a great influence on Bion".[3] Certainly he, like Bion (and Valéry whom Bion mentions), saw mathematics and poetry as somehow complementary disciplines, alternate epistemological vertices straining to provide a notation for the ineffable. My father also taught the therapeutic and truth-seeking powers of storytelling for all ages. Had he lived to read the *Memoir*, he would have been among the few who admired Bion's courage, perspicacity, and humour in his last venture, rather than among the many who saw it as evidence of senility. My father's own self-analytic writings, by contrast, stem from his youth, and consist of a large body of poems written in his twenties,[4] when he had no experience of psychoanalysis and only a brief acquaintance with psychoanalysts. However, as with many— probably all—poets, the very "intensity of working out conceits"[5] leads through musical inevitability to the expression of a vision which is, in a sense, beyond the individual's life experience, and which never changes thereafter but simply reapproaches the same vision from another pathway. So, even when those whom the gods love die young, they may have left their mark. This vision is essentially the Keatsian one of "beauty is truth, truth beauty" with its complex emotionality of mourning, joy, and pain, and its philosophical penumbra of existentialism—"what *is* being?" (Byron). The poetic mentality puts us in touch with our ancestors in the dual sense of ancient, somatic realities, and of internal objects whose wisdom is founded on their integration within the personality.

After Klein and Bion, the main personal psychoanalytic influences on my mother and stepfather were Esther Bick and Roger Money-Kyrle. Esther (Nusia) Bick, famous for her papers on "second-skin" attachments, specialized in child psychoanalysis and started the infant observation course at the Tavistock, later taken over and developed by my mother.[6] She was a family friend. She was also, incidentally, Meltzer's supervisor in the early stages of my own analysis as a child. It was Bick and Meltzer together who started the Klein Study Group after Mrs Klein's death. She inherited Mrs Klein's consulting room couch and armchair, which then passed into our family.

Roger Money-Kyrle was the only man apart from my father whom I knew Meltzer to describe as "wise"; for

> like Socrates who knew how little he knew, no man is wiser than he. The pleasure of working closely with him . . . has brought a little of this wisdom to my work for where I learned psycho-analytic theory and technique from others, I learned the meaning of psychoanalysis as a thing-in-the-world from him. [Meltzer, 1978b, p. ix]

The wisdom of Money-Kyrle is, notably, described in Bionian–Platonic terms of the underlying Idea of psychoanalysis, and distinguished from learning about psychoanalysis through theory and technique. Of his own analysis with Mrs Klein, Meltzer has written:

> It makes me think about my own life experience and what lies behind the one talent that I have discovered in myself, that is the ability to read dreams, and how it came about as the result of falling in love with Melanie Klein and approaching her like an arrow from the bow, determined to have analysis with her. Not a matter of desire—a matter of life and death . . .

With me, a patient, she was very formal but not cold, attentive and observing and talking quite a lot, always to the point and full of her observations. At times of collapse, catastrophe or misery she seemed very strong and fearless. I knew from public situations that she could be aggressive and contemptuous but she was neither with me in the sessions. She seemed immune to seduction or flattery but could be very ambiguous about personal feeling for the analysand. The result was that through years of analysis I never really felt that she liked me nor should ... Her memory seemed remarkable to the end.[7]

My mother's relationship with Mrs Klein was different; she was a supervisee, not an analysand. As a child, I was sometimes taken along to these supervisions and left to play in the background. I remember the atmosphere of interest, calm, and affection that emanated from these meetings, in contradistinction to Klein's reputation as a formidable opponent in public confrontations. Both Harris and Meltzer declined to contribute reminiscences for the biography of Klein by Phyllis Grosskurth (1986—Bick having already died), since they did not like the way the story was being handled, and felt the authentic spirit of Klein was unlikely to be represented.

Meltzer points out that my mother "read voluminously; but only very unwillingly of the psycho-analytic literature" (Meltzer, 1987, p. viii). As a lifelong reader of imaginative literature, as evidenced by her recollection of reading *Wuthering Heights* aged eight while stirring the porridge on consecutive days for family breakfast, she found psychoanalytic literature boring.[8] In general, she also found psychoanalytic groupings and politics tedious, despite being a talented politician herself and contriving to quash outbreaks of infantile tyranny at the Tavistock much as she managed the weeds in her garden or the various sports teams and acting troupes she had led in her schooldays as Head Girl. Pomposity could not thrive in the ambience she created, and shrivelled to nothingness. "The slight soft Scottish furriness of her voice tempered her vehemence in debate and her laugh chimed out in a most infectious way" (Meltzer, 1987, p. vii). She died in 1986, following a car accident two years previously. Meltzer said they had been the fifteen happiest years of his life, and "there was never anybody as much loved as she was". He described her educational methods and their inspiration as follows:

By both background and inclination, Mattie was a scholar of English literature and a teacher. Nothing was more foreign to her nature than the administrative requirements that eventually devolved upon her at the Tavistock. If ever anyone had "greatness thrust upon them", it was the reluctant Mattie at the time when Mrs Bick left the Clinic and it was either up to Mattie to take over or let the infant Child Psychotherapy Course fade away.

The way in which she came to terms with this crisis in her life—and here Roland's encouragement and help was essential—was by framing a radical pedagogical method. Many of the central ideas came from Roland, who was at that time deputy headmaster of a large comprehensive school in London, prior to his going to the Ministry of Education and later to Brunel University. The central conviction, later hallowed in Bion's concepts of "learning from experience", was that the kind of learning which transformed a person into a professional worker had to be rooted in the intimate relations with inspired teachers, living and dead, present and in books. Roland himself, as poet and scholar, was an inspired teacher and the many textbooks he wrote concentrated on the development in the student of the capacity to read in both a comprehensive and a penetrating way.

The second central thesis was that learning takes place in a group context and that the management of the atmosphere was an essential task of the teachers. The prevention of elitism, the avoidance of competitiveness, and the replacement of selection by self-selection through hard work-tasks were the essential components of this task. But Mattie's experience as a teacher, during the war years and after, before she trained as a child psychotherapist and psychoanalyst, had taught her the importance of meeting the formal requirements of the Establishment if there was to be established a profession of Child Psychotherapy with positions in clinics and schools for the graduates of the Course. Here again Roland's extensive administrative knowledge was an invaluable aid to Mattie, not naturally given to orderliness, let alone to giving orders. Eventually she became an impressive negotiator and even, some claimed, politician in the interests of the Course and of the Association that was later formed in conjunction with the Hampstead Clinic and the Margaret Lowenfelt group.

Here again Bion's teaching about groups, and later about the structure of the personality, with its endoskeletal structure and its social exoskeletal carapace, played a central role in her thinking. In keeping with the differentiation between Christ and Caesar, Mattie worked out her method for meeting the requirements of the Establishment without sacrificing the ethos of the learning workgroup. But it cost her a lot, which only the support of Roland made it possible for her to sustain. When he died suddenly in 1969 of a ruptured cerebral aneurism, she developed an acute aplastic anaemia from whose fatal consequences she was saved by timely diagnosis, medication with cortisone, and a dream in which Roland told her she still had work to do for the family and the Course. [Meltzer, 1989, pp. 10–11]

My mother told me, after her marriage to my stepfather, that a colleague had expressed regret, saying that she was the only person who could have united the Kleinians, but that an alliance with Meltzer—who had become a controversial figure—precluded such diplomatic resolutions. She did not need my confirmation, but, nonetheless, I voiced my opinion that she had done the right thing. Perhaps she also felt that in all psychoanalytic institutions there was a danger of time being hijacked by those whose training analyses had resulted in their having

fairly successfully resisted a real experience and grasp of their more unpleasant parts (the unwanted O), perhaps having learned *about* them and become cleverer consciously or unconsciously in disguising them. These may return filled with enthusiasm about analytic work and training, having achieved some sort of collusion of mutual idealization with their analyst—enthusiasm about analysis for others, not for themselves. [1978; Harris, 1987b, pp. 329–330]

Her inspiration and support in attempting to turn basic assumption groupings into situations where teaching and learning was possible was less Meltzer, who was too confrontational, than her internalization of both Bion and my father, with his wide experience of school teaching and administration (and she, also, had begun her career as a schoolteacher). These strands were brought together six years after my father's death, spurred by an opportunity provided by Beri Hayward of the UN to write an educational tract called "A psychoanalytic model of the child-in-the-family-in-the-community" that was founded on Bion's ideas and on the experience of my parents' counselling service in schools (1976; Meltzer & Harris, 1994).[9]

In a paper that details the problems of dealing with the individual and the group in the Tavistock training, my mother writes:

> To recount a personal recollection of Dr. Bion when confronted with the anxieties of a candidate with a first training case: "What do I do if the patient asks me if I am a student?" "What *are* you when you *cease* to be a student of psycho-analysis?" Every teacher must be continually learning or he has no immediate experience to share. Every therapist must be learning something in the heat of every session or he has nothing of interest to say. [1978; Harris, 1987b, p. 327]

She recognized full well, however, the constantly recurring temptation in any group to turn Bion's own teaching on its head in order to create new orthodoxies and hierarchies; as she continues in the same paper:

> According to Bion's premises, all groups are subject to basic assumption activity which interferes with the capacity of the members to work severally and together. We must assume that no training group or society of psycho-analytical workers is going to be free from these phenomena ... The dependent group structure so often manifests itself in the reliance upon a crystallized selection of the theories of Freud (the original Messiah), sometimes pitted against a similar extrapolation from Melanie Klein (a latter day saint). Bion is unlikely to escape the same fate. Their theories in such a climate of polarization are suitably selected and presented to eliminate the essential questioning, contradictions and progressions inherent in the formulation of pioneers who are constantly struggling to conceptualize the clinical observations they are making. Bion's postulation about the impossibility of knowing or describing truth, about the existence of thoughts which do not require a thinker (and of psycho-analysis as one of these thoughts) may help us to try to relinquish the idea of owning our own particular brand of psycho-analysis. [p. 328]

She said it required "constant vigilance" to avoid becoming passively enrolled into whatever the latest fashionable psychoanalytic club might be perceived to be—without going so far as to actually name it the Claustrum. The antidote is to direct attention to the underlying Idea of psychoanalysis as a real experience: psychoanalysis (after Bion) being "one of those thoughts which do not require a thinker" and which pass through our convoluted mental digestive tract with a lot of questioning, contradiction and progression, rather than being owned by our own group, whichever that may be. For, as she concludes this paper, "Bion in *Experiences in Groups* indicates that in this field the label on the bottle can be no guarantee of the contents" (p. 338).

Which brings me to the label "post-Kleinian". The term (now somewhat diffuse and club-like as my mother predicted) arose in the 1980s in the light of Meltzer's radical exegesis of Bion's ideas.[10] Meltzer accepted the label somewhat wryly, while commenting in a lecture of 1989:

> Any account of "post-Kleinian" ideas at this turbulent point in time must inevitably be a subjective one, all the more since it will be based on the personal application of Bion's ambiguously stated ideas. [Williams & Waddell, 1991; Williams, 2005b, p. xvii]

He saw the term as valid in so far as it located the ancestry of "new" theories in the implicit vision of Mrs Klein herself, and, at the same time, because it linked Kleinian thinking with its philosophical, artistic, and literary forebears, in the way advocated by Bion. This did not mean the Kleinian *interpretation* of art and literature, as Bion emphasizes, but, rather, a meeting of minds and a tracery of roots, on the lines of Keats and his spider's web. It means eschewing the various shells of orthodoxy in favour of what Bion calls the "growing germ of thought" (1985, p. 55) and striving towards a more poetic mentality in the transference–countertransference situation. This means (says Bion) reigniting the "spark of sincerity" that fuelled the psychoanalytic pioneers and that is every human being's birthright—Wordsworth's "trailing clouds of glory". Like the Sleeping Beauty, this is liable to be obscured by "debris" but it still lies dormant, "a spark amidst the ashes" waiting to be "blown into a flame" (Bion, 1985, p. 31).

The archetypal poetic mentality is modelled very clearly by Keats: not just because, of all the major poets, he was most conscious of its significance and less dismayed by criticism (*pace* Byron and Shelley), but also because his vision was least contaminated by projections of the selfhood. Its key feature is the *link* between pain, beauty, and knowledge: as Bion always insisted, we must focus on the tension created *between* vertices. For Meltzer, before his own emotional contact with poetry took root, this ideal was formulated in relation to the visual artist. In a dialogue with Adrian Stokes, first published in 1963 (see Meltzer & Stokes, 1988), he described the artist's psychological placement within the social group as a "new baby" situation, arousing both hope and envy among his peers. The artist's "impulse to sermonise" to siblings is different from moralizing, in that it attempts to project not just the good parental object as a psychic entity, but also the capacity to bear depressive pain (Money-Kyrle, 1961). The artist (as Keats said of the poet) is one for whom "the miseries of the world / Are misery, and will not let them rest", striving to be "a sage, / A humanist, physician to all men" (*The Fall of Hyperion*, I: 148, 190).[11] The poetic mentality is driven not by personal guilt and reparation but by "*concern* with the present and future of the world", whose beauty is daily ravaged, such that:

> Every act of violence which he sees go unpunished and, above all, smugly unrepented, every cruel stroke of fate in the external world, threatens his internal harmony because of the pain and rage stirred. [1963; Meltzer & Stokes, 1988, p. 222]

This description of the "mature" artist's heightened internal struggle differs from the softhumanist view of creativity-as-omnipotent-illusion as much as it does from the classic view of creativity-as-guilt-and-reparation. In the 1963 dialogue, Meltzer was working out, by means of his lifelong admiration for the visual arts, the qualities of "the artist" in a more general sense: equivalent to the ideal of the philosopher for Plato, or the poet for Keats or Milton. He retained the central principle, but contact with the poets refined the language and clarified the implications. By the time the dialogue was reprinted twenty-five years on, the "good object" had become the "aesthetic object", and "depressive pain" the pain of the Aesthetic Conflict.

The new-baby situation epitomized by the artist in society is the "spiritual yeast" that makes for the "ferment of existence" (Keats) or the messianic idea that stimulates catastrophic change. This poetic mentality—in all fields—derives from the altruistic, not the narcissistic, aspect of the artist-as-a-person, the part that is most sensitive to communications from internal objects and most in touch with the apprehension of beauty thereby aroused. This is the meaning of "beauty is truth, truth beauty". Concern for the world, and Negative Capability in relation to knowledge, fuse in follow-ing "the principle of beauty in all things". Yet the world itself has always had difficulty in tolerating this complex mentality; in the context of pain or tragedy there is an almost superstitious recoil, since the "beauty that must die" quality ("Ode on Melancholy") that is in any case inherent in it, here becomes accentuated. It demands a developmental response—internal catastrophic change. Recoil is itself a failure to suffer aesthetic conflict (hope and envy) in relation to the aesthetic object: the new poet, baby, idea. As Eliot famously put it, "Human kind cannot bear very much reality" ("Burnt Norton", 1944).

Meltzer wrote in *The Claustrum*: "Out of literary companion-ship . . . the conception of aesthetic conflict arose to alter consider-ably my view of personality development and the human con-dition" (1991, p. 61). He wrote in 1970 that he was "commencing [his] literary education" (personal communication) and became inspired by the potentialities of the new direction that he hoped psychoanalysis, as well as himself, might take. This direction entailed, essentially, a focus on the primacy of the problems caused by the beauty–truth equivalent, and the trials of normal develop-ment in the face of the ambiguity of the aesthetic object (the reli-gious vertex). The aesthetic object is both within and without, and our striving is to create a more fitting match: "In nature we can find reflected the beauty we already contain. But art helps us to regain what we have lost" (Meltzer & Williams, 1988, p. 225).

Each of my three parents had their own projective setting for aesthetic conflict in the natural world. For my father it was a white-sailed boat on a grey sea or eastern estuary, as captured perfectly in words put by Bion into the mouth of his Roland of the *Memoir*: "Ah, the sea at last. The salt marshes and the pee-wees calling and the great clouds billowing past far above. Is the war over? . . . Oh Daddy—stroke me, Daddy!" (Bion, 1991, p. 75). For my stepfather, the aesthetic setting was a chestnut horse in a field, or, preferably, an ancient redwood forest; for my mother, it was a multi-flowered garden where she could "wreathe the trellis of a working brain" in microscopic reflection of the counterpane of the Scottish hills of her childhood.

Unlike Bion, Meltzer was not a poetry-reader, but living in the Harris family illuminated the opportunity which poetry provided for authorizing the innate poetry of Mrs Klein's own model: something which he felt to be not entirely evident from the wording of her theories, but which nonetheless underlay her practice and her working methods. Of *The Apprehension of Beauty*, he wrote:

> This volume has grown over the years almost as a family project of Martha Harris, her two daughters Meg and Morag, and her husband Donald Meltzer. It therefore has its roots in English literature and its branches waving wildly about in psychoanalysis. It is earnestly hoped that it will reveal more problems than it will solve. Its roots in English literature—Shakespeare, Milton, Wordsworth, Keats, Coleridge and Blake—are as strong as the psycho-analytical branching from Freud, Klein and Bion. Its philosophical soil is certainly Plato, Russell, Whitehead, Wittgenstein, Langer, Cassirer and, in aesthetics, Adrian Stokes. (Meltzer & Williams, 1988, book jacket]

"The aesthetic conflict", the core concept of this book, paves the way for the reparation of what Bion called the "victimisation" of literature by psychoanalytic interpreters. I had always been disturbed by the reductive nature of psychoanalytic literary criticism of all types[12] and looked instead for ways to develop a "symbolic congruence" with the underlying ideas in literature: one of these being to make use of literary criticism's capacity for reading deep grammar (not just intentionalism) to try to investigate the literary origins of the psychoanalytic model of the mind.[13] Another was to observe the art of literary criticism in terms of a countertransference dream or conversation between internal objects: that is, as self-analysis in response to the aesthetic object, observation in both directions being (as Bion always stressed) "of the essence" (Bion, 2005b, p. 13). Following this, it became easier to see the complementary picture—the sense in which psychoanalysis is an art form.

Awareness of the potential interdigitation of psychoanalysis with poetry helps to regain this lost source of inspiration, and, at the same time, to overcome timidity in confronting and metabolizing the pain which is intimately linked with the poetic mentality. Perhaps psychoanalysis may be gradually moving towards a position where it can begin to pay its debts to its ancestors and so make an exponential leap forward. Sanity, as Stokes suggested, may come to be considered an aesthetic achievement. For the post-Kleinian development as originally identified and the aesthetic development in psychoanalytic thinking, are the same thing. And the "new aesthetic dimension", in Meltzer's view (2005c, p. xii), places Mrs Klein herself as "the first 'post-Kleinian'".

Notes

1. Bion takes the opportunity the *Memoir* gives him to say what he really means, to "praise men who ought to have been famous", his true internal teachers (1991, p. 560, also p. 396).

2. *Poetry for You* was published posthumously in a version much abridged from the original manuscript, which had been more appropriately titled *The Craft of Verse*.

3. A character called Roland (though not a portrait of my father) plays a significant part in the *Memoir*. Bion's escape to California in 1968 from the "tank" of the British Psychoanalytic Society in order to free his own thinking may have incurred feelings of guilt for those in a transference relationship whom he had left in London. In his autobiographies, he describes how he was haunted by Sweeting and others whose deaths he could not prevent; including that of his first wife, which became associated in dream-memory with "something false [in the] psychiatric pressure waves" (Bion, 1985, p. 62).

4. He was in the process of collecting and arranging these, and his intention had been to start writing poetry again after his children were grown up. A selection was published in 1970 to inaugurate the Clunie Press.

5 Keats writing about Shakespeare in a letter to Reynolds, 22 November 1817; 1970a, p. 40.

6. See Williams (1987b) for papers by both Bick and Harris.

7. This passage amalgamates two sources: a lecture transcription on *"Weltanschauung"* and a letter (see www.harris-meltzer-trust.org.uk/ About Donald Meltzer).

8. For a brief biography of Martha Harris's early years see www.harris-meltzer-trust.org.uk/Martha Harris.

9. See also "Consultation project in a comprehensive school" and "Teacher, counsellor, therapist: towards a definition of the roles", in Williams (1987b, pp. 283–310).

10. Michael Rustin coined the term in a socio-political context (developed in Rustin, 1991).

11. These passages are complicated by Keats's despairing distinction (in view of his own illness) between true poet and "dreamer" who "venoms all his days / Bearing more woe than all his sins deserve" (*The Fall of Hyperion*, I: 175–176). This is not to say that infantile destructiveness does not *exist* in the creative artist; rather, that it is not the aspect responsible for his creativity.

12. First set down in an article "Knowing the mystery: against reductionism" (Williams, 1986).

13. The philosophy of non-intentionalist criticism was first formulated by the American New Critics: see Beardsley and Wimsatt (1946). Subsequently, both psychoanalytic and postmodern theories of criticism distorted the Shelleyan idea of the poets' prophetic vision into a parasitic assumption that the reader "understands" better than the poet.

REFERENCES AND BIBLIOGRAPHY

Aristotle (1996). *Poetics* (c. 330 BC). M. Heath (Trans.). London: Penguin.

Bacon, F. (1985). *Essays* (1625), J. Pitcher (Ed.). London: Penguin.

Bal, M. (2006). Dreaming art. In: G. Pollock (Ed.), *Psychoanalysis and the Image*. Oxford: Blackwell.

Beardsley, M., & Wimsatt, W. K. (1946). The intentional fallacy. Revised in *The Verbal Icon: Studies in the Meaning of Poetry* (pp. 3–18). Kentucky: University of Kentucky Press, 1954.

Bernstein, L. (1969). *The Joy of Music*. London: Panther.

Bion, F. (Ed.) (1985). Envoi. In: W. R. Bion, *All My Sins Remembered*. Abingdon: Fleetwood Press.

Bion, F. (1995). The days of our years. *Journal of Melanie Klein and Object Relations*, *13*(1). Weblink: http://www.psychoanalysis.org.uk/days.htm.

Bion, W. R. (1961). *Experiences in Groups*. London: Tavistock.

Bion, W. R. (1962). *Learning from Experience*. London: Heinemann.

Bion, W. R. (1963). *Elements of Psycho-analysis*. London: Heinemann.

Bion, W. R. (1965). *Transformations*. London: Heinemann.

Bion, W. R. (1967). *Second Thoughts*. London: Heinemann.

Bion, W. R. (1970). *Attention and Interpretation*. London: Tavistock.

Bion, W. R. (1973–1974). *Brazilian Lectures*, 2 vols. Rio de Janeiro: Imago.

Bion, W. R. (1977). *Two Papers: The Grid and Caesura*, J. Salomao (Ed.). São Paulo: Imago.

Bion, W. R. (1980). *Bion in New York and São Paolo*. Strath Tay, Perthshire: Clunie Press.

Bion, W. R. (1982). *The Long Week-End*. Abingdon: Fleetwood Press.

Bion, W. R. (1985). *All My Sins Remembered*, F. Bion (Ed.). Abingdon: Fleetwood Press.

Bion, W. R. (1991). *A Memoir of the Future* (3 Vols. 1975, 1977, 1979). London: Karnac.

Bion, W. R. (1992). *Cogitations*, F. Bion (Ed.). London: Karnac.

Bion, W. R. (1997). *Taming Wild Thoughts*, F. Bion (Ed.). London: Karnac.

Bion, W. R. (2005a). *Italian Seminars*, P. Slotkin (Trans.). London: Karnac.

Bion, W. R. (2005b). *The Tavistock Seminars*. London: Karnac.

Bishop, P. (2008). *Analytical Psychology and German Classical Aesthetics*. London: Routledge.

Blake, W. (1966). *Complete Writings*, G. Keynes (Ed.). Oxford: Oxford University Press.

Borges, J. (2000). *This Craft of Verse* (Charles Eliot Norton Lectures, 1969). Cambridge, MA: Harvard University Press.

Brontë, E. (1941). *Poems*, C. W. Hatfield (Ed.). New York: Columbia University Press.

Brontë, E. (1972). *Wuthering Heights* (1847), W. M. Sale (Ed.). New York: Norton.

Budd, M. (1998). Aesthetics. In: Craig (Ed.), *Routledge Encylopaedia of Philosophy*. London: Routledge.

Byron, G. G. (1974–1980). *Letters and Journals*, L. Marchand (Ed.), 6 vols. London: Murray.

Caro, A. (2003). Art and the moral imperative. In: S. J. Newton & B. Taylor (Eds.), *Painting, Sculpture and the Spiritual Dimension* (pp. 203–206). London: Oneiros.

Cassirer, E. (1953). *Language and Myth* (1946). New York: Dover.

Cassirer, E. (1961). *Rousseau, Kant, Goethe*. Hamden, CT: Archon.

Catan, J. R. (1990). *A History of Ancient Philosophy: Plato and Aristotle*. New York: State University of New York Press.

Clark, K. (1956). *The Nude*. Harmondsworth: Penguin.

Coleridge. S. T. (1956). Letters (6 vols.), E. L Griggs (Ed.). Oxford: Clarendon Press.

Coleridge. S. T. (1957). Notebooks (3 vols.), K. Coburn (Ed.). London: Routledge.

Coleridge. S. T. (1969). *The Friend* (1818), B. E. Rooke (Ed.). London: Routledge.

Coleridge. S. T. (1972). *Lay Sermons* (1816), R. J. White (Ed.). London: Routledge.

Coleridge, S. T. (1981). *Logic* (*Collected Works*, Vol. 13), J. R. de J. Jackson (Ed.). London: Routledge.

Coleridge. S. T. (1997). *Biographia Literaria* (1817), N. Leask (Ed.). London: Dent.

Dante (1971). *The Divine Comedy* (3 vols.), J. Sinclair (Trans.). Oxford: Oxford University Press.

Dickinson, E. (1955). *Complete Poems*, T. H. Johnson (Ed.). Boston: Little, Brown.

Donne, J. (1976). *The Complete English Poems*, A. J. Smith (Ed.). Harmondsworth: Penguin.

Edwards, A. (2003). *Images of Eden: an Enquiry into the Psychology of Aesthetics*. Welwyn: Skylark Press.

Ehrenzweig, A. (1967). *The Hidden Order of Art*. University of California Press.

Eliot, T. S. (1935). *Murder in the Cathedral*, new edn, Faber, 1976.

Eliot, T. S. (1944). *Four Quartets*. London: Faber.

Gaut, B. (2004). The ethical criticism of art. In: P. Lamarque & S. H. Olsen (Eds.), *Aesthetics and the Philosophy of Art: The Analytic Tradition* (pp. 283–294). Oxford: Blackwell.

Glover, N. (2008). *Psychoanalytic Aesthetics: the British School*. London: Karnac.

Golding, W. (1955). *The Inheritors*. London: Faber.

Gosso, S. (2004). *Psychoanalysis and Art: Kleinian Perspectives*. London: Karnac.

Grosskurth, P. (1986). *Melanie Klein: Her World and Her Work*. London: Hodder & Stoughton.

Grotstein, J. (2007). *A Beam of Intense Darkness: Wilfred Bion's Legacy to Psychoanalysis*. London: Karnac.

Hahn, A. (Ed.) (1994). *Sincerity: Collected Papers of Donald Meltzer*. London: Karnac.

Harris, M. (1987a). Bion's conception of a psycho-analytical attitude (1980). Reprinted in: M. H. Williams (Ed.), *Collected Papers of Martha Harris and Esther Bick* (pp. 340–344). Strath Tay, Perthshire: Clunie Press.

Harris, M. (1987b). The individual in the group: on learning to work with the psychoanalytical method (1978). Reprinted in: M. H. Williams

(Ed.), *Collected Papers of Martha Harris and Esther Bick* 1987b, (pp. 322–339). Strath Tay, Perthshire: Clunie Press.

Harris, M. (1987c). Towards learning from experience in infancy and childhood (1978). Reprinted in: M. H. Williams (Ed.), *Collected Papers of Martha Harris and Esther Bick* (pp. 164–178). Strath Tay, Perthshire: Clunie Press.

Harris, R. J. (*ca* 1938–1951). Poems, unpublished.

Harris, R. J. (1970). *Poems*. Strath Tay, Perthshire: Clunie Press, 1970.

Harris, R. J. (1986). *Poetry for You*. London: Hutchinson.

Hazlitt, W. (2007). On the living poets (1818). Charleston, SC: Bibliobazaar.

Herbert, G. (1968). *The Temple: Sacred Poems* (1633). Menston: Scolar Press.

Hinshelwood, R. (1988). *A Dictionary of Kleinian Thought*. London: Free Association Books.

Hobbes, T. (1908–1909). Answer to Davenant (1650). In: J. E. Spingarn (Ed.), *Critical Essays of the Seventeenth Century*, Vol. II (pp. 54–66). Oxford: Clarendon Press.

Holmes, R. (1982). *Past Masters: Coleridge*. Harmondsworth: Penguin.

Hulks, D. (2001). Painting, atom bombs and nudes: symbolism in the later psychoanalytic writings of Adrian Stokes. *Psychoanalytic Studies*, 3(1): 95–109.

Jain, N. (1991). *The Mind's Extensive View: Johnson and the Origins of Language*. Strath Tay, Perthshire: Clunie Press.

Keats, J. (1970a). *Selected Letters*, R. Gittings (Ed.). Oxford: Oxford University Press.

Keats, J. (1970b). *Poems*, M. Allott (Ed.). London: Longman.

Kierkegaard, S. (1940). Guilty? Not guilty? A passion narrative. In: *Stages on Life's Way* (pp. 179–446) (1845), W. Lowrie (Trans.). Princeton, NJ: Princeton University Press.

Kierkegaard, S. (1985). *Fear and Trembling*, A. Hannay (Ed.). Harmondsworth: Penguin.

Klein, M. (1930). The importance of symbol-formation in the development of the ego. *International Journal of Psycho-Analysis*, 11: 24–39.

Lamarque, P. (2004). How can we fear and pity fictions. In: P. Lamarque & S. H. Olsen (Eds.), *Aesthetics and the Philosophy of Art: the Analytic Tradition* (pp. 328–336). Oxford: Blackwell.

Lamarque, P., & Olsen, S. H. (2004). The philosophy of literature: pleasure restored. In: P. Kivey (Ed.), *The Blackwell Guide to Aesthetics* (pp. 195–214). Oxford: Blackwell.

Langer, S. (1942). *Philosophy in a New Key*. Cambridge, MA: Harvard University Press.

Langer, S. (1953). *Feeling and Form*. London: Routledge.

Langer, S. (1957). *Problems of Art*. New York: Scribner.

Longinus (1965). *On the Sublime (ca 50BC)*. In: *Classical Literary Criticism*, T. S. Dorsch (Trans.). Harmondsworth: Penguin.

Maclagan, D. (2001). *Psychological Aesthetics*. London: Jessica Kingsley.

MacLeish, A. (1960). *Poetry and Experience*. London: Bodley Head.

Margolis, J. (1962). *Philosophy Looks at the Arts*. New York: Scribner.

Marvell, A. (1952) [1681]. *Poems*, H. MacDonald (Ed.). London: Routledge.

Meltzer, D. (1967). *The Psychoanalytical Process*. Strath Tay, Perthshire: Clunie Press.

Meltzer, D. (1973). *Sexual States of Mind*. Strath Tay, Perthshire: Clunie Press.

Meltzer, D. (1975). *Explorations in Autism*. Perthshire: Clunie Press.

Meltzer, D. (1978a). *The Kleinian Development*, 3 Vols. Strath Tay, Perthshire: Clunie Press.

Meltzer, D. (1978b). Introduction. In: D. Meltzer & E. O'Shaughnessy (Eds.), *Collected Papers of Roger Money-Kyrle*. Strath Tay, Perthshire: Clunie Press.

Meltzer, D. (1983). *Dream Life*. Strath Tay, Perthshire: Clunie Press.

Meltzer, D. (1986). *Studies in Extended Metapsychology: Clinical Applications of Bion's Ideas*. Strath Tay, Perthshire: Clunie Press.

Meltzer, D. (1987). Portrait. In: M. H. Williams (Ed.), *The Collected Papers of Martha Harris and Esther Bick*.

Meltzer, D. (1989). Mattie as an educator. *Quaderni di Psicoterapia Infantile No. 18* (pp. 10–11). Rome: Borla.

Meltzer, D. (1992). *The Claustrum*. Strath Tay, Perthshire: Clunie Press.

Meltzer, D. (1994a). Three lectures on W. R. Bion's *A Memoir of the Future* (1985). In: A. Hahn (Ed.), *Sincerity: Collected Papers of Donald Meltzer* (pp. 520–550). London: Karnac.

Meltzer, D. (1994b). 'The diameter of the circle' in Bion's work (1980). Reprinted in: A. Hahn (Ed.), *Sincerity: Collected Papers of Donald Meltzer* (pp. 469–474). London: Karnac.

Meltzer, D. (1994c). Does Money-Kyrle's concept of "misconception" have any unique descriptive power? (1981). Reprinted in: A. Hahn (Ed.), *Sincerity: Collected Papers of Donald Meltzer* (pp. 496–513). London: Karnac.

Meltzer, D. (1994d). Temperature and distance as technical dimensions of interpretation (1976). In: A. Hahn (Ed.), *Sincerity: Collected Papers of Donald Meltzer* (pp. 374–386). London: Karnac

Meltzer, D. (1994e). Routine and inspired interpretations (1973). Reprinted in: A. Hahn (Ed.), *Sincerity: Collected Papers of Donald Meltzer* (pp. 290–306). London: Karnac.

Meltzer, D. (1995a). Thought disorders. Unpublished lecture.

Meltzer, D. (1995b). Talk on Bion's grid. In: C. Mawson (Ed.), *Bion Today*. Routledge (in press).

Meltzer, D. (1997a). Concerning signs and symbols. *British Journal of Psychotherapy*, 14(2): 175–181.

Meltzer, D. (1997b). The evolution of object relations. *British Journal of Psychotherapy*, 14(1): 60–66.

Meltzer, D. (2003). Good luck. In: D. Meltzer, with R. Castellà, C. Tabbia, & L. Farré, *Supervisions with Donald Meltzer* (pp. 315–324). London: Karnac.

Meltzer, D. (2005a). Thought disorder: a distinct phenomenological category? *British Journal of Psychotherapy*, 21(3): 417–428.

Meltzer, D. (2005b). Creativity and the countertransference. In: M. H. Williams (Ed.), *The Vale of Soulmaking* (pp. 175–182). London: Karnac.

Meltzer, D. (2005c). Foreword: Psychoanalysis acknowledges its poetic forebears and joins the artistic family (1991). Reprinted in: M. H. Williams, *The Vale of Soulmaking* (pp. xi–xix). London: Karnac.

Meltzer, D., & Harris, M. (1994). A psychoanalytical model of the child-in-the-family-in-the-community (1976). Reprinted in: A. Hahn (Ed.), *Sincerity: Collected Papers of Donald Meltzer* (pp. 387–354). London: Karnac.

Meltzer, D., & Stokes, A. (1988). Concerning the social basis of art (1963). Reprinted in: Meltzer & Williams, 1988, pp. 206–226.

Meltzer, D., & Williams, M. H. (1988). *The Apprehension of Beauty: The Role of Aesthetic Conflict in Development, Art and Violence*. Strath Tay, Perthshire: Clunie Press.

Milton, J. (1966). *Poetical Works*, D. Bush (Ed.). London: Oxford University Press.

Milton, J. (1974). *Selected Prose*, C. A. Patrides (Ed.). Harmondsworth: Penguin.

Mithen, S. (1996). *The Prehistory of the Mind: A Search for the Origins of Art, Religion and Science*. London: Phoenix.

Money-Kyrle, R. (1961). *Man's Picture of his World*. London: Duckworth.

Money-Kyrle, R. (1978). Cognitive development. In: D. Meltzer & E. O'Shaughnessy (Eds.), *Collected Papers of Roger Money-Kyrle* (pp. 416–433). Strath Tay, Perthshire: Clunie Press.

Negri, R. (1994). *The Newborn in the Intensive Care Unit*. Strath Tay, Perthshire: Clunie Press.

Negri, R., & Harris, M. (2007). *The Story of Infant Development*. London: Karnac.

Nordheim, A. (2006). CD cover notes to *The Tempest Suite*.

Oelsner, R., & Oelsner, M. (2005). About supervision: an interview with Donald Meltzer. *British Journal of Psychotherapy, 21*(3): 455–461.

Pater, W. (2005). *The Renaissance: Studies in Art and Poetry* (1893). London: Dover.

Plato (1955). *The Republic*, H. D. P. Lee (Trans.). Harmondsworth: Penguin.

Plato (1956). *Protagoras and Meno*, W. Guthrie (Trans.). Harmondsworth: Penguin.

Plato (1975). *Phaedrus* (c. 370 BC), W. Hamilton (Trans.). Harmondsworth: Penguin.

Plato (1987). *Theaetetus*, R. Waterfield (Trans.). Harmondsworth: Penguin.

Podro, M. (2003). Kant and the aesthetic imagination. In: D. Arnold & M. Iversen (Eds.), *Art and Thought* (pp. 51–70). Oxford: Blackwell.

Pollock, G. (Ed.) (2006). *Psychoanalysis and the Image.*

Rhode, E. (1994). *The Image in Form*, retrieved from www.pstokes. demon.co.uk.

Rhode, E. (1997). *On Hallucination, Intuition and the Becoming of "O"*. New York: ESF.

Rhode, E. (1998). The enigmatic object: the relation of understanding to being and becoming. *Journal of Melanie Klein and Object Relations, 16*(2): 257–272.

Richards, I. A. (1989). *Principles of Literary Criticism*. London: Routledge & Kegan Paul.

Ricoeur, P. (1977). *The Rule of Metaphor: The Creation of Meaning in Language*. Toronto: University of Toronto Press.

Ricoeur, P. (2004). *Memory, History, Forgetting*. Chicago: University of Chicago Press.

Rimbaud, A. (1871). Letter to Georges Izambard, 13 May. Accessed at: Letters known as "Of the Visionary", www.mag4.net/Rimbaud/DocumentsE1.html.

Rustin, M. (1991). *The Good Society and the Inner World*. London: Verso.

Rycroft, C. (1968). *Imagination and Reality*. London: Hogarth Press.

Sanders, K. (2006). Meltzer and the influence of Bion. *British Journal of Psychotherapy, 22*(3): 347–362.

Sandler, P. C. (2005). *The Language of Bion: a Dictionary*. London: Karnac.

Sapen, D. (2008). *Freud's Lost Chord* (dissertation, Adelphi University, USA; in press).

Segal, H. (1957). Notes on symbol formation. *International Journal of Psychoanalysis, 38*: 391–397. Reprinted in: *The Work of Hanna Segal*, New York: Aronson, 1981.

Shakespeare, W. (1964). *The Tempest*, F. Kermode (Ed.). London: Methuen.

Shakespeare, W. (1982). *Hamlet*, H. Jenkins, (Ed.) London: Methuen.

Shelley, P. B. (1977). A defence of poetry (1840). In: D. H. Reiman & S. B. Powers (Eds.), *Poetry and Prose*. New York: Norton.

Sidney, P. (2004). The defence of Poesy (1580). In: G. Alexander (Ed.), *Sidney's "The Defence of Poesy" and Selected Renaissance Literary Criticism*. London: Penguin.

Sparshott, F. (2004). Dance: bodies in motion, bodies at rest. In: P. Kivy (Ed.), *The Blackwell Guide to Aesthetics* (pp. 276–290). Oxford: Blackwell.

Spitz, E. (1985). *Art and Psyche: a Study in Psychoanalysis and Aesthetics*. New Haven, CT: Yale University Press.

Stephenson, R. H. (1995). *Goethe's Conception of Knowledge and Science*. Edinburgh University Press.

Stokes, A. (1951). *Smooth and Rough*. London: Faber.

Stokes, A. (1961). *Three Essays on the Painting of our Time*. London: Tavistock.

Stokes, A. (1963). *Painting and the Inner World*. London: Tavistock.

Stokes, A. (1965). *The Invitation in Art*. London: Tavistock.

Stone, M. (2006). The analyst's body as tuning fork: embodied resonance in countertransference. *Journal of Analytical Psychology, 51*(1): 109–124.

Tolstoy, L. (1982). *War and Peace*, R. Edmonds (Trans.), 2 Vols. London: Penguin.

Upanishads (1879). M. Muller (Trans.), 2 Volumes. Richmond: Curzon Press. Reprinted 2001.

Williams, M. H. (1982). *Inspiration in Milton and Keats*. London: Macmillan.

Williams, M. H. (1986). "Knowing" the mystery: against reductionism. *Encounter, 67*: 48–53.

Williams, M. H. (Ed.) (1987b). *Collected Papers of Martha Harris and Esther Bick*. Strath Tay, Perthshire: Clunie Press.

Williams, M. H. (1987c). *A Strange Way of Killing: the Poetic Structure of Wuthering Heights*. Strath Tay, Perthshire: Clunie Press.

Williams, M. H. (1988a). The undiscovered country. In: D. Meltzer & M. H. Williams, *The Apprehension of Beauty: The Role of Aesthetic Conflict in Development, Art and Violence* (pp. 84–133). Strath Tay, Perthshire: Clunie Press.

Williams, M. H. (1988b). Holding the dream. In: D. Meltzer & M. H. Williams (Eds.), *The Apprehension of Beauty* (pp. 178–199). Strathtay, Perthshire: Clunie Press.

Williams, M. H. (1990). Looking with the mind: psychoanalysis and literature. *Encounter, 74* (May): 33–38.

Williams, M. H. (1994). A man of achievement—Sophocles' Oedipus. *British Journal of Psychotherapy, 11*(2): 232–241.

Williams, M. H. (1997). Inspiration: a psychoanalytic and aesthetic concept. *British Journal of Psychotherapy, 14*(1): 33–43.

Williams, M. H. (1998). The aesthetic perspective in the work of Donald Meltzer. *Journal of Melanie Klein and Object Relations, 16*(2): 209–218.

Williams, M. H. (1999). Psychoanalysis: an art or a science? *British Journal of Psychotherapy, 16*(2): 127–135.

Williams, M. H. (2005a). The three vertices: science, art, religion. *British Journal of Psychotherapy, 21*(3): 429–441.

Williams, M. H. (2005b). *The Vale of Soulmaking: The Post-Kleinian Model of the Mind*. London: Karnac.

Williams, M. H. (2008a). The hieroglyphics of Catherine: Emily Brontë and the musical matrix. In: S. Hagan & J. Wells (Eds.), *The Brontës in the World of the Arts* (pp. 81–99). Aldershot: Ashgate.

Williams, M. H. (2008b). The role of incantation: life drawing as an analogue to psychoanalytic process. *The Psychoanalytic Review, 95*(3): 463–472.

Williams, M. H. (2008c) A post-Kleinian model for aesthetic criticism. *PsyArt Online Journal*. http://www.clas.ufl.edu/ipsa/journal/2008_williams01.shtml

Williams, M. H. (2009). Psychoanalysis as an art form. *British Journal of Psychotherapy, 25*(3): 381–392.

Williams, M. H., & Waddell, M. (1991). *The Chamber of Maiden Thought*. London: Routledge.

Winnicott, D. (1971). *Playing and Reality*. London: Tavistock.

Woodhouse, C. M. (1982). How Plato won the west. In: M. Holroyd (Ed.), *Essays by Divers Hands: Transactions of the Royal Society of Literature* XLII. Woodbridge, Suffolk: Boydell Press.

Woolf, V. (2002). *Moments of Being; Autobiographical Writings*. London: Pimlico.

Wordsworth, W. (1979). *The Prelude: 1799, 1805, 1850*. J. Wordsworth, M. H. Abrams & S. Gill (Eds.). New York: Norton.

Yeats, W. B. (1982) [1933]. *Collected Poems*. London: Macmillan.